AS SHE LAY SLEEPING

AS SHE LAY SLEEPING

*A Shadowy Figure, a Brutal Murder,
an Anonymous Tip. Will Justice Prevail?*

A TRUE STORY

BY MARK PRYOR

New Horizon Press
Far Hills, New Jersey

Requests for permission should be addressed to:
New Horizon Press
P.O. Box 669
Far Hills, NJ 07931

Pryor, Mark
As She Lay Sleeping:
        A Shadowy Figure, a Brutal Murder, an Anonymous Tip. Will Justice
        Prevail? A True Story

Cover design: Wendy Bass
Interior design: Scribe Inc.

Library of Congress Control Number: 2012941578
ISBN-13: 978-0-88282-428-4

New Horizon Press

Manufactured in the U.S.A.

17   16   15   14   13   1   2   3   4   5

For Johnny and Tom

Author's Note

I have tried to paint an accurate and fair picture of the pre-trial proceedings and trial in this case. As much as possible I have quoted directly from the transcripts to allow readers a more unbiased view. Quotations from court are from the official trial transcript, although occasionally I have taken the liberty of editing with the sole aim of making the story more readable.

During the trial portion, I reference the jury as one body or collectively as "the jurors" without identifying the jurors individually. My reason for this is simple: I have always felt that jury service is a valuable but onerous task, one where people are press-ganged into a job they don't want and forced to abide by restrictive rules that the rest of the people involved in a trial can ignore. One mistake can put them in contempt of court and/or cause a mistrial. As Judge Mike Lynch put it, "Next to military service in a time of war, being a juror is the hardest job we ask our citizens to do."

I agree with Judge Lynch and, in this case particularly, I feel that the jurors were plucked from their lives and thrust into a difficult situation. I have chosen to allow them to return to and stay in their private lives and not have to relive it through my naming or otherwise identifying them.

This book is based on my experiences and reflects my perception of the past, present and future. The personalities, events, actions and conversations portrayed within this story have been taken from interviews, research, court documents, letters, personal papers, press accounts and the memories of some participants.

In an effort to safeguard the privacy of certain people, some individuals' names and identifying characteristics have been changed. Some of the minor characters may be composites. Events involving the characters happened as described. Only minor details may have been altered.

Contents

Prologue

Her destination was Sixth Street, Austin's liveliest nighttime address, packed with bars, restaurants and live music clubs. Natalie Antonetti first headed to a club called Toulouse and then, toward midnight, moved on to Club Steamboat, a venue that lived at the very heart of Austin's vibrant music scene. Some argued that it *was* the heart of the city's music scene, right up until it closed. As Andy Langer, a reporter for the *Austin Chronicle* wrote: "Over the years, Steamboat has been the home of all-star bands, late-night jams, and yes, even a few cover bands. It's where Stevie Ray Vaughan's *In the Beginning* was recorded, where Dino Lee took a shotglass to the head, where Gibby Haynes unknowingly relieved himself on an S.R.O. crowd, and where comedians Bill Hicks and Sam Kinison honed their timing."

Natalie danced at the club, moving easily between groups of friends. At one point, she ran into her ex-boyfriend Dennis Davis. Even though he'd been the one to end their relationship, Davis seemed unhappy that she was talking so animatedly with another man. He seemed more than unhappy; he seemed angry with her and showed it. Davis's best friend, Jimmy Rose, witnessed Dennis's tirade at Natalie but attributed it to his buddy's jealous nature, something he'd seen before and would see again. Eventually he led Davis away and thought nothing more of it that night.

At 2:30 A.M., Natalie returned home and found her roommate Jolene still awake. They chatted for a few minutes; then Natalie went upstairs and changed into blue jogging shorts and a pink T-shirt. She told Jolene that she was going to take a brief walk outside by the apartment complex's swimming pool. Jolene warned her to be careful. Walter Griffin, a neighbor who was on his way to his apartment after taking his family's babysitter home, saw Natalie walking to the pool.

After about ten minutes, Natalie came back into the apartment and found Jolene watching television. Natalie lay down on the couch and started to doze off, so after a few minutes Jolene turned off the television and prepared to go up to her own bed. Before she went upstairs, she walked over to the front door and pushed it, to make sure it was shut. She asked Natalie if she'd locked it and Natalie grunted in reply, which Jolene took to mean yes. Jolene didn't check the lock.

Two hours later, Jolene woke up and went downstairs to fetch a glass of water. She saw Natalie sleeping peacefully on the couch so she made sure not to wake her.

At 5:15 A.M., barely forty-five minutes later, Jolene woke again. She heard moaning and thumping noises from downstairs. She also heard a door shut. She thought this was strange, because she still heard someone moaning downstairs even after she heard the door close.

Jolene went to investigate and, to her horror, she found Natalie sitting on the couch covered in blood "from head to foot." Jolene rushed over and Natalie tried to speak but was unable. Jolene ran upstairs and woke Natalie's teenage son, Johnny, bringing him down to his bloodied and incoherent mother. Jolene grabbed the phone and dialed 911, calling for the police and an ambulance. After hanging up with the emergency dispatcher, Jolene tried talking to Natalie again, but when she couldn't understand her friend's mumblings, she picked up the phone and called Dennis Davis, "a mutual friend of ours."

Together, Jolene and Johnny did what they could to communicate with Natalie, Johnny pleading for his mother to explain what was going on and who had done this. She didn't tell him, couldn't tell him, but the sixteen-year-old boy recognized something in his mother's eyes that he later described to police in a simple sentence: "I can't say for sure, but judging from the look in my mother's eyes, she knew what had happened to her."

Though her ability to speak was destroyed, Natalie got up from the couch and started moving about the apartment, ignoring her son's pleas to remain still. She staggered as she walked, trailing blood over the floor and leaving bloody handprints on the walls as she steadied herself.

Natalie went into the downstairs bathroom, taking tissues and wiping her nose and lips, smearing blood around the room in the process. Then she walked to the staircase and started climbing. Johnny walked with her, staying right by her side, and Natalie kept going until she reached her bedroom. Once there she sat on the bed, quiet and still for a minute before reaching over and opening one of her drawers. She took out a purple baby doll nightgown, then stood and went into her bathroom. Johnny tried to stop her, but Natalie wanted to change and closed the door on him, seemingly oblivious to her wounds, to the trail of blood she was leaving. She didn't want her son to watch her change clothes. Johnny, terrified and confused, didn't want to push on the door or to fight his battered mother, so he ran downstairs and told Jolene to go up and be with her while he waited outside for the ambulance.

Chapter 1

MUSIC AND VIOLENT DEATH

The city of Austin lies in the heart of Texas, a midpoint for the traveler on his way between two of the state's largest cities, Dallas to the north and San Antonio to the south. On the east-west axis, Austin is the gateway from the green flatlands that stretch toward Louisiana to the east and the drier, hillier land to the west.

It was the verdant, rolling landscape upon which Austin now sits that caught the imagination of the vice president of the Republic of Texas, Mirabeau B. Lamar, in the early 1800s. He was on a hunting trip in central Texas, where the buffalo ran aplenty, and was reminded of the tradition that began with Rome: that all great cities be built on hills. Thus, when he took over the presidency from Sam Houston just a few months later, he began the transition of the government from Houston to Austin. Work on a new capitol building began in May 1839.

Since then, Austin has continued to inspire loyalty and praise from the visitors who are drawn to the natural pools of the artesian-fed Barton Springs and to fuel the imaginations of generations of artists moved by the purplish haze that settles in the evening sky. Short story writer O. Henry was one such artist, describing Austin as looking as though it wore "a violet crown."

Many writers have called Austin their home, but it is for music that the city became known. Dubbed "The Live Music Capital of the World," the city is host to the Texas Music Hall of Fame headquarters and the Texas Music Museum. Every year thousands flock to its two live music festivals, South By Southwest and the Austin City Limits Music Festival.

The city has also been home to a horde of musicians, famous and infamous, who began their careers and, in some cases, ended them here. Janis Joplin played the folk circuit in and around Austin and Willie Nelson enjoyed a revival of his career when he moved here in the 1970s. Townes Van Zandt called Austin home and Pinetop Perkins still does. One of the oldest Mississippi bluesmen around, Perkins played piano in several of Austin's clubs well into his nineties. And the musical talent has never stopped, with Stevie Ray Vaughan, two of the three Dixie Chicks and Cornell Haynes Jr., better known as rapper Nelly, all Austinites. It's even said that the city helped popularize bands like the Police and Elvis Costello, giving them a foothold in America and allowing their music to flow north into the American Midwest.

With all that creativity comes drama and tragedy. That colorful crown so beloved by O. Henry is best viewed from the highest point within the city limits, the 780-foot Mount Bonnell, a place shrouded in mystery, romance and death. One legend relays that a young woman jumped off the peak to escape the Indians who had killed her fiancé, which is why Mount Bonnell is also known as Antonette's Leap. Another legend tells of a woman named Golden Nell and her husband, Beau, who leaped off the peak to avoid being captured and tortured by Native Americans. Such stories have inspired the lore that the first time a couple climbs the ninety-nine steps to the mount's peak, they fall in love. On the second trip, they get engaged. But beware, the story goes that the third climb could prove fatal.

Even Austin's music scene has seen its share of tragedies. Cult figure Blaze Foley was gunned down in Austin in February 1989 and a year later the legendary Stevie Ray Vaughan died in a helicopter crash in Wisconsin. Townes Van Zandt, who wrote a song about Foley, succumbed to years of hard living at the age of fifty-three, dying of heart arrhythmia in January 1997.

In 1985, Austin was near its musical zenith. The punk scene had swept through the city and, in its wake, dozens of bands thrashed their guitars at the many clubs along Sixth Street, the music scene's main artery. Other venues entertained a more sophisticated, or at least older, crowd with blues and jazz.

Wide-eyed freshmen at the University of Texas at Austin wandered the few blocks south from their dormitories and, so many of them new to town from the country, encountered every form of music they ever imagined. Then, as now, Austin sat as a cultural icon for those looking to experiment, be it with music or something a little more ingestible. A liberal beacon in a sea of conservativeness, Austin has always pulled in those at the fringes, people seeking to discover themselves and others like them.

It was this scene that drew Natalie Antonetti away from the suburban life she'd been living outside of Houston. Born in Cuba, Natalie moved to Miami with her parents when she was thirteen. Two years later the family moved to Wichita Falls, Texas, but within a year was back in Florida, living in Coral Gables, one of the nation's first planned communities.

The fiery and beautiful Natalie, with her petite frame and bright smile, never had trouble attracting admirers and she was just twenty when she met and married her first husband. A year later they had a son, Johnny Goudie, and the next year the three moved to Houston. The marriage didn't last, the couple splitting after four years together.

Natalie and son Johnny bounced around together, moving to Mexico, California and back to Houston. Their longest stay was in the Woodlands, a suburban development and bedroom community located twenty-eight miles north of downtown Houston along Interstate 45. When they moved there, Natalie found a job as a school teacher. But eventually she tired of the quiet suburban life and decided to take her beloved Johnny and flee. She tapped into her network of artist friends—writers, painters and musicians—and Natalie and Johnny moved to Austin.

They settled into a small apartment in the Barton Hills area and Natalie took a job with a nursery as a landscaper. She also worked hard to keep Johnny, now a teenager, happy and entertained, encouraging his powerful interest in music but making sure he was also exposed to sports, books and the other arts. Natalie became more social, too. As

Johnny described it, the move to Austin was a rebirth of sorts, giving Natalie the chance to "spread her wings" and meet new people.

One of the first people she met was Jolene Wells, in her mid-twenties, a friend of Dennis Davis who owned a recording facility called Studio D. They met because Dennis and Natalie had started dating. Studio D was also where Johnny started to spend a lot of time; the teen stared wide-eyed at the state-of-the-art equipment Davis was using, glad to hang around and meet the many musicians who booked time at the studio.

And in those heady, hedonistic days, where music and marijuana drove so much of Austin's social networking, it came as no surprise to anyone when Jolene and Johnny, despite their age difference, started dating. It was a relationship Natalie did not necessarily approve of but felt unable to prevent.

Chapter 2

A BLOODY SCENE

On the afternoon of Saturday, October 12, two days before Johnny's seventeenth birthday and a few days after Natalie and Dennis Davis broke up after several months of dating, Natalie was at home, waiting to help Jolene move into the two-bedroom apartment on Barton Hills Drive.

It was while there that, at about 4:20 P.M., Natalie spoke to Johnny by phone, telling him that she had no plans for the evening, at least until 10:30 or so when she was going to go downtown. She talked to a couple of other friends on the phone and, true to her word, was still at home at 9:15 when Jolene Wells arrived with Johnny.

He'd spent the evening at Studio D and, despite his tender years, Johnny had been drinking gin and tonics, enough to make himself sick. With Jolene's help, Natalie put her son to bed and spent a few minutes rubbing his back before putting a waste basket beside the bed, in case he threw up. Once she was sure he was safe and in need of nothing more than sleep, she left him in the care of Jolene and headed to downtown Austin.

Just hours later, Johnny awoke to Jolene's cries. Haltingly, she explained his mother was injured. Johnny got out of bed and rushed down the stairs behind Jolene. He discovered his mother on the couch, covered in blood. Desperately he asked her questions about what happened, but she was unable to respond. Jolene made phone calls as Johnny followed his mother, who began wandering around the apartment, pleading with her to remain still.

Paramedics arrived at the apartment complex at approximately 6 A.M. and Johnny, hysterical, ran out to meet them. Their first task was to make sure that any danger had been removed, that it was safe to enter the apartment. As soon as Warren, one of the paramedics, calmed Johnny enough to get that reassurance, Warren and his partner Leo walked into the apartment. Immediately they were struck by how much blood there was, on the wall by the front door, up the stairs and throughout the living area, drenching the couch.

Warren began to look for the patient and saw her walking down the stairs toward him, bleeding heavily from the top of her head. He could see blood that had clotted in her hair, on her face, in her ears and on her nightgown. Warren tried to stop her, to talk to her, but she seemed not to notice, walking straight past him. As he watched, she moved into the downstairs bathroom and Warren tried unsuccessfully to keep the door open, to keep an eye on her. He heard the toilet flush before she reappeared, walking over to the couch where she sat down.

As soon as Natalie was still, Warren started to examine her wound, seeing a "large multi-faceted laceration" on the top of her head. While he was examining her, Natalie was "crying, mumbling, talking," yet he was unable to understand what she was saying. He assumed she was speaking in Spanish.

At some point while Natalie was still being treated inside the apartment, Dennis Davis arrived. He later told police that Johnny stopped him from going inside, saying Natalie wouldn't want him to see her that way, but Johnny remembered it differently, saying that Davis was the one who hung back, keeping himself and Johnny away from Natalie while she was being treated. Either way, Dennis Davis did not go to Natalie's side while she was conscious.

The police also arrived during Warren's examination. Warren and Leo soon moved Natalie onto a stretcher and into the ambulance, letting Johnny join them for the ride to the hospital. On the way, Warren later wrote, Natalie "became less responsive to verbal stimuli and upon arrival to Brackenridge less responsive to painful stimuli."

Natalie Antonetti was admitted to Brackenridge Hospital on the morning of October 13, barely conscious.

Chapter 3

WHODUNNIT?

In almost every criminal case, police, prosecutors and jurors have sought the smoking gun, the piece of evidence that puts the perpetrator directly at the scene at precisely the right time, with the weapon in his hand and the victim dead at his feet.

The men and women in blue always hope for a big break, the piece of evidence that points the investigation in the right direction, on its inexorable trajectory toward catching the criminal responsible.

In this investigation, that big break was a possible eyewitness sighting of the killer. The sighting was by a neighbor who lived in the same unit as Natalie, at the other end of the building. His name was Donn Chelli and his statement was not only the detectives' big break, but also just about their only piece of evidence. Like a beacon glowing in the night, Chelli's statement informed and guided the ensuing investigation.

Given the importance of Chelli's observations, it was appropriate that the lead detective made sure they were put in writing. The lead detective in this case was a young man, just thirty years old, named Eddie Balagia.

Balagia's family hailed from Lebanon and he retained the olive complexion of his forefathers, enhancing his natural good looks with a slender frame and sharp clothing. Within the department he had a formidable reputation as a detective and was known to play his cards close to his chest. Unless you knew him or that aspect of his personality, you could read one of his reports and miss something, see a recitation of facts when in reality there were clues to his opinion regarding a case or a suspect.

Balagia was acutely aware of the importance of Chelli's statement, not just for what it contained, but also because many of the avenues he'd normally explore were closed off from the very start: the lack of a break-in and the violence of the assault made it likely that the killer was someone Natalie knew. That meant fingerprints were useless. If the victim knew her attacker one would expect to find his prints at her home or, at the very least, a defense lawyer would be able to argue their presence had an innocent explanation. The crime scene itself had been tainted, too. With Natalie moving about and EMS workers treating her on-scene, there was no chance of accurately reconstructing what had happened. Balagia knew, too, that no one else had seen or heard anything that would lead him to the killer: not Johnny, not Jolene, nor any other eyewitness. Just Donn Chelli. Right from the first, Eddie Balagia viewed him as their most important witness.

On October 13, Balagia met the thirty-nine-year-old Chelli at the police station downtown and immediately noted those details cops are trained to notice: Chelli was about six feet tall, burly, an articulate speaker and neatly attired. Reassuringly, as far as Balagia could tell, Chelli had no reason to lie or invent details. And he was positive about what he'd seen.

Balagia began the statement by noting a few details about the man's life, putting in the sworn statement that Chelli was a self-employed swimming pool contractor who had lived at the apartment complex for about ten months with his girlfriend, Fran Alcozer. With perfunctory details and his phone number duly noted, Balagia moved on to asking what Chelli had seen.

Early on Sunday morning, Chelli said, between 4:30 A.M. and 4:45 A.M., he'd noticed a white male, about six feet tall, broad-shouldered, with a big belly and straight, dishwater blonde hair that didn't quite touch his collar.

"Can you say what he was wearing?" Balagia asked.

Chelli could. "He had on a gray or dark green T-shirt with 'The Lotions' written on the back. He also had on a pair of shorts. I'm not sure what color they were, but they might have been tan. He appeared to be in some kind of rage."

"Rage?"

"What I mean by this is that while he was calm, he appeared to have a lot of built-up tension inside of him. This man was carrying what looked like a child's baseball bat. It was wood and approximately twenty-four inches long."

Balagia was curious about why Chelli had been outside his apartment at that hour. Chelli explained that he'd been up that early because he was supposed to leave for a business trip to Las Vegas. He had gone to the convenience store that backed up to the apartment building, which could be accessed via a path that ran right behind his and Natalie's apartments, to get milk for his girlfriend. "I had been walking back from the store and noticed this man looking into my living room window facing the south side of my apartment. When I saw him he said something to me. I can't remember his exact words, but it was something like, 'You're the second person that's gotten into my shit.'"

Chelli said that he asked the man what he was doing and the man said he'd been looking at Chelli's cats on the second floor balcony, above the living room. Chelli told Balagia that he walked alongside the man toward the parking lot, at which point Chelli turned right toward his apartment and the mystery man walked off in the direction of the swimming pool and clubhouse.

Back in his apartment, Chelli debated telling his girlfriend, Fran, about the man and did so about an hour later, right before calling 911 to report the incident. The dispatcher, Chelli told Balagia, asked whether his sighting was related to the incident that had just been called in by Jolene Wells. "I told him that I didn't know and he told me that someone was just beaten at my complex and that he would have a police officer come talk to me."

When Chelli hung up, he and Fran went outside and met Johnny who told them about his mother and that he was waiting for the ambulance.

Donn Chelli swore to the truth of his statement, just a few hours after the assault on Natalie Antonetti. And as good cops are aware, those first few hours are vital—evidence can be tainted or destroyed, witnesses can disappear and suspects can cover their tracks.

This meant that Balagia's first task was to find the mystery "Lotions man." Quickly he discovered that the Lotions were one of Austin's hottest musical acts, a reggae band. Their popularity meant that many people would have access to their T-shirts, but even so, it was a lead, as was the detailed description Chelli gave. But who in Natalie's circle might fit it? Using Donn Chelli's statement, Balagia and his team first looked at a recent boyfriend of Natalie's, Andy Stout.

Stout's name surfaced the day after the attack, when Balagia and Sergeant Russell Schmidt headed to Sixth Street to retrace her last steps. They first went to the club Toulouse, where Natalie had danced just hours before the attack. The club's manager said he knew Natalie and Andy Stout. More importantly, the club manager said that Stout fit the description provided by Donn Chelli. Balagia then spoke to a man named Marshall, who made his living on the street selling flowers to those with romantic inclinations and loose change. Marshall said he, too, knew Natalie Antonetti and that he saw her on Saturday night on East Sixth Street, where he worked. Marshall agreed with the club manager that Stout fit Chelli's description of the man with the bat.

On October 14, Johnny Goudie's seventeenth birthday, thirty-one-year-old Andy Stout met with detectives at their offices. He told police that he'd met Natalie six or eight months previously, when Jolene Wells introduced them. While they were dating steadily, he said, they saw each other a few times a week and kept their relationship "pretty informal." She kept him from getting too serious, because she was interested in dating Dennis Davis.

Stout told detectives that he had last seen Natalie the previous Monday evening, October 7. He'd been playing with his band at the club Toulouse. Natalie stopped by the club at about 11:30 P.M. to say hi, because she knew he'd be playing there. They talked some, mostly about the landscaping business she was helping run, and then she headed home. The next time he heard from her, he said, was on Saturday, the afternoon before the attack. She telephoned and left a message for him: "Hi, it's Natalie. Give me a call; I want to talk to you." He tried returning her call that day, sometime in the late afternoon or early evening, but got no answer.

He told police he wasn't the man Donn Chelli saw. Not possible, Stout said, because he was playing with his band until 2:30 A.M. that Saturday night and after his set he went straight home. Stout's two roommates confirmed with Balagia that after arriving home, the three of them went out to eat, returning to the apartment at about 4:30 A.M. They went to bed, he said and all slept until the early afternoon.

The only other information that Stout offered was hearsay. He had talked to a bassist named Isaac who had been playing at club Toulouse. Isaac had spoken to Natalie on Saturday night and afterwards told Stout that Natalie seemed "nervous and upset about something." But if Isaac knew why he didn't tell Stout and Stout himself had no idea.

Andy Stout seemed like a dead-end lead, but just to be sure Balagia photographed him and went back to the Barton Creek apartment complex. He found Donn Chelli at home and showed him a photo lineup that included Stout. Chelli studied the pictures and then told Balagia that the man he'd seen the night of the attack was not one of them.

That same day, another former boyfriend of Natalie Antonetti gave a statement. Dennis Davis described himself to detectives as the "owner of Studio D," which he had operated for a year. He said that he'd known Natalie for about a year, said he was a close friend of hers and of her son's, adding: "We dated on and off for about nine months. Just recently, about a month ago, we started being 'just friends.' I saw and talked to Natalie no fewer than two or three times a week over the past year."

Davis then went on to describe his last encounters with Natalie. He said he'd seen her on Thursday, October 10, in the evening. She'd visited Studio D and "we sat outside and talked for a couple of hours. I had a date at ten but we talked until about 10:30 P.M."

The next time he claimed to have seen Natalie was the day before she was attacked, Saturday, October 12. They had gone out on Friday night, Davis said, with some other friends. After their night on the town they went to another friend's house. They slept until late on Saturday, Davis said, close to two in the afternoon. Then Davis dropped Natalie off downtown, where she'd left her car the night before. He told police: "I dropped her off and she seemed fine aside from being tired."

He went on to say that Natalie talked to him later that day, when she called Studio D trying to get ahold of Jolene. "This was the last time I spoke to Natalie," he said.

Then Davis gave police his alibi. He said he worked at the studio until about eleven, maybe midnight:

> After I got off work two friends of mine, (Amparo "Ampie" Garcia and Rose L.N.U. [last name unknown]), and myself were going to go out someplace but we had gotten off too late. Rose then went home and I took Ampie home to my house. While we were watching TV she fell asleep on the floor. I watched a couple of movies and then I woke her up to go to bed. I woke her up around 5:00 A.M. so that we could go to bed. It seems like I was in bed only a couple of minutes when the phone rang.

The phone call, he said, was from Jolene Wells who was "hysterical and screaming and didn't make a whole lot of sense."

Davis said that Jolene described the horrifying scene at Natalie's apartment and that he left Ampie at his house to go to Natalie's. He said that it took him about twenty minutes to get to Natalie's apartment and that he found the scene in chaos. He learned that EMS was treating Natalie who was on a stretcher inside. Johnny, Davis said, told him not to go in because "she [Natalie] wouldn't want me to see her that way."

Balagia did not suspect Davis although he was a former boyfriend of Natalie's. Not only had he given a specific alibi, but also, still using Donn Chelli's statement as a guiding reference, it seemed certain that the slim, relatively slight Dennis did not fit the description of the man lurking outside Chelli's apartment. Thus, not considered a suspect, Davis was not asked to take a polygraph test. Nor was his alibi checked.

The next day, October 15, Sergeant Balagia tracked down Davey Kane, who worked with Natalie at the landscaping business. Kane told Balagia that he and Natalie were close friends as well as business associates but that the two of them had never dated.

As for the fateful weekend, Kane said that he'd seen and spent time with Natalie on Saturday night. It was at about midnight at Steamboat, he said, when she came into the club with Mark "Buster" Lewis, whom Kane described as being five feet four inches tall and of medium build. Balagia immediately noted that this description was quite different from Chelli's description of the mysterious lurker. Kane said that he and Natalie were at Steamboat for about thirty minutes, then left to get pizza at a nearby restaurant, where they stayed for a half hour before returning to Steamboat. At about 1:15 A.M., Kane was busy talking to someone else when he looked around for Natalie and realized she'd gone. He himself left the club at two in the morning and didn't see Natalie again. He spent the night at a friend's house, he said, an alibi that Sergeant Balagia later confirmed.

About Natalie's demeanor that night, Kane said: "Natalie did not appear to be bothered by anything that night. Mostly we talked about the business. The only problems I knew that she was having were with her on-again, off-again boyfriend Dennis Davis. This wasn't really a problem; the relationship just wasn't going as smoothly as she would like it to be."

When asked about Natalie's dating habits, Kane described them as "reserved," saying that she was not the type to pick a man up at a bar and take him home. Detectives never suspected that she had picked up her attacker at a bar, but it was one potential avenue that Kane helped narrow and one that diminished further when Natalie's sister, Olga Antonetti, confirmed that while Natalie was a trusting individual, she was also "conservative with her romantic interests."

After speaking with Olga, Sergeant Balagia brought Donn Chelli to the station and had him sit down with a sketch artist, Austin Police Department Officer William Beechinor. Beechinor had graduated from Southwest Texas State University, where he'd trained and received a degree in commercial art. He'd become a cop, though, starting with the San Marcos Police Department and joining the Austin Police

Department two years later. He had quickly developed a reputation for the cartoons he drew in the corner of the briefing room's whiteboard in the patrol building. And he was a master sketch artist, receiving his training from Texas A&M University, the University of Southern Alabama and the FBI Academy. Together, Beechinor and Chelli constructed a composite of the man Chelli had seen outside his apartment. It was to be released to the media to try to prompt some good citizen's memory. That job done, Balagia and Beechinor then went to Natalie's apartment and made a detailed diagram of the crime scene.

While they were there, Balagia decided to stop at Walter Griffin's apartment and made him promise to come to the station and give a formal statement about seeing Natalie walking by the pool on the night of the attack. Griffin assured him he would.

Their next stop was Sixth Street, where they spoke to Deanna Cooley, who lived in the Barton Creek complex. She'd contacted police after hearing about the assault. She told Sergeant Balagia that on the night of October 12 she'd been partying downtown. She returned home at about four in the morning, heading over to the all-night market behind Natalie's apartment. On the way, she told detectives, she saw a sedan, "beaten up, gray in color." It was parked sideways, parallel to the curb instead of perpendicular, and so was taking up two spaces in front of the building that included Natalie's and Donn Chelli's apartments. Two people were inside the car, Cooley said, a man and a woman. She didn't get the license plate number, nor could she identify the people inside.

The presence of the car and its occupants could have been coincidental, detectives knew. But the way it was parked bore noting. Was it parked ready for a fast getaway? It certainly wasn't the way a resident would park and even if its occupants had no connection to the murder, they might have seen something or someone who was.

On October 16, Sergeant Balagia went back to the crime scene with Sergeant Dusty Hesskew to try to analyze the blood spatter. When they got there, though, Hesskew told Balagia that any firm conclusions would be hard to reach simply because Natalie had moved about so much after the attack, smearing blood and distorting existing patterns. The fact that the EMS crew had worked in the cramped little apartment also tainted an already inexact science. Hesskew told Balagia that before he reached any conclusions, he'd have to look at the couch covers taken from the apartment and all photos taken of the scene.

In the days that followed, Sergeants Eddie Balagia, Howard Hall and Russell Schmidt continued to work the case, interviewing Natalie's friends and family. But on top of the evidentiary issues in the assault, their reliance on Chelli and the dearth of other leads, Eddie Balagia and the detectives had other problems. Five, to be precise.

Five murders in six days. The Austin Police Department's detectives were stretched thin before they even showed up at Natalie's apartment the day of her attack, because they were deep in three of these cases: On October 11, Odessie Dale, Jr., thirty-six, was murdered with a shotgun in east Austin. The next day, Saturday, saw two more murders: Robert Espinoza, seventeen, was stabbed to death in the early hours of the morning and, at about the time Natalie was enjoying herself downtown, alleged drug dealer Curtis Meeks was shot to death just a mile from the Espinoza crime scene. His murder has never been solved.

As Balagia and his team were juggling those investigations and Natalie's, the city suffered two more homicides. On October 16, in the middle of the morning, twenty-three-year-old Linda Guerra was shot and killed in north Austin. Her case, like that of Curtis Meeks, remains unsolved and on the books of Austin's Cold Case Unit. Twenty-four hours after Guerra was killed, Ana Maria Lima, twenty-four, was shot to death in a field in southwest Austin.

This maelstrom of murder pulled the homicide division apart, producing a staggering amount of work, requiring far more from the division's detectives than they could possibly give. The police department's homicide unit had just six detectives.

There was one other major difference, too, that added significantly to the workload of Balagia and his men: When they worked a case, it was their job to collect, bag and tag evidence. This is a painstakingly slow process when done properly and, depending on the scene, can take hours. The importance of that job, in terms of time and dedication, is recognized these days because police departments now employ highly-trained specialists to photograph and take video of crime scenes and handle the collection of evidence. Nowadays, detectives can concentrate on the investigation process itself, a luxury that Eddie Balagia would have surely appreciated. As it was, Balagia himself stuffed the blood-soaked couch cover into a bag.

For all these reasons, the unusually deadly week and the extra tasks ascribed to detectives, Austin's homicide unit was stretched far too thin to do justice to Natalie and to the other people whose lives had been cut short so violently. Natalie's case was an assault, maybe an attempted murder, but not a homicide. That some lead or clue should fall through the cracks was almost inevitable: an alibi not checked, a piece of evidence lost, a witness statement not written down. Tasks small enough to slip by unnoticed, but whose significance would later, so very much later, become apparent.

Balagia and his team did all they could, welcoming clues and calls from wherever they came, even fielding one call, via the police tips hotline, claiming that Johnny had killed his mother for insurance money. No one took this particular tip seriously, as there was no insurance money and Johnny had no other reason to harm Natalie. Every witness police talked with said the same thing: Johnny and Natalie adored each other.

As busy as they were, detectives were grateful for volunteer help. Natalie's former boyfriend Dennis Davis offered to use his music scene contacts to collect as many Lotions T-shirt designs as he could and deliver them to police, which he did. Davis also called in a couple of phone tips, suggesting people for Balagia to interview.

As the detectives kept working, they continued to compare suspects to the description given by Chelli of the mystery man wearing a T-shirt with the Lotions' logo. They talked to a part-time boat captain named Brent Smith who knew Natalie casually and examined the alibi of another man who roughly matched the description of the "Lotions man" and had previously caused a disturbance at Natalie's apartment complex. They also interviewed a known burglar who had been operating in the area. All to no avail.

Natalie remained in critical condition for more than two weeks, until October 31, when she died. She was never able to tell anyone what had happened or who had attacked her.

On November 1, Dr. Roberto J. Bayardo conducted an autopsy. His conclusions strongly indicated murder:

> It is my opinion, based on investigation of the circumstances and the findings at autopsy, that the decedent, Natalie Antonetti, came to her death as a result of skull fracture and contusions of cerebrum. Homicide. Delayed death.

Natalie Antonetti's passing was noted in the city's newspaper. On November 1 a headline on page B12 of *The Austin American Statesman* read: "Austinite beaten in Oct. 13 attack dies at hospital." And the paper laid bare a harsh truth: "Investigators say they have no suspects."

Chapter 4

A NEW LEAD

Detectives thought they had caught a break when, on November 2, they received a call from Donn Chelli. He told them that he'd just seen the man he saw outside his apartment the night of Natalie's attack. They raced to pick up Chelli and went looking. They searched the Barton Springs area and eventually found Seth Pickett, a middle-aged transient hiding in a baseball dugout just off West First Street.

They placed him under arrest and took him downtown where they checked his criminal history. Plenty of arrests for public intoxication, but nothing to indicate a violent, let alone murderous, streak. Nevertheless, they took his fingerprints to compare them to any that might be found at the scene. They also administered a polygraph exam, where he was asked if he knew anything about the assault and if he had done it. He denied everything and passed the polygraph.

He wasn't their man.

The subsequent days and weeks were filled with interviews for the investigators. In one significant twist, Jolene Wells stopped cooperating on the advice of her attorney and no new leads had come their way to counterbalance that loss of information. Yet detectives kept going, talking to more friends of Natalie, taking written statements but learning nothing new. They wanted, just to be thorough, to have Johnny take a polygraph test. He'd left Austin within a week of his mother's death, returning to Florida to be with his father. Investigators learned he was coming back to Austin sometime over the Christmas period, so they arranged to meet with him then.

On December 27, Johnny took a polygraph test. It was no surprise to anyone when he repeated what he'd already told detectives and when his responses came back as "truthful" on his polygraph. While he was there, though, Sergeant Balagia pressed Johnny about why Jolene might have gone silent on them or, as Balagia wrote in his offense report entry, displayed an "uncooperative attitude." Johnny confessed to detectives that he had no idea. He couldn't understand why she would start acting that way. He told them that he'd asked her himself and immediately she'd become defensive and refused to talk about it.

The New Year came and went with no new leads, but on January 27, Sergeant Eddie Balagia got a telephone call. Austin Police Lieutenant James Baker told him that he had a man in custody with whom Balagia might want to speak. The man had been arrested for breaking into a woman's apartment and raping her. And that wasn't all.

The man, Lieutenant Baker said, was John "Marty" Odem and not only did he fit the description of Chelli's lurker, but also Odem lived in the same apartment complex as Natalie. Something about the man, his attitude, his demeanor, had triggered suspicion that maybe he knew something about Natalie's murder. With too much time already wasted, Eddie Balagia moved quickly. He found out that although Marty Odem was facing two counts of burglary and one of sexual assault, he was still willing to talk to detectives.

Before paying Odem a visit, Balagia pulled the file of Odem's fingerprints and compared them to those found at the scene. No match. He also called Bruce Boardman, a sergeant in the sex crimes unit. Boardman confirmed that Odem lived in the same apartment complex as Natalie and then offered to contact Odem's roommate to see if he'd talk to the detectives.

On January 28, Glen Sloan sat down with Sergeant Eddie Balagia. He said that he'd lived with Marty Odem since August, but had known him for twelve years, because they grew up in the same neighborhood.

He described Odem as "the type of person who is extremely hot tempered" and, when angry, went into "an uncontrollable rage." He also said that Odem was a habitual liar who fantasized his lies to the point where he believed them to be reality and, if confronted about a lie, flew into a rage and turned on whoever was questioning him, even a close friend.

Sloan went on to say that in the past four years he'd seen Odem change in the way he treated women. Odem, Sloan said, had turned more violent. Even though Sloan had not seen it himself, his wife, Odem and other friends had told Sloan that Odem had seriously assaulted most of the women he'd dated.

As for Odem's nocturnal activities, Sloan said that Odem liked to hang out on Sixth Street and when he did, it was with the intention of picking up girls. But Sloan added: "It usually turns out that he just hangs around down there and doesn't pick anyone up."

But Odem was bringing home new things for their apartment and Sloan had no idea from where. A watch, a video recorder, stereo equipment and even a computer "all appeared after I got back from Houston over the Thanksgiving weekend." A neck chain and watch had "popped up" since then. When Sloan asked Odem where they came from, Odem told stories about mafia theft rings and gave other equally outlandish explanations.

On the weekend of Natalie's attack, Sloan said, he and Odem had gone to New Braunfels on Friday, returning on Saturday at about five in the afternoon. They headed to Sixth Street just before nine to meet friends, Odem driving, and they spent most of the evening at a Sixth Street restaurant.

At about midnight, roughly the time Natalie went to the same restaurant for pizza, Odem took one of their friends home because the friend felt sick. Sloan didn't think that Odem returned to the bar, because he remembered having to find another ride home. And when he got home, he saw the ill friend asleep on the couch, but not Odem. Sloan headed out again, to Eleventh Street this time, and arrived home several hours later. He didn't see Odem in the apartment, though he told Balagia he didn't search the apartment to see whether his roommate was there. He might have been, Sloan said, and he just didn't see him.

Sloan then gave Balagia an interesting piece of information, something directly related to Natalie:

Sometime around the beginning of October Marty mentioned the fact that he had met a woman who lived at the
complex. He stated that he had met her at the [self-service
laundry center] located behind the convenience market and
that her apartment was located right next to the market on
the side of the [center]. He further stated that she offered
to share a bottle of wine with him. Marty said that he had
sex with her but that she then made him leave. His reason
for her making him leave was because he thought that she
had a boyfriend. He seemed dumfounded, like he couldn't
believe it that she would make him leave. When Marty told
me this I got the impression that it had occurred probably
the night before he had told me about it. Later on Marty
pointed out the apartment to me that the woman lived in.
The apartment that he pointed out was downstairs, next to
the [laundry center] and was behind the market. I am absolutely positive that the apartment he pointed out to me was
one of the two end apartments.

The story was intriguing on several levels. It didn't necessarily
fit with the descriptions of Natalie's sexual behavior, as described by
Davey Kane and Natalie's sister Olga. But the description of the apartment was right; it certainly seemed like it was Natalie's. To be sure,
Sergeants Balagia and Boardman drove Sloan to the complex and asked
him to point out the exact apartment Odem had identified to him.
Immediately he pointed to Natalie's. He told the detectives that until
they had told him, he had no idea Natalie Antonetti had lived there.

Sloan also had no idea the detectives were investigating a murder.
He'd assumed it was just an assault. When detectives corrected that
impression, Sloan asked if the victim had been stabbed. Balagia said
no. Sloan then asked if she'd been beaten with fists and again was told
no. Balagia later noted in his report that "he then looked at me in a
sort of peculiar way and asked if a baseball bat had been used." When
Sergeant Balagia wanted to know why he asked that, Sloan responded
that Odem wasn't into playing sports but used to keep a baseball bat
around the apartment. Sloan added that he hadn't seen it recently.

Back at the police station, Glen Sloan ended his statement by offering an opinion, one that stood out to Sergeant Balagia, because Sloan and Odem had known each other for so long, had grown up together and were now roommates. Sloan said: "I do think that Marty is capable of killing a person. When he loses his temper he loses total control. I would not be surprised to learn that Marty had killed someone and I did not realize that he was a time bomb waiting to explode."

Chapter 5

MORE QUESTIONS, FEW ANSWERS

Later that same day, Sergeants Balagia and Boardman sat down with Marty Odem, who was brought to the homicide interview room and agreed to waive his right to remain silent. He wanted to talk about what police phrased to him as an "assault" on Natalie Antonetti.

He began by saying that he'd never heard of her, didn't even know the name. Sergeant Balagia showed him Natalie's picture. Odem studied it for a moment and then said: "She's a lot better looking in this picture than the person I know." Still holding the picture, he told the detectives: "Prove I did it. You won't find my prints, saliva or blood in her apartment." He then told them that they wouldn't find a single witness who saw him at or leaving her apartment the night of the assault.

Sergeant Balagia noted in his report of the interview that while Odem was talking, Odem stared intently at the photograph of Natalie and that "Odem had an answer to every question asked and that the answers simply rolled off his tongue, as if they were coming off the top of his head without thinking."

Without saying what the inconsistencies in Odem's story were, Sergeant Balagia did note that when confronted with the inconsistencies, Odem exploded with anger. Sergeant Balagia didn't believe a lot of the things the man was saying. His report stated:

It seemed to me that Odem is the type of person to constantly tell lies about all aspects of his life and that he can't handle it emotionally when he's forced to confront his lies. He then retreats into his anger and tries to camouflage his getting caught lying by using intimidation and making a show of his rage.

Sergeant Balagia then offered Odem the chance to take a polygraph exam. Odem agreed, saying he wasn't scared, because police had no hard evidence with which to convict him. That was his theme for the interview, almost taunting the two cops with their lack of evidence against him.

Odem's violent nature and his admission to the rape charge and burglaries made him a strong suspect, as did his claim to Glen Sloan that he'd slept with Natalie, who had then insulted him by kicking him out. But some of his comments during the interview caused Sergeant Balagia to wonder if Odem was all bluster. Most notably, Odem kept asking to be confronted by Natalie, to see if she could identify him.

Balagia and Sergeant Boardman paid another visit to Glen Sloan and asked permission to search the apartment for the baseball bat. He let them in, but after a thorough search they were unable to find it or anything else to link Odem to the crime.

But they weren't done with Odem yet. They went to the city jail to pick him up and took him to a polygrapher who asked Odem the same questions he had asked all of the witnesses in Natalie's case, including whether or not Odem was involved in the murder, whether he knew who was and whether he was lying about his involvement. From beginning to end, Odem denied having anything to do with Natalie's death.

The polygraph test's results told a different story, coming back as "deceptive." The polygrapher told police he felt Odem was responsible for the attack.

The detectives took Odem back to the station and sat him down for another interview. He continued to deny his involvement and called the polygrapher a liar, working himself into a rage and laying all the blame for the police's interest in him on the polygrapher.

Odem then changed his story, telling Sergeant Balagia and Sergeant Boardman that he'd never even met Natalie and that he'd made up the story about sleeping with her. He said he'd met a girl that fit her description but he'd only chatted with her, never had any kind of relationship. Odem then clenched his fists, closed his eyes and began yelling, "I didn't do it!"

Suddenly he calmed down and smiled at Sergeant Balagia. "You'll never be able to prove it and you know it," Odem said.

Balagia knew Odem might be right. Not just because of the lack of evidence putting Odem at the scene, but also because he might be innocent. His roommate, Glen Sloan, hadn't been able to give Odem an alibi nor would anything Sloan had said prevent Odem from claiming he was in his bed the night of the assault. Also, his car didn't match the one Deanna Cooley had seen outside the apartments.

Sergeant Balagia left the interview room to call Odem's girlfriend, Hollie Meeks. Sergeant Balagia began by asking if she would come immediately to the homicide unit to give a statement. She agreed and Sergeant Balagia waited patiently for her to arrive. Once she arrived, Balagia asked about her contact with Odem on the weekend of the attack on Natalie. Meeks said she hadn't seen Odem that weekend, not spending time with him until the Monday afterwards, perhaps later.

Sergeant Balagia left her for a moment and returned to Odem's interview room, where he again asked Odem about his movements that weekend. Odem insisted he'd been in New Braunfels the whole weekend, a story the detectives believed to be untrue.

As they were talking, Odem changed his demeanor again. He told them that he'd spun a few lies to them, but he was now telling the truth. He hadn't killed Natalie, he said, but if Sergeant Balagia could show him some evidence of his guilt, he'd confess. And until he was shown some proof, he wasn't going to talk to them. Odem then smiled at Sergeant Balagia and added: "You can't pin the murder on me and there's nothing you can do about it."

Sergeant Balagia decided to rattle the smugness right out of Odem. He left the interview room and returned a few minutes later with Hollie Meeks. She repeated what she'd told Sergeant Balagia about not seeing Odem that weekend.

Odem stared at her for a moment and then told her, clearly and unequivocally, that she was mistaken and that he had been with her.

Apparently intimidated, Meeks turned to Sergeant Balagia and told him she'd been confused and maybe Odem was right that they had been together. Seeing that Meeks was about to lose all composure, Sergeant Balagia took her out of the interview room and away from Odem, who was himself taken out in handcuffs and sent back to the city jail.

Then Sergeant Balagia sat down with Hollie Meeks for a formal statement.

She told him in some detail about Odem's violent nature. He began getting rough with her, she said, in May of the year Natalie was killed, showing an obsession with being the boss and not feeling like a man. Meeks said that at first he just yelled, threw things and pushed her. She started fighting back and after a while he moved out and headed to Houston. Three weeks later, she said, he came back saying that he missed her. But there was another reason he'd left Houston, according to Meeks: He'd gotten into a fight and bitten off someone's nose.

She said that the "rough stuff" with Odem picked up where it left off. She told Sergeant Balagia about an incident at a Willie Nelson concert when they got into an argument and Meeks tried to get a ride home with some friends. Odem grabbed her and dragged her through the parking lot. When some male bystanders tried to help her, he told them she'd given him herpes. Most of the men left him alone at that point but one, an off-duty cop, told Odem to lay off her. Odem told the man to "fuck off and mind his own business." Odem dragged Meeks into his car and sped off, driving wildly until they got home. There, he hauled her from the car by her hair and attacked her. He blackened her face, she said, and broke her left arm. He then dragged her into the bedroom, pulled out a knife and threatened to cut off her nipples. To show he was serious, Odem began stabbing the bed around her.

Eventually he passed out and Meeks said she waited thirty minutes before calling a friend to come get her. They went to the hospital, but she lied about how she'd gotten her injuries, too scared to tell the truth.

The violence didn't stop. She told Sergeant Balagia that Odem had beaten her twice since, "once breaking my nose and the other time possibly breaking my jaw and giving me a blood clot."

She also echoed Glen Sloan's fears about Odem: "When Marty is in one of his rages I think he could accidentally kill someone but never intentionally. When he gets into one of his rages I sometimes have the feeling that he could get out of control."

Meeks's statement didn't say anything about a baseball bat, nor did it clarify her or Marty Odem's whereabouts the weekend Natalie was attacked.

At Sergeant Balagia's request, Sergeant Howard Hall drove to Barton Hills with a photo lineup that included Marty Odem. He found Donn Chelli at home and showed him the pictures.

Chelli stared at the faces for a moment and then pointed to Marty Odem. He said that Odem looked something like the man he'd seen outside his apartment on October 13, but he couldn't be sure. He said if he saw the man in a real lineup, in person, he might be surer. The offense report indicates that an in-person lineup was never done.

Leads continued to trickle in and detectives followed up on each one, no matter how unlikely it seemed at the time. As new crimes filtered into the homicide division, detectives looked at those cases with an eye toward solving Natalie's murder.

One such possibility was an early suspect in the murder of Connie Jane Bibb, a senior at the University of Texas who was found strangled in her home on Thanksgiving Day. The man police were interested in at the time had met Bibb at a club on Sixth Street and had been linked to clubs in the area at about the same time Natalie was spending her evenings on Sixth Street. But nothing else, as it turned out, suggested the man as Natalie's killer. The murder of Connie Jane Bibb remains unsolved, though detectives at APD's cold case squad have not forgotten her.

Similarly, one day a police officer pulled over a vehicle and while talking to the driver noticed a length of lead piping that was tucked by the seat of the female passenger. One end of the pipe was wrapped in tape as a makeshift handle and the other appeared to be stained red. When the officer seized the weapon, it looked to him like hair was matted in the red blood-like substance. It was never connected to

Natalie's murder, though police assumed it was used as a weapon in some other bloody dispute.

These tips and others were passed on to Sergeant Balagia, who ran each lead until it ended and he was forced to turn his attention to his other cases.

Eventually the leads dried up altogether.

The file was left virtually untended as time passed, with just one brief notation as a reminder should someone find the bags containing Natalie's clothing or the blood-stained sofa cover and want to dispose of them:

> As of this date, 3/21/95, this is still an unsolved murder. Do not destroy evidence.

There is also a reminder of the importance police placed on Donn Chelli as the only man believed to have seen, even spoken to, the killer. On July 31, 1997, homicide detective Hector Reveles updated the files with Chelli's new Nevada driver's license number and his new phone number.

And for the next nine years, that was that.

Plenty happened to those who were touched by the investigation. Natalie was buried in the Forest Park Westheimer Cemetery in Houston, Texas.

Johnny moved back to Austin and became a musician, fulfilling the dream he'd carried with him as a child, a dream his mother had nurtured. He remained in Austin and grew into a confident and good-looking man, playing to the crowds and the pretty girls with delight. He married one of them and it was one of the momentous occasions in his life that made him feel very keenly the absence of his mother. But he kept busy. For Johnny, the nineteen-nineties and early two-thousands became a whirl of recording, live performances, tours, concerts and band changes. A talent on the guitar, keyboards and many other instruments, he also wrote, co-wrote and sang. Ten years later Johnny experienced another of those times when his mother should have been there, when her absence hurt more than usual: the end of his marriage. With Natalie unable to provide comfort, Johnny quite naturally expressed his emotions in his music.

Sergeant Eddie Balagia continued to work in homicide, handling several other high-profile cases until, just a few years later, he went for a routine physical as required by the department and came away with a diagnosis of cancer. He died soon after, on November 25, 1990.

Donn Chelli, Eddie Balagia's eyewitness, moved to Las Vegas, Nevada, and later to Los Angeles. Balagia would never know about some of the odd reports that Chelli began to file, nor of the paranoid behavior that led him to conceal his physical address like a master criminal. Eventually, Chelli himself developed cancer, but unlike Balagia he fought it off.

As for Sergeant Balagia's prime suspect, Marty Odem, he was offered a plea deal if he admitted to killing Natalie, but he refused, stolidly maintaining his innocence. He admitted, though, to the other burglaries and rape of which he was accused and was sentenced to thirty years for aggravated sexual assault. He was released from prison on October 30, 1996.

Chapter 6

FROM COLD TO WARM

Years passed, but all it took was a phone call. One phone call to a homicide detective and the case came alive. Barely moving at first, the vital signs faint until a cold case detective was called in to see if it could breathe again, to see if, with care and attention, it could be brought back from the dead.

The call came on July 7, 2006 and was received by homicide detective Manuel Fuentes, who recorded it.

The voice was female, the caller saying that she was a friend of Dennis Davis. She said that Davis had told her about a previous girlfriend of his named Natalie who had been killed and that the murder was unsolved. The caller relayed several facts of the case, including the correct year as well as the delay between the attack and Natalie's death. She said that Davis was a recording engineer at the time of the murder.

Then the caller said that Davis had told her that he had "sinned against God and man." She also said that Davis had demonstrated violent tendencies, but she did not elaborate. She said he was now living in Pennsylvania and that his health was less than perfect. The caller admitted that she had no direct knowledge of Davis's involvement in Natalie's death and that he had never confessed his involvement. But his statement that he'd "sinned against God and man" bothered her and she thought police ought to know about it.

A copy of the recording of the phone call was put in the official file. And the case went back to sleep, for just a little while.

Thomas Walsh was one of five detectives in the Austin Police Department's Cold Case Unit, one of a select band of men and women chosen to sift through evidence and transcend time, to do what the hard-working detectives of the Austin Police Department's Homicide Division were unable to do the first time around: catch a killer.

The cold case unit, founded in 2000, always worked closely with the homicide unit. Since 2005, cold case had been run by Sergeant Ron Lara, who was a slight man, energetic and friendly, with dark eyes that watched you carefully when you spoke. His desk was always tidy and it carried two picture frames. One held photos of four teen girls killed in Austin's most famous murder, known as "the yogurt shop murders." Next to them was the face of a six-year-old girl, Volith Long, who was sexually assaulted and murdered, her body wrapped in a curtain and thrown into a dumpster. Lara solved the case fifteen years later. He was a champion for all his cold cases and because he ran an elite unit, he got to handpick his detectives.

That meant Austin's cold case unit was staffed by the best of the best, experienced detectives, usually from the homicide division, who were happy to leave the sprint to solve new homicides for the marathon that is a cold case. Many marathons, actually, because each detective handled approximately thirty cases, though when one heated up, when a detective got close to the killer, they banded together to help, to make sure the job was done and done right. The oldest case they had dated to 1967 and at any one time the unit had files on about 140 unsolved cases.

Detective Tom Walsh, at forty-nine years old and a nineteen-year veteran of the police department, went through the same interview process every applicant did for the cold case unit, but he was one of the rare ones: most came from the regular homicide unit, whereas Walsh was a robbery detective. Even so, Sergeant Lara felt that Walsh would be a perfect fit. "Patient, up-beat and enthusiastic. He was just so passionate about working these cases," was how Lara described Walsh. "He had just the right mentality and I knew he'd fit right in; I never had a doubt."

The passion that Lara spotted was always channeled; Walsh carried with him an air of calm intensity. He was a deeply spiritual man and had a quietness to him, but when he spoke about his cases, in a voice that was soft and low, he quickly became animated and his commitment burst forth. Intelligent, as all these detectives must be, he was patient while on the trail of a murderer, using logic and facts as his best allies. But he was not one to ignore his intuition and he believed that some things were meant to be, that some cases were meant to be solved. He gave the impression that he'd be a loyal ally and a formidable adversary.

The unsolved murder of Natalie Antonetti was Tom Walsh's case and although she could never know it, Natalie had a very good friend in him.

In January 2007, several months after the anonymous tip from the female caller had been filed away, Tom finished another case, turned to Natalie's and found the recording.

He discovered that the caller was Rebecca Davis. The last name, he quickly found out, was no coincidence—she was Dennis Davis's ex-wife. Walsh called her at her home in Nashville, Tennessee, on January 8, making sure to record their conversation.

Rebecca was surprised and not very happy to be contacted and Walsh reassured her that he would not reveal her identity to anyone. With his soft voice and earnest tone, he got her talking and she repeated what she'd told Manuel Fuentes about Davis, adding that it was her feeling that her ex-husband was referring to Natalie's death when he said he'd sinned. Once again she said he'd never admitted that much to her, though his words about sinning had weighed on her.

After speaking with Rebecca, Walsh looked into Davis's criminal record and found that Rebecca was right about his being violent—he had a conviction for assault nearly two decades earlier.

Walsh recognized the name Dennis Davis. He remembered coming across it while looking into another cold case, that of Debra Jan Baker.

Debra Baker, aged thirty-five, was last seen the night of January 12, 1988. She failed to report for work on January 13 and was found dead in bed by a family member who went to the residence to check on her. Debra had been beaten multiple times with a blunt object and there was evidence of possible forced entry into her residence. Detectives believed that her killer took an electronic device and possibly additional belongings from the residence. They also thought that sexual assault was a possible motive.

Davis's name had been suggested by someone who moved in his circle, someone who was scared of him back then and who still didn't want it known she'd spoken to police. Walsh called and spoke to that woman. She told him that she'd had a bad feeling about Davis back in the mid-eighties, though was unable to say exactly why. She said it was the way Davis treated Natalie; she felt he was just using her.

It wasn't much to go on and it wasn't very specific. But it was something and now that the case was reopened, Walsh started poking around some more.

He began by looking at the suspects at the time the case went cold and decided there were three main leads to follow up on: First was Dennis Davis. He'd get to him in due course.

Second was Marty Odem. Walsh looked over Odem's file and saw him to have been defiant, angry and a confirmed rapist. Not to mention that he failed the polygraph.

Third, in Walsh's view, was Stan Rivera.

During the initial investigation, police had briefly looked at Rivera, but he barely warranted a mention in the official offense report. He had been a friend of young Johnny Goudie. He was also a confirmed and incorrigible flasher. Rivera had numerous arrests for indecent exposure and admitted to a sergeant that at one time he exposed himself two or three times a week, every week.

Tom Walsh noted that Rivera's name had been brought into the original investigation by Dr. Cunningham, a psychiatrist. The call had been taken and noted by Sergeant Howard Hall who wrote that Dr. Cunningham called the night Natalie died in the hospital. The note in Walsh's hand told him that Rivera was "upset and emotional" that night but didn't elaborate further.

On August 23, Walsh paid a visit to Dr. Cunningham, who still lived in Austin. He found her recovering from a heart attack, weak and frail. At first she had trouble remembering the incident, but when Walsh read her the note and showed her Rivera's photograph, it all came back to her. She told Walsh that she'd never called the police about a patient before, but when she heard about Natalie's death and

saw the way Rivera was behaving, she felt obligated to call. As well as
Rivera knowing the son of the victim, Dr. Cunningham said she knew
Rivera kept a baseball bat for protection.

Walsh pushed her to remember more about why she might have
called the police, why she might have thought Rivera had something
to do with Natalie's murder. He asked whether he'd confessed to her,
whether it was just a gut feeling she had or whether something about
her professional encounters with him made her think there was a connection. She said it was her professional background and her working
with Rivera, but she was unable to be more specific.

Walsh thanked her for her time, wished her a speedy recovery
and left. As he drove back to the office, Walsh thought about what
he'd learned. Coincidences, in his opinion, always warranted investigation, but this one hardly made for compelling evidence. Soon after
he got back to the office, the phone rang. It was Dr. Cunningham.

She'd been speaking to her husband about Walsh's visit and he'd
reminded her that, when she and her husband first met, she'd been
sleeping with a gun under her pillow. Walsh asked if that was because
she was afraid of Rivera and she said it was.

Walsh checked deeper into Rivera's background and found a report about his being arrested for the possession of illegal drugs on
Sixth Street the year after Natalie's murder. The following year Rivera
was arrested again for a "disturbance" downtown. Walsh called several
people mentioned in the reports to get more information, but memories had faded in the intervening years. He learned nothing new.

Chapter 7

SEARCHING FOR THE KEY

Having cleared his desk of several other cases, Walsh decided it was time to look deeper into his first suspect in the murder of Natalie Antonetti: Dennis Davis. Walsh decided on a direct approach. He first searched for Davis in Pennsylvania, where his ex-wife said he was living. He found nothing. Eventually he learned that Davis had a brother in Austin and contacted him. But the brothers had not spoken in over a year and the last the brother knew Dennis was working for a company in California.

Walsh tapped into the various law enforcement tools for locating people but again came up empty.

On August 30, he called Rebecca Davis. She told Walsh she'd not had any contact with Davis but would not give him the names of others who might help find him. She denied knowing where Davis was or knowing anyone who did. Walsh, an experienced detective, felt she was lying.

While he was out of the office he received a message to call her. He did so and she told him she was with her sister in Louisiana, helping her recover from surgery. She hesitated and, sure enough, told him what he already knew: She'd lied when they had spoken earlier. She told Walsh that she and Davis had started a reconciliation of sorts and that she knew exactly where he was: at her house. She gave him Davis's cell phone number.

But before Walsh could call Davis, Davis called him. He said that his ex-wife had told him the police wanted to talk. Walsh asked him if he knew what it was about and he simply said: "Natalie Antonetti." Walsh explained that he was working the case, her murder.

"Oh my gosh," Davis said. "I know a lot about that."

Walsh made no accusations, merely telling Davis that he was contacting everyone involved in the case. He asked Davis whether he had been in contact with anyone from that time. Davis said no and gave the same answer when Walsh asked if he'd been in contact with Jolene Wells. He'd last seen her, Davis said, about six months after Natalie died.

Walsh started to talk about the advances in investigative technologies since Natalie's death. "Would you be willing to give us a sample of your DNA?"

Davis hesitated for four or five long seconds and then said: "Sure." He also agreed to give a sample of his hair.

Walsh asked him to keep it confidential that investigators had DNA from the scene and Davis agreed.

They began talking about the time of the murder and Davis said he and Natalie had just broken up and he'd been dating Ampie Garcia.

"How long?" asked Walsh.

"Not long," replied Davis. He said that Garcia had gotten "freaked out" about the assault and they didn't see each other again after that. Walsh sought clarification for what seemed, to him, like an odd statement.

"Freaked out? Why would she be freaked out?"

"Well, it was a murder and all and she didn't want to have anything to do with it."

That didn't clarify much for Walsh, but he let it go. "How long had you been broken up with Natalie?"

"Two days."

"That's not very long."

"I know," Davis agreed.

Walsh then asked about the last time Davis had seen Natalie. Davis said it was two nights before the attack, probably at the club Steamboat and probably when he was with his usual circle of friends.

"Are you coming at this in the dark?" Davis asked. "I have an advantage in that I know all the friends, the people from back then."

He went on to talk about how things were after the attack, how he "got crazy" for a while, because he wanted to know who'd done it and how he'd started following people. At a benefit they had for Natalie's family, the media covered it and he'd hinted to them he knew who the killer was.

Walsh asked when Davis had last slept with Natalie, but Davis said he couldn't remember. He admitted they didn't break up on particularly good terms, saying that Natalie was "sad" and he'd left her because he wanted his freedom.

Walsh moved on to the topic of Jolene Wells. Davis said that they were good friends, but that they had never had any kind of sexual relationship. He thought that Jolene and Johnny had been very much in love.

When asked, Davis said that he knew Stan Rivera; they'd been friends. He and Rivera had tried doing their own investigation into what happened, which included approaching Donn Chelli who, Davis said, had refused to tell him anything.

Finally, Walsh asked Davis for his thoughts on the attack and who he thought was responsible. Davis said that he had no idea, though he mentioned the name Marty Odem and said that both Jolene Wells and Ed Balagia had figured out who the killer was.

Walsh thanked Davis for his time and, before hanging up, asked Davis again if he'd provide a DNA sample. Davis repeated that he would.

Looking back at the file, Walsh realized that no one had double-checked Davis's alibi. After a thorough search through the offense report and the many papers that made up the official investigation files, Walsh realized that no one had ever tried to locate or speak to Ampie Garcia or to identify the friend named Rose that Davis said had picked Garcia up from his house. Davis hadn't been a real suspect in the case, but now his alibi needed to be verified or disproved.

This would not be easy, Walsh knew. One of the biggest problems in solving cold cases is the fading memories of the witnesses. What were the chances of Ampie Garcia remembering whether Davis had been with her that night? She might not even remember the name of her friend, Rose.

But he had to try.

Walsh located Ampie, now Amparo Garcia-Crow. She was still living in Austin and working while also pursuing her musical and acting career. He met her on September 7 and heard what he'd feared: She remembered Dennis Davis but couldn't possibly say, almost twenty-five years later, whether she was with him on a particular night.

"How could I be expected to remember something like that?" she asked. "But," she continued, "I did keep diaries back then. If I spent the night with him, it'd be in there."

Hardly daring to ask, Walsh whispered the question: "Those diaries, is there any chance you still—?"

She did.

After digging them out of her attic she read through them carefully, then prepared and shared with Detective Walsh a summary of her entries relating to Dennis Davis:

Sept. 18: Davis called her for a date.
Sept. 24: She spent the night with Davis.
Oct. 1:   She had a date with Davis.
Oct. 11: This entry related Davis's complaint that Ampie didn't have enough time for him, that she was too busy for him. She commented to Walsh that Davis had previously told her that Natalie had this same complaint about *him*.
Oct. 27: She tried to contact Davis and got no response.
Nov. 12: She made contact with Davis and she thought sometime after that maybe Davis took Rose out on a date.

Amparo Garcia-Crow's diary was a key piece of evidence, because it seemed to contradict several things Davis had said in his initial sworn statement and in his recent conversation with Walsh. It indicated Davis was *not* with Garcia-Crow the night Natalie was assaulted. Which meant that Dennis Davis's alibi had just disappeared.

Another contradiction, albeit minor, was that Davis had accused Ampie of "freaking out" after Natalie's death, of not wanting to see him after that. Walsh felt pretty sure that Ampie was not the "freaking out" type. Quite the opposite: She was calm, put together and quite confident in her demeanor.

But to stand up as evidence, good evidence, Amparo Garcia-Crow would have to be certain about her and Davis's whereabouts. So Walsh asked her again about being with Davis that night and she repeated that she didn't remember being with him in those hours. She *was* sure, however, that if she had been with him at the time of the attack on Natalie, she would remember something so momentous and would have written about it in her diary.

She also addressed the part of Davis's statement that said her friend Rose had picked her up from his home later that morning. Amparo doubted that Rose would have picked her up there, because she didn't think Rose would have known where Davis lived. She added that she'd also remember if she'd woken there alone, because Davis lived with his parents and she would have been unhappy about being left alone with them. As she put it, being abandoned in a hurry, in a strange house, with no explanation and no way to get back to town, would be memorable twenty-five years later, because she would have been *pissed*. And if he'd abandoned her *with* an explanation, told her where he was going and why, that would also have been pretty memorable. Even if she had somehow forgotten, either set of circumstances would absolutely have made it into her diary. After all, she'd logged *every other* interaction with Davis. How could she possibly omit something so momentous? She wouldn't. No way, she told Walsh.

It looked to Walsh like Davis's account of events was a fabrication. And he knew of very few reasons for a man to risk fabricating his alibi in a murder investigation.

Finally, Walsh asked Garcia-Crow if she'd been "freaked out" by what happened to Natalie, as Davis had told him. She said that no, she hadn't been. That was what Walsh had suspected and, when pressed, Garcia-Crow had no explanation of why Davis might say that.

That same day Walsh searched the name *Rose Knowles* that Garcia-Crow had provided him and found her in Queensbury, New York. They spoke on the phone that evening and Rose said she didn't remember a Dennis Davis. She went on to say that she couldn't remember ever picking up Amparo Garcia-Crow from a house in Onion Creek and didn't know where the area was. Even when Walsh described the location it didn't help—she was pretty sure she'd never been down that way, having lived near the university in central Austin. Knowles told Walsh that she didn't remember the attack on Natalie, but said she would have expected to remember something like that if she'd been even remotely connected to it.

With Davis's alibi severely damaged and given his apparent penchant for violence in relationships, he was looking a more likely suspect. But whoever ended up being charged with Natalie's murder, if anyone at all, would have to fit the description given by Donn Chelli. And Davis, Walsh knew, didn't fit the image of the man Chelli had seen. He was about the right height but too slight and he didn't have a belly.

Was it possible Chelli's statement itself was questionable? Walsh looked at it again and compared it with the one given by Fran Alcozer, Chelli's girlfriend at the time. He noted the discrepancies in timing, that Chelli had said he'd told Fran about the man outside when they were downstairs eating breakfast, but she had said they'd been upstairs when he mentioned seeing the man. Walsh listened to Chelli's 911 call and noticed that Chelli referred to the object in the man's hand as a "club," not the "child's baseball bat" he later wrote about in his statement.

Walsh wondered why someone would wait a full hour between seeing an angry man with some sort of weapon looking through his window and calling the police. Something about that just didn't make sense.

He ran a check on incidents in which Chelli had been involved and got two hits. Both were incidents of harassment. Walsh located Chelli in Nevada and found two more similar incidents, one in Henderson and one in Las Vegas. He contacted the police in both cities and requested copies of those reports.

Walsh wanted to talk to Fran Alcozer before confronting Chelli but discovered that she was dead. He managed to find her widower and called him to ask if she had ever said anything to him about Donn Chelli.

"Yes," he said. He told Walsh that his wife had told him that she and Chelli had split up because, as he got older, Chelli became more and more "eccentric." Worse, he developed a wicked temper and had even gotten violent with Fran.

Despite this information, Donn Chelli appeared to have no criminal history and Walsh was not ready to write off his statement or discount him as a witness.

His background work done, Walsh called Chelli in Las Vegas, Nevada. Walsh told him he was looking at Chelli's statement from after Natalie's death and asked Chelli if he could remember anything else he hadn't discussed with police at that time. Chelli responded that it would be best if Walsh could fax a copy of his statement so he could remind himself what had gone on, what he'd seen. But Walsh was after what Chelli remembered, not a recitation of the same facts read from his statement. So he asked him again what he could remember.

Chelli told Walsh he remembered getting up early to get ready for a trip to Las Vegas, for a swimming pool convention. He said he went to the convenience store and came back through the hole in the fence, walking along the back side of the apartments. He stopped at the back of his apartment to say hello to his cats, who were peering down at him from the balcony on the second floor of his apartment. That's when he noticed someone looking into his apartment, he said. He said the man had a small baseball bat in his hand. He didn't remember if the two talked, but he remembered walking around to his front door and going inside to have breakfast. He said he thought about telling the girl he lived with at the time about it and eventually did before calling 911.

Walsh asked him if he really saw someone there. "Yes, absolutely," Chelli said and reminded Walsh he helped construct a drawing of the suspect.

Walsh tried a different approach, asking Chelli about a man named in the Henderson, Nevada, harassment report. Walsh wanted to evaluate Chelli's reliability, even his mental stability. He asked Chelli if he thought the man was still after him. Chelli didn't answer the question directly but his answer was telling. The man, he said, was a bodyguard for someone who was into "illegal stuff." Chelli didn't know him that well but, even so, he said, the man had been out to get him.

Walsh brought the conversation back to the morning of the attack on Natalie and asked Chelli again whether he'd told Fran Alcozer about the lurking man. He repeated that yes, after a while he did.

Walsh had played nice throughout the conversation but decided to put a little pressure on Chelli. "I don't believe that you saw anyone out there that morning," Walsh told him. "You made the whole thing up."

Chelli denied it adamantly, but he was clearly rattled. He started to tell Walsh that he'd have never done anything "to that girl." Walsh agreed, telling Chelli he never was and still wasn't a suspect in the case. For twelve minutes the phone call rambled on, Chelli altering his story and saying he'd phoned police just minutes after reentering the apartment. A little bizarrely, he began referring to a report about organized crime and the FBI. Eventually Walsh and Chelli finished and hung up.

One week later Walsh received a call from Gary Shernak, an attorney in San Antonio who said he was representing Donn Chelli. Walsh told Shernak that Chelli was not a suspect in the case but that he didn't believe Chelli's account of that morning. The two men talked and Shernak agreed with Walsh that Chelli might have some mental or emotional issues. In a second conversation with Shernak, the lawyer said that whatever happened, Chelli believed that he saw someone outside his apartment. Walsh suggested a polygraph but Shernak said he wouldn't recommend his client agree to that. He did promise, however, to talk to his client again and see if he could get any further information from him. Before hanging up, Shernak mentioned that he'd spent two hours on the phone with Chelli, listening to the man rant about the mob being after him. This confirmed Walsh's view that Chelli was an unreliable witness, then and now, and was quite probably clinically paranoid.

With no new information after speaking with Chelli, Walsh turned his attention to the other witness who was at the apartment with Natalie the morning of her attack: Jolene Wells.

One thing Walsh wanted to address was the phone call Jolene had made to Dennis Davis soon after finding Natalie. It was clear to Walsh that the timing of that call needed to be narrowed down as tightly as possible. Was there time for Davis to assault Natalie and get home in time to receive Jolene's call? The first step in answering that question was finding out when in the chaos of that morning Jolene had phoned him. The second would be to make the drive himself to see just how long it would take.

Detective Walsh tracked Jolene to an address in Austin, where she lived in a house that sat about a half mile from the apartment complex on Barton Springs Drive. On two consecutive days, September 17 and 18, Walsh called and left messages at Jolene's home. She returned his calls on the evening of September 18, leaving her own message that she did not want to talk to Walsh and that her lawyer would be in touch with him.

Walsh noted in his report that Jolene Wells "is not a suspect at this point" and that he would wait to hear from her lawyer before considering getting a grand jury subpoena to compel her to testify.

In the meantime, Walsh turned his attention back to the man who had come to be a prime suspect: Dennis Davis. He needed to run the man's "handled bys." These are the reports where someone has been in contact with or "handled by" police as a suspect, victim or witness. For someone's name to come up there did not even need to be an arrest, just a police report written at the time of the incident.

Walsh pulled all reports involving Dennis Davis and started to read. His eyes opened wider and wider and Walsh wondered if maybe, just maybe, Davis could be the one for whom he was searching.

Chapter 8

VIOLENT PAST

The first report, made two years after Natalie's death, listed Dennis Davis as the victim and Kellie Torres as the suspect. The officer wrote of a disturbance at their house where they both had been drinking and she'd gotten upset and started to break things. Davis assured the officer he didn't want to press charges, so the patrolman put Kellie in his squad car to drive her to a friend's house. En route, Kellie told the officer that Davis had a live hand grenade at his house and that she'd hidden it in her room to stop Davis from using it. The officer returned to Davis's house and found what turned out to be a smoke grenade. No charges were filed against either of them.

The next report, dated six months later, listed Kellie as the complainant. She told the officer that Davis had hit her and kicked her out of the house. Davis wasn't present when the police arrived and, despite Kellie having a witness, she chose not to press charges.

The next report involving Davis was filed more than a year later. It did not seem to involve Kellie, at least as far as Walsh could tell from the narrative. The report said that Davis had followed a pickup truck out of the parking lot of the strip mall where Studio D was located, chased after it in his car and rammed it into a telephone pole. The driver ended up punching Davis in the mouth and several witnesses confirmed what the victim told police. Though Davis himself didn't give a statement, his lawyer offered a "hypothetical" as to why a man might ram the vehicle of a complete stranger. That hypothetical involved the man seeing a woman he thought was his girlfriend getting into the vehicle of another man. In other words, a case of misplaced jealousy. Again, no criminal charges were filed against Davis, the matter being settled in the civil courts.

Less than a month later, though, Davis was arrested for assaulting Kellie. Apparently he'd seen her at a club on South Congress in Austin, roughly three weeks after they'd broken up. He offered her a ride home and she accepted, but they stopped at Studio D on the way. There, she said, he started ranting and raving so she left and walked to her apartment, which was close by. Davis followed her and she made the mistake of letting him into her apartment. Almost immediately he worked himself into another rage but this time took it further, attacking her and punching her in the head and back. The officer noted in his report that he could see "visible bruises and abrasions on her body." Kellie told the officer that it was only after she'd collapsed on the floor that Davis stopped the attack and left the apartment. He was gone by the time police arrived. The officer called EMS and an ambulance took her to St. David's Hospital for treatment. This time Kellie did press charges. Subsequently Davis was arrested and charged with assault, a Class A misdemeanor. He pled guilty to the charge.

These incidents with Kellie Torres were the first indications to Detective Walsh that Davis had a mean, even violent, side. He particularly noted the attack that came after the couple had broken up, very suggestive given that Davis and Natalie Antonetti had ended their relationship just before the assault on her.

Walsh traced Kellie Torres to an address in the Southeast and called her on September 24. He introduced himself and began by asking if she had any idea why he might be calling. Immediately she responded: "It's about Natalie." She told Walsh she hadn't known Natalie but had lived with the guy whom people accused of killing her.

"By 'people,' who do you mean exactly?" Walsh asked.

"Everyone," she replied.

Kellie went on to talk about the incidents that had been recorded by the patrol officers at that time, saying that Davis was "literally nuts" and describing how she'd woken one day to find him holding a gun to her head.

Then she recounted details about Davis that weren't in any police report.

Kellie told Walsh about the incident in which she went to the hospital, filling in a few details that were not included in the official report, but which told Walsh plenty. Davis had snuck into Kellie's house as she was sleeping and started beating her. The injuries had been so bad, she told Walsh, because Dennis Davis had assaulted her with a small baseball bat. They were, as Walsh thought, no longer a couple at that time.

The story astounded Detective Walsh and, as far as he was concerned, looked like it might just be the key to the case.

Then she discussed further information which Walsh noted as even more potent. When she and Davis were living together in Austin, within walking distance of Natalie's apartment, Davis went into a "three day binge of a rage." Kellie was so scared she hid in the attic for much of his rampage, almost eighteen hours. When she eventually came out she found Davis in the front yard "in a fetal position crying or bawling like a big baby."

He kept repeating that he was sorry, so sorry and Kellie first assumed he was apologizing to her for his outburst. But when she asked him what he was sorry for, he replied that he didn't mean to do it.

"Do what?" Kellie asked.

His response shocked her: He said he was sorry for killing Natalie, that he didn't mean to do it. He also said, oddly, that Natalie had been pregnant with his baby, which was not true. Kellie told Walsh that she asked Davis over and over, for thirty minutes, what he meant, what he was talking about, but he just kept saying that'd he'd killed Natalie but didn't mean to.

As if that bombshell wasn't enough, Kellie also provided Walsh with other important details. She told him that while living with Davis, she found a small wooden box in the house. She opened it and saw women's jewelry, "a couple pair of women's panties and a special rabbit's foot." Davis walked in and caught her with the box, she said, and he snatched it away from her. He told her that the items were his "trinkets." While he didn't say which trinket, he told her one of them had belonged to Natalie.

All of this was stunning information from Walsh's perspective. He now had a witness who could testify that Davis had confessed to the crime. While some confessions are suspect, he knew, the ones that usually came under the greatest scrutiny were those offered under pressure from the authorities, given under the influence of some drug or as the result of braggadocio. This one didn't fit any of those categories: It was completely unprompted, offered while sober and to someone who couldn't possibly have intimidated a false confession from Davis.

Walsh asked Kellie why she'd not come forward before. The answer was a mix of disbelief that someone she knew would do such a thing, fear of retaliation by Davis and denial.

After hanging up with Kellie, Walsh reflected on their conversation. On top of the startling confession, Kellie had also confirmed that Davis kept a baseball bat, a small one, just like the one that could have been used to beat Natalie. And it sounded like Davis had also kept a souvenir.

During their telephone conversation, Kellie mentioned to Walsh a man named Jimmy Rose, describing him as one of Dennis Davis's best friends. Walsh looked him up and found him still living in Austin. Walsh called him and Rose told Walsh he'd been waiting a very long time for someone to talk to him about Dennis Davis. So on October 17, 2007, he willingly gave an official sworn statement.

Rose began by saying he met Davis sometime around twenty-six years earlier but hadn't heard from him in almost twenty years. During that time, Rose said, "I considered him by best friend and loved him like a brother." He told Walsh that the loss of contact, he believed, came from Davis's guilt over Natalie's death. "I think he knew I suspected that he had killed Natalie."

Rose told Walsh what happened the night before Natalie was attacked. He'd been on Sixth Street at Club Steamboat, he said, and at one in the morning witnessed a big fight between Davis and Natalie. The argument started when Davis saw her talking to another man, Rose told Walsh, and was "mostly verbal but was very emotional."

The argument began as Rose was about to leave the club and so he took Davis with him, leaving Natalie behind.

Rose had plenty to say about his former best friend's temperament. "I knew Dennis to be a very jealous and very violent man...I say that Dennis was a violent and jealous man because I have witnessed this. I have witnessed him losing his temper and go into a rage and breaking things. Once he would lose his temper and go into a rage I could not calm him down."

But could he have killed Natalie? Rose seemed to think so. "I remember thinking that Dennis could have possibly done this because of the argument I witnessed several hours earlier at the club and knowing his jealous and violent nature. I think I was too close to Dennis at the time to really believe it was him."

According to Rose, not only did Davis have the temperament to kill Natalie, but he had the means, too.

"When I lived with Dennis, I found a wooden baseball bat under my bed. The baseball bat was a souvenir type, maybe eighteen inches long. I assumed that it belonged to Dennis. I thought that Dennis put the bat there. I later felt that Dennis put it there so I would find it. This was about a year after Natalie died...This is when I really started believing that Dennis killed Natalie." Not knowing what else to do, Rose said he hid the bat between his mattress and box springs. He never found out what happened to it, because he moved out of the apartment soon after without ever seeing it again.

Rose also commented on Davis's demeanor after Natalie's death, saying that at first Davis appeared to be grieving but quickly started acting in a way that seemed out of character, taking large amounts of aspirin or stalking Sixth Street acting like he was going to find Natalie's killer. Rose said he wondered at the time whether Davis's behavior was prompted by a guilty conscience.

Walsh was now building a clearer picture of Dennis Davis and his treatment of women. Every witness he spoke with filled in the picture a bit more. Rose's former girlfriend Linda Bless was one. She'd never dated Davis, she told Walsh, but she felt like he'd wanted to and stalked her a few times. He often "talked bad about and degraded" the men she dated and while she couldn't prove it was him, she suspected Davis of leaving violent and pornographic material on the windshield of her car on several occasions.

Even more disturbing, Bless said, was that when Rose was living with Davis at his parents' house in Onion Creek, Davis sometimes walked into Rose's bedroom while she was visiting Rose. Sometimes it was while they were asleep and sometimes he came in while they were making love. He just stood there, watching and staring, until Rose yelled at him to leave.

Bless also confirmed what Kellie Torres had told Walsh about Davis:

> Kellie would call me on the phone and tell me that Dennis had freaked out again and assaulted her. She told me that he would punch her in the face, kick her and lock her out of the house. At first I thought that Kellie was exaggerating, but over time I witnessed some of the abuse and knew that she was telling the truth.

And Bless, too, saw Davis with a baseball bat. She was at Dennis and Kellie's home in Barton Hills when something seemed to upset Davis. She told Walsh that Davis disappeared from the living room but came back a few minutes later with the bat in his hand. She couldn't recall his exact words, but he insinuated that he'd used the bat before and would happily use it again. Bless said that Davis continued to stand there intimidating them with the bat until she got up and talked to him, calming him down.

She added that this wasn't the first time she'd seen him with the bat, which he kept under his bed. Somewhat ominously, Davis once told Bless: "You never know when you might need a bat."

Bless herself received one specific threat from Davis that was witnessed. It came in the form of a phone message left at the apartment where she was living at the time with Davey Kane.

Detective Walsh contacted Kane, who told Walsh in a statement that just a few short months after Natalie's death the phone had rung during the night, but they hadn't answered it. In the morning they discovered a message from Davis. In his statement, Kane told Walsh: "He said something to the effect of he was going to come in and break her legs and bash her head in if she didn't stop seeing who she was seeing. I think the reason was because of his jealousy."

At the time, Kane was concerned enough to take out the tape and give it to his brother, asking him to listen to it for himself. Kane didn't report it to the police or confront Davis, Kane said, because they'd been friends. When Walsh followed up with Kane's brother, the brother remembered being told about the tape's existence and its contents, but he couldn't remembering having it or listening to it himself.

And after twenty-two years, the tape itself was long gone.

Further affirmation of Davis's volatile and jealous nature came when another ex-girlfriend of Davis came forward. Her name was Laurie Emerson and she told Walsh that Davis had told her all about Natalie's death, for some reason distorting what happened. She remembered Davis saying that Natalie had been stabbed multiple times while he was out at the store and he'd returned to find her with blood spattered everywhere. He was even wrong, at the time, when he told Emerson that he was the number one suspect in her murder. Emerson told Walsh that she felt like Davis was "unloading" and "dumping information to get it off his chest." Not surprisingly, she stopped seeing him soon after that.

She also told Walsh about Davis's jealous nature, once again exhibited after he'd stopped dating someone. Emerson had parked her car outside a friend's house soon after she stopped dating Davis and returned the next morning to find all the tires flat. On the windshield she found several of Dennis Davis's business cards. When she saw Davis on Sixth Street not long after, he brought up the incident, freely admitting he'd done it. He was smug, she said, "as if he was taunting me with it."

Detective Tom Walsh now was armed and ready. He consulted with his colleagues and with Assistant District Attorney Darla Davis. They agreed: It was time for an in-person interview with Dennis Davis.

On April 1, 2008, ADA Davis waited outside the room as Walsh and Detective Steve Meaux sat down with Dennis Davis at the Venango County Courthouse in western Pennsylvania. Davis was serving a short jail sentence for driving under the influence and was brought into the room wearing an orange jumpsuit. Although Walsh was planning to take the interview slow, not necessarily letting Davis know he was a suspect, he wanted to make sure Davis's words could be used in court, so he began by reading Davis his rights and also videotaping the interview.

They chatted for a while, settling on pizza and soft drinks for their interview meal, continuing the informal banter while they waited for the food to be delivered. And then slowly, like an engineer tweaking the buttons of a recording deck, Walsh tuned the conversation to the right frequency. For the next couple of hours they talked about Natalie's murder, Davis standing by the written statement he had given to Detective Eddie Balagia, swearing it to be the whole truth. But when Walsh pressed, Davis began to concede ground. He admitted leaving a nasty note for Natalie but claimed he couldn't remember when he'd taped it on her door. He agreed that he used to go into rages but told Walsh that he was always in control when he did so.

He insisted throughout that he'd been with Ampie Garcia the night of Natalie's attack, that he'd left her behind and raced over to Natalie's place after Jolene had called.

"Did you own a baseball bat?" Walsh asked at one point.

Davis looked surprised at the question and immediately denied it, denying it a second time later in the interview. Walsh knew that Davis was lying about this, because Davis's best friend, among several others, had said he'd owned a child-sized baseball bat. Davis's denials, including his confession to Kellie Torres, were quiet but emphatic that afternoon. Neither man raised his voice, Walsh wanting Davis to unburden his heart, admit his crime on his own.

More than five hours after they'd walked into the room they ended the interview. Davis had not confessed, but he'd said something that Walsh would remember. In a calm, almost resigned, voice, Davis told him: "Very compelling, yes... jealous boyfriend writes note, puts it on the door, has a big argument, alibi no good. Next thing you know there it is, black and white, it's all laid out."

Over the next year, Walsh crisscrossed Texas and beyond collecting statements and interviewing everyone connected to Natalie's case. He looked deeper into Marty Odem's alibi to be sure he wasn't missing something, interviewing all associates of Odem he could find. But nothing changed Walsh's mind that Odem, although a superficially attractive suspect, was innocent of killing Natalie.

Finally, with his other suspects excluded and all the evidence pointing to one man, he felt the case was ready.

On June 30, 2009, Assistant District Attorney Darla Davis presented the case to the grand jury. Kellie Torres and Tom Walsh were the only witnesses and the grand jury returned a true bill of indictment. Davis was arrested at his home on July 3 and he decided not to fight extradition to Texas.

The *Austin American Statesman* ran a story with the headline: "Suspect in 1985 Austin homicide arrested." The story read:

> Dennis Davis…was the ex-boyfriend of Natalie Antonetti, 38, who died from injuries after an assault in October 1985, police said…Investigators interviewed Davis after the death, but he was never listed as a suspect. The Austin Police Department's Cold Case Unit re-examined the case in 2007 after detectives received an anonymous tip that produced other leads, police said.

Beside the article was the book-in photograph of Dennis Davis, not looking at the camera, his eyes focused up and to the left.

Chapter 9

INTO MY HANDS

At this point, I was on my second tour of duty in the district attorney's office. It had been a long road, but this time I was there to stay. I'd been intensely curious about murderers. Not just because I wanted to know what made them tick, why they killed, but also because I wanted to know how they lived with themselves afterwards. At least those who had consciences.

This interest was nurtured during my first career in England, where I worked as a newspaper crime reporter. Eventually my travels brought me to America, where my mother was born and where cops carry guns. As do the criminals. I wrote an article for *The Independent*, a newspaper based in the Raleigh-Durham area, about a man on death row, a short piece about the art he was producing. His name was John Conaway and we were the same age, nearly to the day. Otherwise, we could not have been more different. He was the child of rape, his brothers all dead through street violence, his own young life a disaster of drugs and alcohol that led him to kill two people, in cold blood, in the middle of a deserted wood. Through thick glass with raised but hollow voices we spoke. I wanted to understand him—not just his crime, but also the man himself. How he could kill like that and how he could live like this, under the weight of a death sentence and amid others who'd killed?

Six years of my monthly visits and our growing closeness as friends inevitably led me toward the law. A volunteer stint for a criminal defense attorney opened up a whole world of possibilities before me. I slogged through Duke Law School and had my head turned by prestigious law firms. I worked for one for three years, quiet hallways and plush offices high above the Dallas skyline, before remembering my desire to be in front of a jury, to get back into exploring the criminal world in the tense but civil environment of a courtroom.

Then I moved south with my family, lucking into a job at the Travis County District Attorney's Office in Austin, Texas, where I was put straight into the trial division, negotiating, pleading out and trying felony cases to my heart's content. I worked there for a year before returning to a higher-paying job at a civil firm in town after my wife and I had our third child. It wasn't a move I was happy about, but I couldn't support my family on an assistant district attorney's salary. It was a move I always intended to reverse.

In March 2009 I was assigned to the 167th District Court and I was put back in the trial division. I was one of four lawyers handling hundreds of cases a year in front of Judge Mike Lynch. I was a little nervous meeting him, because a judge can make a lawyer's life miserable, tolerable or pleasant. Any worries were swiftly eliminated. Judge Lynch, a slight man in his sixties, sported a close-cropped beard and had a twinkle in his eye. He'd been on the bench seventeen years when I arrived in his court and I discovered that those years had made him wise, tolerant and humble. He shared my passion for crime fiction and, in his Texas drawl, reveled in reminding me to speak English "properly" in the courtroom.

By the summer, I was comfortable practicing in his court but impatient to get a case with some significance, to handle the kind of case that would tell me and others whether I really had what it took to be a good prosecutor. In short, I wanted to prosecute a murder case I could believe in and fight hard for justice for the victim.

And so I went looking. The cases I was handling were all felonies, where dealers were caught with crack in their pants, where burglars left fingerprints inside the house, where drunk drivers gave blood and promised sex to the cops for leniency, taking turns to cry and get angry like drunks do. There were closer cases, but not many, and usually we went to trial because the evidence pointed to guilt but wasn't admissible. By the fall I had not taken a single case to trial where I had even a slight fear that the defendant might be innocent.

What I didn't know, because I had not even sat second-chair on one, is that murder cases are different. Not only are the stakes higher, but also the prosecutor will always be without his or her most important witness, the person who saw everything happen and who, in any other case, would be present and able to testify: the victim. If two people have a fight in a room and only one walks away, how do you prove it was murder?

In the narrow hallways of the DA's office I heard about a cold case. A cold murder case involving the brutal attack on and subsequent death of a woman named Natalie Antonetti. I did a little research, read a newspaper story about it and became fascinated. I went looking for Darla Davis, thinking I could maybe just sit second-chair with her. A tall, elegant woman, Darla was the chief of the 390th district court, a senior prosecutor with a soft voice and an open and friendly face but a reputation for winning tough cases.

She'd recently adopted a little girl and, she told me, was quite willing for someone else to handle the case. The case was one she'd hesitated to present to the grand jury. No DNA, she said, no witness to put the defendant at the scene. She smiled kindly and said, "It's a circumstantial case. A circumstantial cold case, at that."

I didn't know enough to mind, so as willing as she was to pass on the case, I was eager for the hand-off. But it wasn't mine yet, because cold cases are important, not just to the family of the victim, but also to society as a whole. The successful prosecution of a cold case is a statement to the community: If you kill, we will catch you. Which meant that better prosecutors than myself had a chance to handle the case, if they so desired.

The other prosecutor looking at this particular case was Robert Smith, who was as seasoned as Darla. Judge Lynch once told me that Smith was the most intelligent prosecutor he had ever worked with and the best trial lawyer. I didn't know him well and we hadn't said much more than "hello" at this point, as he was a quiet figure around the office. In his early fifties, he carried himself like a twenty-year-old and was athletically lean. I'd heard that he often went sky-diving and rock-climbing.

He decided to pass on this case and said to me some of the same things Darla had said about it being a tough case. But those words didn't mean the same things to me as to those who've tried murder cases or cold cases.

Prosecutor Jim Young delivered the case file to me. It was now my case, but I was told I needed an experienced lawyer sitting second. I knew enough about my limitations to be grateful for that directive. Jim was older than I was, small and trim, with gray hair and a gray mustache. He smiled a lot and behind glasses his eyes twinkled. He'd been a prosecutor for many years and had tried numerous murder cases. We talked about this one and he said he believed we could prove it, but doing so would be like jumping from lily pad to lily pad. The pieces of evidence were close enough to create a path to a guilty verdict, but some creativity and a few acrobatics would be needed to get there. And, like a flimsy lily pad, he said, no one piece of evidence would stand the weight of the entire case. As time continued, I realized that these were very astute observations.

The case file was on my desk but before I opened it, I read the newspaper story again. "Anonymous tip…other leads…" Months from now, maybe even a year or more, I would need to educate twelve jurors about the case, guide them through a quarter century, lead them from then to now. So I cast my mind back to when I knew nothing of the case, not so long ago, and I told myself that I had to remember this moment, the time when my knowledge was the same as my future jurors. If I could persuade myself of my case then I should be able to persuade them, too.

I had an advantage over them in the persuasion, though, because over the coming weeks I would learn things I couldn't share with them, evidence I would like to introduce but couldn't because it was hearsay or legally irrelevant. But for me, that was all the more reason to remember the starting line, the moment the jurors and I stood side-by-side, ready to learn. I would go faster, yes, but no matter what evidence and details I needed to convey, I knew I could not let them lag too far behind. And I could not lose sight of them, ever.

The very first thing most prosecutors do when opening a new file is to scan the probable cause affidavit. This is the legal document presented by a police officer to a judge in order to get an arrest warrant issued. The PC affidavit, as it's called, is one-sided, laying out in a few brief paragraphs, maybe one page, who did what to whom, where and when. No nuances, no conflicting stories and very rarely is the defendant's side presented. That comes later.

ADAs look at this document before any other for two reasons. The first is to satisfy their natural curiosity—they get to learn about the case in a few sentences. The second reason is for reassurance—they can make sure that no one filed a worthless case. The PC affidavit is like a prosecutor's blanket, warming them to the case and keeping out those cold, unpleasant facts that might creep in and chill their spirits.

But there comes a time when prosecutors have to read the full offense report, the detailed account of everything that transpired, good and bad. It is at this moment that their minds click into a new gear and become more analytical; convinced that the defendant committed a crime, prosecutors now have to convince themselves they can prove it. So they look at the offense report, referred to as "the OR," with a more critical eye, often playing the role of defense lawyer to spot the weaknesses in the case and balance them against the strengths.

This is where the doubts can rise like specters and haunt the case.

And so it was with Dennis Davis, because I knew that within the paperwork lurked a demon waiting to stop me in my tracks. As much work as the detectives did two decades ago, as hard as they tried, there was one issue I could not escape: This case went cold for a reason.

Before I could convict Davis I needed to know why the investigation ceased. I had to know all the things that were wrong with the case, every hole, mistake, fact, inference and coincidence that lurked within the file, waiting to make a fool of me at trial and set a possible killer free. I needed to know why Davis was arrested now and not then, what led to his arrest and what might lead to his release.

So I returned to the OR and I kept reading.

The offense report was fifty pages long and began with a two-line entry by Officer Daniel Reyes: "On call to Barton Hills Drive at an apartment to a sexual assault on 10/13/85, arrived at the scene."

Sexual assault. Not the most accurate beginning to a police report. I steeled myself and read on.

The OR covered the discussions with Donn Chelli and his girlfriend, Fran Alcozer, and included Officer Reyes's inspection of the scene: blood everywhere, handprints on the wall and nothing that looked like it had been used as a weapon. Reyes assumed control of some physical evidence: the shorts and pink T-shirt Natalie had removed when she changed, a note with the words "I'll be at Steamboat probably" and a wet pair of men's underwear, waist size thirty inches, that officers found by the swimming pool. Reyes also called in a crime scene expert to process the scene for fingerprints.

The next entries in the OR were from the detective who was assigned the case, Eddie Balagia, a man I'd never get to talk to and a man who died without knowing who killed Natalie Antonetti. He wrote about returning to the scene of the crime.

I had read about the attack, about Natalie's bizarre wanderings upstairs and down. I had read about the neighbor, the convenience mart nearby and the swimming pool. Now I wanted to see it for myself, just as Eddie Balagia did.

I talked with Tom Walsh on the phone and he confirmed that the apartment complex was still there and that he had not been to it yet. But like me, he wanted to go. We arranged a day for him to pick up Jim Young and me and drive us there.

The day before we planned to visit the scene of the crime I reread the statements of the two people who had been there, Jolene Wells and Johnny Goudie. Their stories seemed to dovetail, with just one discrepancy: Jolene said that she found Natalie, called emergency medical services, then called their friend Dennis Davis and afterward woke Johnny. But Johnny's statement was clear that Jolene woke him right after she called the police and that he was with his mother in the bathroom as Jolene was calling Davis. Given what had gone on that morning, such a difference didn't seem all that surprising or especially important.

The following day, right after lunch, Tom Walsh picked us up in his own car and we took little time over formal introductions. It was clear at this first meeting that he knew a lot about the case and wanted to share all of it. He didn't mind explaining and re-explaining to help us catch up. Slowly and carefully he drove away from downtown to Barton Springs, talking all the way.

The Bluffs of Barton Creek was now known as Barton Hills Park Place, but it was the same apartment complex, a sprawling property with a dozen different buildings. We wound through the maze of a parking lot before pulling into a vacant space and climbing out into the August sunshine. All three of us moved instinctively across the black tarmac to the shade of a large oak tree.

As we stood there, a middle-aged man driving a golf cart pulled up, curious about the three men with badges and, in Tom's case, a gun strapped to his hip. We introduced ourselves and the man told us he had worked there for a dozen years and knew the area well even before that. Everything, he said, was pretty much the same as it ever was. New paint for the apartments and outside lights affixed to the roofs, plus a new fence at the back between Natalie's old apartment and the small mart, which we could see right behind it. He explained that where there was once a gap in the fence, there was now a gate. He knew the gate was in the same place as the gap, through which Chelli went to get his milk years earlier, because a pathway had been worn into the soil there. We could see for ourselves he was right about that.

We walked a circle around the apartments and the conversation dropped away as we finished pointing out everything on the outside that could be seen. I felt the tension increase. As casually as possible, I suggested we try knocking on the door of Natalie's former apartment. We started down the pathway.

Tom knocked on the door and, after a few seconds, we heard movement inside. Then voices. The door opened and I did a double take. The woman in the doorway looked so much like Natalie's picture that the similarities were, for me, momentarily disconcerting. The woman was petite and very slender, with her brown hair pulled back. She was pretty in the same way Natalie was pretty, with dark, tanned skin and white teeth. Right behind her was a toddler, a little girl peering out at us.

Tom did the talking and did it well. The woman seemed worried by the posse of men on her doorstep, especially since one was armed. But Tom hurriedly reassured her that nothing was wrong, no one was hurt or in trouble and that we were only there to investigate a very old case. Tom was vague, accurately describing the crime as an assault and he asked if we could come in, just to look around, to help us get a mental image of what happened. A little wary, she seemed reassured that the crime was an old one but to my surprise she never, not then or later, asked what the crime was. She stood to one side and watched as we talked quietly with one another, recreating the layout of Natalie's furniture in the apartment.

I had visited crime scenes before, but not many and none that led to homicide charges. So I had no expectations when I stood in the living room, looking at the space where Natalie's couch had sat, looking down at the spot where her sleeping head had been beaten by a person in a rage. I stood where the killer stood, yet imagining this peaceful place as a murder scene was nearly impossible. The experience was, perhaps for the best, turning out to be a more clinical, almost scientific plugging of gaps in my knowledge and understanding of the case.

We asked permission to go upstairs and the woman granted it. Photographs of the woman and her equally handsome husband lined the staircase walls, a happy couple in exotic locations all over the world. Impossible to see the blood, the horror, that had possessed the place when Natalie was beaten.

In the main bedroom we stood for a moment, then wondered aloud about Jolene's ability to hear the assault as she'd originally claimed. Jim and I went back downstairs and Jim clapped his hands five times. Tom came downstairs and confirmed that he heard each clap clearly.

We took one more look around, smiled at the little girl and thanked the young woman for accommodating us. As we left the apartment, a thought occurred to me. A potentially serious problem with the case and one I put to Jim and Tom.

"If Jolene's statement is right and she heard the door close right before finding Natalie, then called the cops and immediately after that called Dennis Davis, we have a problem."

"Meaning?" asked Jim.

"Meaning they didn't have cell phones. How did Davis assault Natalie, get back to his car and drive to southeast Austin where he lived in time to answer Jolene's phone call?"

"Not just that," Jim added. "He showed up at the scene pretty quickly so he had to clean himself up, too."

We looked at Tom for reassurance, but he just smiled. He was ahead of us; he had thought of this already. "The case has warts," he shrugged. "No doubt about it."

We talked some more, settling on Johnny's account that would buy Davis more time to get home. Not because we wanted it to be the truth but because if he'd heard Jolene make the call, then he'd have to have been up. At five in the morning on a Sunday, Davis would have had no traffic with which to contend. If Jolene had come downstairs a minute after Davis had closed the door, then spent a few minutes with Natalie before calling 911, then another few minutes waking Johnny, then a couple minutes more with mother and son before finally calling Davis, then it was possible Davis could have made it home in time to receive Jolene's phone call. It would have been close, but it might have worked.

That weekend I visited Natalie's grave for the first time. It didn't start as a sentimental thing. I had a camera in my hand and a plan for the murder trial that I knew would play out on television and the newspapers a year later. I was there at the height of a Texas summer to visit the first murder victim I would represent.

I was also there because I didn't trust the passage of time. It worried me that over two decades had passed since the murder and that the woman for whom I sought justice had been gone so long. I feared that a jury would wonder, just a little and maybe subconsciously, if perhaps they should let the past lie, if they should let the man on trial live out the rest of his life, grow old and die unmolested by the police, the prosecution and the Texas Prison system.

No matter that he bludgeoned a woman repeatedly, pounded her skull with a bat as she lay sleeping.

I was there because I didn't find that view acceptable and because I wanted to show each juror why the passage of time shouldn't affect his or her vote in the jury room. I would argue that if he did it, then he was guilty. He shouldn't be given credit for getting away with it for so long.

Her headstone was nothing more than a rectangle of granite on the ground, as minimal as a memory can be. The newer ones that surrounded hers gleamed in the Texas sun, clean, almost whitewashed.

This was Houston, where oven-like heat and oppressive humidity combined every summer, the reasons why the city center is riddled with underground tunnels for commuters and shoppers alike.

The air was close and the sun overhead was ferocious. I could almost feel the older stones crumbling under the twin assault of heat and damp. She had been buried here for twenty-four years.

I kneeled and touched the stone once, brushing my fingertips over the letters and numbers. I looked at the ground under my feet, a filled-in hole where a once-vibrant woman lay, a tumble of bones in a box. At that moment I made a swift and silent promise to bring her justice and if there was no spirit or soul to hear me then my promise was to the man who did this. To the man who put her here. *He* would see justice.

Pictures taken, I stood beside her grave for a moment. Not for the first time, I wondered if maybe I was doing her an injustice of my own. I had never handled a murder case and I had been an assistant district attorney for fewer than eighteen months. I was assigned this case because I asked for it, because I bugged several senior lawyers for it, promising I'd do a good job.

And because they didn't want it themselves.

The case was devoid of all the types of evidence prosecutors and jurors love to see: I had no fingerprints or DNA. I had no murder weapon. I had no eyewitnesses. A cold case, nearly a quarter of a century old and I had no physical evidence whatsoever.

There were too many things I could not control in this case, most importantly the passage of time and the quantity and quality of the evidence, so I was determined that my own ignorance would never undermine Natalie's case. Whatever there was to know, I would know it.

Maybe I just didn't know enough to be put off.

But as I traced my fingers over her name, carved into stone a quarter century ago, I knew enough to be worried. I had spent hours with the file, a thick black notebook with Natalie's picture on the front, prepared by Detective Tom Walsh of APD's Cold Case Unit. He had done a thorough job, put hundreds of hours into the case and, like any cold case, put in so much more than hours.

I walked back to my car, promising Natalie that I would try my hardest to obtain justice for her.

Chapter 10

IMMUNITY

At my desk I was reenergized, able to picture everything so much more clearly. The smallness of the apartment that I'd not gotten from the diagram in the file, the closeness of the convenience mart to Natalie's apartment and the way the concrete paths ran in front and behind her place. The report made mention of the front door, how it might not have been locked, but no one had said anything about the sliding glass doors that were at the back of these apartments. Didn't it make as much, maybe more, sense for the attacker to have watched Natalie sleeping on the couch through the back window, then slid open the glass door and attacked her? After all, it was on the back side of the apartments that Chelli saw his mystery man, not the front. It was another unknown and perhaps an unknowable.

I returned my attention to the offense report and read that no fingerprints were found on the note that read: "I'll be at Steamboat probably." That wasn't a surprise, nor particularly harmful to my case. Even had Davis's prints been found on the note, he could point out that he'd dated Natalie and touched that piece of paper before, maybe even left the note. Similarly, no prints were found on a beer bottle from the scene. That would have been more difficult to explain away, but again I was not surprised.

And then a bombshell seemed to explode in front of my eyes.

On page thirteen, right at the bottom, was an entry referring to a polygraph exam given just three days before Natalie died.

Detectives polygraphed several witnesses, just as homicide cops do today, as much to rule out suspects as to rule them in. It was, and is, a way of putting an investigator's mind at ease, reassurance that he's on the right track. But it doesn't always work out that way. Texas law is clear that the results of a polygraph cannot be used in court.

This offense report, like all of those in the Austin Police Department system, was sometimes hard to read, because it was written all in capital letters. This can confuse the eye and make it easy to misread words or miss them altogether. But the last word in this entry seemed to leap out at me:

Q: Did you say anything in your sworn statement that you know is a lie?
A: No.

Q: Did you purposely and intentionally put anything in your statement that you know is untrue?
A: No.

Q: Do you actually know who hurt Natalia?
A: No.

Q: Did you yourself cause Natalia's injuries?
A: No.

Results: Deceptive.

The subject of the polygraph exam was Jolene Wells.

I continued reading and learned that Sergeant Eddie Balagia sat down with Jolene Wells a second time on November 5 in an Austin Police Department interview room. She again denied any involvement in Natalie's murder and said she'd already told police everything she knew. When pressed, she maintained that she wasn't withholding any information and that her statement was the truth.

Unsure, Balagia asked her to take another polygraph exam, telling Jolene that it was the perfect opportunity to back up her words, to make the police believe her and get them off her back. She refused, saying that she was "not emotionally ready" to take another test at that time.

Toward the end of the interview, which had yielded nothing to help the investigation, Jolene told Balagia that she was heading out of state to visit her parents and would be gone more than a few days. She agreed to leave contact information though and the interview ended.

Four days later, Balagia contacted Jolene, but she refused to speak with him about the case. She told him that any future communication with her needed to be through her attorney, Frank Malone.

This was a significant hurdle for Balagia and a mystifying one. Significant because Frank Malone was one of the most respected criminal defense lawyers in Texas, the kind of lawyer hired to defend murder cases by those who could afford him. Mystifying because Jolene Wells had never been a suspect in the case and, despite refusing to talk to police, still wasn't a real suspect. She had no motive to kill Natalie, for one thing. Quite the opposite—with Natalie gone, Jolene no longer had a place to live. So why would she clam up?

The mystery deepened a few days later, I read in the report, on November 22. That was the day Sergeant Howard Hall, a homicide detective with APD, received a subpoena from the Travis County District Attorney's Office to serve on Jolene. The subpoena required her presence in front of the grand jury where she would be questioned under oath by an assistant district attorney. She appeared as required by the subpoena but, with her lawyer by her side, refused to answer questions, invoking her rights under the Fifth Amendment not to incriminate herself.

Of interest in later years, but little more than a mention in the offense report, was an entry that noted that Sergeant Hall served the subpoena on Jolene at a home in an Onion Creek subdivision which was the residence of Dennis Davis.

Another entry, a few lines further down, things became murkier still:

Based on information that has been gathered by Sgt Howard Hall, which cannot be set forth at this time, Jolene Wells will definitely be considered prime suspect in this case.

Although I had not been a prosecutor all that long, I had read hundreds, maybe thousands, of offense reports. I had never seen a detective write that he or she had information which "cannot be set forth at this time." The whole point of an offense report is to catalog and record all of the evidence, good, bad and indifferent. It is not a document for whimsy or conjecture, for speculation or veiled implications of someone's guilt. If it's a fact, it goes in the report. If it's a theory, it stays out until it's proven as fact.

I made a special note of that entry and determined to talk to Jim Young about it and then, assuming he was still alive, to Howard Hall himself.

Then I thought about Jolene Wells. I didn't know what she looked like, then or now, and I didn't know what her mental state was the night Natalie was killed. I didn't know nearly enough about the woman who was the last to see Natalie before she was attacked and the first person to find her afterward. Despite Hall's cryptic note and Jolene's refusal to cooperate, I still didn't think she was the killer.

I continued reading Hall's entry about Jolene and came across another oddity. Hall had listened to the 911 calls and, according to him, Jolene told the dispatcher something different from what was in her statement. According to Hall, Jolene told the 911 operator, "She just came in from outside and she is very pale—help me!" Jolene was then transferred to another operator who asked: "You said that she was outside and that she came in like that?" And Jolene's reply was: "Yes."

I sat back and tried to make sense of this. It occurred to me that a woman, who might or might not be predisposed to overreacting, came downstairs and saw her friend covered in blood. Her mind, barely awake, tried to process the bizarre scene and remembered that one of the last times she saw her friend was right after her friend had been outside. In a state of confusion, dismay, horror, perhaps Jolene spoke without thinking, relayed the information about Natalie being outside, because she *had been* outside, earlier, and maybe because it was inconceivable to Jolene that something like this could have occurred in her home. Additionally, she only said it once, merely responding "yes" without thinking or analyzing when the second operator sought to confirm the information.

As I wrestled with the Jolene problem, I started to see, really for the first time, how deep I had gotten myself. I was trying to piece together a coherent story for myself and eventually a jury when I didn't have complete information.

But I decided there was one thing I could do.

It was an idea that was mooted before, as recently as a few months previously when Jolene Wells was again subpoenaed to appear in front of the grand jury and again invoked her Fifth Amendment rights, refusing to testify.

Immunity. I could offer her immunity to get to the truth. A simple piece of paper on which I promised not to prosecute Jolene Wells for any crime revealed to me, directly or indirectly, if she testified truthfully about what happened that night. Immunity was something I could grant her and if I did, I could rely on the court to impose sanctions on her if she refused to testify still. So, at trial, if she took the stand and refused to speak, the judge could jail her.

The trouble was, I didn't want to hear what she had to say for the first time in trial. I wanted very much for her to sit down with Tom Walsh in an interview room and give a statement. One that we would record and one I could watch with my own eyes.

Jim Young and I talked about this option and agreed we had no choice. If we went to trial and didn't present Jolene as a witness, the jury would know something was wrong and it would weaken our case immeasurably, because we would have no timeline for Natalie's movements that night. Similarly, if we put Jolene on the stand and she pleaded the Fifth, our case would be ruined. How could we convict Dennis Davis if we had someone willing to go to jail rather than testify?

So Jim and I agreed. We would offer Jolene immunity and ask for an interview.

Jim knew Jolene's current lawyer, David Botsford. He was a former associate of and successor to Frank Malone and in his own right had become a big hitter in the world of Texas criminal law, experienced, extremely intelligent and very expensive.

Jim called Botsford and they had several conversations. Jim persuaded him to have Jolene come in and give an interview, but not before asking Botsford for one thing, something that was crucial for us: a proffer. This is an informal, non-binding statement from an individual through his or her attorney about the facts of a case or the person's involvement in it. What we wanted, in essence, was reassurance that Jolene did not wield the bat.

During the week that Jim and Botsford were discussing the interview, I reflected on Jolene's possible new statement. I wanted it to change; I wanted to hear certain things that would make my case better. Did she see Davis there that night? Maybe she let him in or even let him out. But I didn't think that likely. Why would she live with him afterward? There had been no indication of an affair between the two of them, so why would she risk her own life to live with a murderer, to be the keeper of so great a secret?

I wanted her to say that Johnny was right—she woke him before calling Davis. Or maybe that she called Davis at his studio, closer to the Barton Creek apartment than his home and thereby giving me more room to argue that he'd committed the murder and then driven to where Jolene reached him on the telephone. I spent days torturing myself hoping for the perfect outcome, should she agree to sit down and try to remember things more clearly.

Every day I worried. How could I, little more than a greenhorn prosecutor, make such a momentous decision? What did I know about these people, their generation, their motivations? *Nothing* was the correct answer, but I needed to find out.

In quiet moments I read and reread the file which sat on my desk. Whenever I went to court I took it with me and read it between pleas, between negotiations with defense lawyers and conferences with the judge.

Eventually, though, I decided I could neither control nor predict what Jolene would say. I needed to chase down other things while I waited for her to talk to us.

More often than not, the hardest part of my job is dealing with crime victims and their relatives. They often have unreasonable expectations and are driven by what they see as a need for justice but is little more than revenge. This is not unreasonable on their part, but revenge cannot be my guiding principle. Issues such as fairness, mitigating factors and judicial economy are considerations I have to work into the conversation and into the cases. The families are too often impatient for the trial and for the sword of vengeance to drop. They don't care about the evidentiary problems, don't understand them and don't want to know the details of case preparation and witness locating.

Johnny Goudie was different.

I met him on August 31 in a conference room in the bowels of the DA's office. All I knew about him was what I had read and a few music videos of his I had watched online. I was not sure what I expected to see.

"He's really nice," said Lynn Cragg as I stopped by her office on the way to the conference room. If he wasn't nice, Lynn wouldn't say so, because she wasn't like that. She might have raised an eyebrow or ignored my "What's he like?" question, but she wouldn't speak badly of someone and she wouldn't lie. She was a victim counselor, the person who updates victims and delicate witnesses on the status of a case, the person who arranges their travel and hotel for trial, the person who keeps them calm when emotions and stress are high. A willowy blonde with pale skin and large, knowing eyes, she was quiet and very hard to get to know, one of the most private people I had ever met, but she was ruthlessly efficient and supremely good at her job. And, quite possibly, one of the nicest people in the world.

She led me and Jim in to meet Johnny and made the introductions. I couldn't help but stare because this man was my age and a musician but had the face of a boy. He was a wonderful listener and it was apparent that he was also intelligent. He had no trouble following the procedural path I laid out and his large eyes watched me as I talked. His questions were few but clever, asked in the soft voice I would get to know so well. Johnny's eyes lit up when I talked about Tom. Clearly they had bonded.

He also looked a little shell-shocked and admitted that he was. His mother had been gone and her killer free and untouched for so long, he told us. Justice for her and closure for him seemed like distant dreams, impossibilities after more than two decades.

But he was also realistic about our chances. Jim and I explained why it was a hard case, but I got the feeling that Johnny knew that already and wasn't so much interested in hearing about the odds as he was in hearing about how hard we would work to gain justice for his mother. Just spending an hour with Johnny proved to be motivation itself.

When we parted I did something I rarely do: I gave him my direct line at the office and also my cell number. Usually I preferred a barrier between myself and my witnesses but this case was different; Johnny was different. I wanted us to be in touch. I wanted to convince him of our fervent commitment to his mother's case.

At the doorway his handshake was firm, but it was the sincerity in his face, the trust he transmitted to me with a look, that resonated the most. This would be a long fight, a hard one filled with twists and drama, but I left our meeting glad to know the man for whom I was fighting, reassured that I had his trust and feeling confident that, win or lose, I could meet his expectation: that we did all we could to find justice for his mother and tried our best to give him the closure he never thought he would see.

Chapter 11

BROKEN MEMORIES

As the cool air of fall nudged away three months of intolerable heat, our outlook shifted. Jim Young and I inspected the trial docket and saw that there was no chance of going to trial this year. We were not close to being ready and neither was the opposing counsel.

I didn't know much about Wade Russell, Davis's defense lawyer, when we first met in court. He had always been one of those attorneys I looked forward to working with; his genial approach and friendly demeanor were in stark contrast to some of his younger colleagues who imagined that thumping the table and decrying the oppressive and vicious nature of the State somehow established the factual innocence of their clients. Personal responsibility to them meant that the prosecutor was responsible for inflicting cruel and unusual punishment on their poor, downtrodden clients. Wade wasn't like that, not from what I could see in my limited experience, and when I talked to other prosecutors they confirmed my preconceived notions about him: bright, articulate, affable.

I learned that his hobbies chiefly involved riding his motorcycle into the hills, frequently accompanied by his friend Judge Mike Lynch. I was not in the slightest bit troubled by their being friends, either. My experience with Judge Lynch continued to show me that personal preferences for individuals were shed the moment he put on the robes and I was, frankly, relieved that I wouldn't have to fight against a lawyer who believed that the best defense he could provide his client was to make my life difficult. I was also beginning to realize that this case would be so very different from anything I had done before and that would mean some cooperation with defense counsel on getting witnesses lined up and evidence admitted.

The debrief of Jolene Wells was to take place on September 14 at the Sex Crimes Unit of the Austin Police Department, because they had a setup that enabled all of us to fit in one room and record the conversation in color.

We met her for the first time in the interview room. She was dressed in a black pantsuit with a light blue blouse. She was nervous, very nervous. Her large eyes darted about and her long fingers fiddled with one another. Tom Walsh and I shook her hand and introduced ourselves to her and to David Botsford, her attorney, who sat beside her. Tom was in a gentle mood, as ever, but especially so with her.

Jolene started by explaining she had a head injury, laughing a little as she told us an object fell off a shelf last September and hit her head. But if she couldn't remember things or stuttered as she spoke, that was probably why.

Before we began, she excused herself to the bathroom and David explained a few other things to us. As we already knew, she was emotional and was profoundly affected by the murder of her best friend. He added that police were heavy-handed with her after Natalie's death, at one point lying to her in an attempt to trick her. Her father was the one who told her to hire a lawyer and put an end to cooperation.

When she returned to the room, Tom reassured Jolene that she had immunity, she was free to talk and she wouldn't get in trouble if what she said today was different from what was in her statement.

She started by telling us that she couldn't remember the first part of her statement; her memory now began when she saw Natalie sitting on the couch. As Tom led her through the statement, it was clear that her memory was far from good. She couldn't recall where she went once Natalie was taken away, nor exactly when she gave her statement. She thought she talked to a detective called Balagia, but the names Howard Hall and Russell Schmidt meant nothing to her.

Tom asked what Eddie Balagia said that upset her so much. She wasn't specific, but her response pointed to odd and constantly repeated questions. As much of her recollection would prove to be, she was vague.

"Where did you stay after the murder?" Tom asked.

"I was too afraid to return home alone," Jolene said, "so I stayed with a lot of friends." She named some of them, but Dennis Davis wasn't mentioned until Tom brought him up, saying that she stayed with him for six months.

"No, I did not!" she said, emphatic. One night maybe, she conceded, but she never lived with Dennis Davis.

Tom wasn't convinced, because he and I both knew the grand jury subpoena from that time listed Davis's house as her address. Even though Tom pushed, asking her to help him out, she couldn't explain it.

She did provide crucial information, though, about something she'd spotted at Davis's home. "I saw a bat in the corner of one of his rooms and I asked him, 'Why do you have a bat?' and he said for protection." That, she admitted, frightened her.

Tom turned the conversation back to the weekend in October when Natalie was attacked. He asked about her relationship with Johnny. "Natalie was fine with it," she responded. "We had both discussed it with her and, yes, it was that weekend I was moving in to live with them both."

They returned to her statement, going through it line by line. She read it, but this was all the memory she had—if it was written there, it must be true. Time had wiped away the details contained on this piece of paper, the minutiae of Johnny being drunk, the conversations with Natalie before they went to sleep.

But when Jolene began talking about finding Natalie, I knew the memory was clearer to her. Her voice trembled and she had a hard time keeping from crying. We learned that she didn't necessarily target Dennis Davis for a phone call, but after she'd called the ambulance she was calling friends' numbers randomly, trying to get someone on the line. She just happened to connect with Dennis, a call she didn't even remember making.

Tom moved on to things we wanted to know.

"Did you speak to Dennis that night, out in the parking lot after Natalie had gone to sleep?"

She didn't seem surprised at the question, but shook her head. "I don't think so," she replied, but it was another thing she couldn't remember.

"What about his car? What was he driving?"

"Something black and sporty," she said. She didn't really recall his car.

I could see that Tom was getting frustrated and he used some of the same tactics he did with Dennis. Confession is good for the soul, he told her. Telling the truth and getting some of these burdens off your chest will make you feel better. The soft voice came back at him, promising she was telling the truth, telling all she could remember, but it was clear to me she was also still worried about being implicated somehow.

"I do know that I was asleep that night…and I do know, one hundred percent, that I had nothing to do with any of this."

"I don't think that you did," Tom responded. "I don't think that you did…if I thought you did, this would take a different course." Tom told her she was a victim of this crime, not just because she suffered through the trauma of the assault itself, but also because she'd had to live her whole life dealing with it. I thought it was a smart move on Tom's part, bringing Jolene closer to his side and aligning her with Natalie, not Dennis Davis.

"I think that you know who was involved and you're just not telling me and I don't know why. I don't know why you just can't get that off your chest."

Her response was emphatic. "I do not know who was involved with this. I swear to you I do not know. If I thought it was Dennis I would absolutely have told you and I would have told them back then, when this incident happened."

This, to me, was important, because I agreed with her that she had no reason to lie or to cover up for him. Not only was Natalie her best friend, but also not one single person had indicated that Jolene and Dennis were involved in anything more than a friendship. I couldn't imagine any reason why Jolene Wells would risk her liberty and maybe even her life to cover for Davis.

The interview ebbed and flowed, Tom asking easy questions, soft questions and then pushing Jolene to tell the whole truth, to remember details and timelines. But we were learning nothing new, nothing that would help us shore up a circumstantial case.

After about an hour, we took a break, because I needed to talk to Tom outside. I wanted to ask Jolene a few questions myself. I had no real expectations of shaking anything loose from her, but I knew that if I didn't at least try I would regret it.

When we went back into the room, David Botsford raised an interesting possibility: hypnosis. Jolene didn't remember anything anymore; that was obvious to us all. And because Eddie Balagia was dead, we had no way of knowing if everything Jolene told the police was in the statement on which we were relying. What if there was something else locked away inside her memories? David had used the technique before in a murder case and I was intrigued by the idea.

But for now, I picked up the questioning and asked about after the assault. "How did Dennis behave in the following days, weeks and months?"

"He didn't seem terribly upset." She acknowledged, as we all knew, that people react differently to an event like this and there simply isn't any one way to behave. But to Jolene, someone who knew Dennis Davis, he seemed oddly unmoved, even callous. And she gave examples.

"He and I were at the hospital visiting her once. I think we went together, but I'm not sure if I met him there or if I went with him. And I remember him saying something kind of weird to her. She was on this bed that was rotating, to keep her circulation going and she was really swollen. Her face was blown up like a balloon and she looked really bad. I mean, she was completely swollen up. And he said to her, he said, 'Oh look, Natalie, your wrinkles are gone.'"

Jolene's voice quavered as she continued, "What a fucked up thing to say to somebody who's hanging by a thread. Why would you say that to somebody? And I knew she was very self-conscious about her wrinkles; she always had been. She was a beautiful girl, but she had some wrinkles under her eyes and I think it bothered her, because she said it did."

The other example she gave was equally strange. Jolene was at Davis's parents' house one night after the assault but before Natalie died. Jolene was trying to talk to Dennis about her friend. She was upset and crying and looking for emotional support and comfort. Dennis said nothing, just went to the television set and put in a movie. A picture came onto the screen and Dennis said, "Look at that, just look at that." It was pornography.

Jolene emphasized that she and Dennis were always just friends; she had no interest in him sexually, nor had he shown any such interest in her. That, she told us, made his response all the more upsetting, made her all the more angry.

I asked her about the sequence of events at the apartment, whether she could remember whether she woke Johnny before calling Dennis or the other way around. She couldn't recall but agreed that if Johnny said he remembered overhearing the telephone call, then he was telling the truth. He had no reason to lie, she reminded us, and I agreed.

Asked about the 911 call, Jolene couldn't remember telling the operator that Natalie had come in from outside. She shook her head slowly at the question. David Botsford interjected, while looking through his own notes, that Jolene had told him a while ago a little about what was going through her mind. On this point, he said that Jolene hadn't really considered the possibility that someone had been in their apartment and that all she could think was that Natalie had been hit by a car and somehow made it back into the apartment. It was an explanation for the call I had already considered and, I thought, a reasonable one.

I asked Jolene about Dennis's temper and she recalled just one incident that happened at Studio D when he'd been drinking and got angry enough to throw a couch across the room. But that was it and as far as Jolene could remember, he had treated Natalie well enough.

The interview lasted another thirty minutes. At the conclusion, I assured Jolene we would meet again, because I knew she would need preparation before trial. As she left, as shaky as she seemed, as poor as her memory was, I felt a sense of relief. For one thing, she did not confess to killing Natalie. For another, I now knew what we were dealing with; I had the confines of her statement that I could rely on to shape a small part of my case.

And she had added a couple of points that a jury might find interesting: Dennis Davis's response to Natalie being in a coma was to make fun of her appearance and show Jolene porn. I didn't think much of that behavior and I was pretty sure that a jury wouldn't like it either.

Christmas had come and gone, with spring arriving early as it did every year in Texas, chasing away the last of the cold days and reminding us with a few warm afternoons that summer lurked just around the corner. I had been very busy with other cases, but the Davis case stayed on my mind. One thing now seemed abundantly clear to me: The defense would most likely insist Marty Odem was the real killer.

He knew Natalie, they lived in the same apartment complex and Odem's own friend said Odem was angry with her for kicking him out after a sexual encounter. Odem was a man with a temper and a criminal streak and was an admitted rapist. He owned a bat and was at the same pizza place as Natalie the evening she was attacked.

I realized that this would be one of the fights I would have with Wade Russell, Davis's lawyer. A legal fight carried out with supporting case law and persuasive logic. But he was fighting for his client's life and Marty Odem was his weapon. Just as Jolene Wells might help me convict Davis, so Wade hoped that Marty Odem would be the key to setting Davis free.

Would Judge Lynch let Wade call Odem as a witness and present him as an alternate suspect? I didn't know, but I couldn't take the chance that he might testify without my talking with him first. I trusted that Tom had properly considered and excluded him as the killer; that was not the question anymore. The question was whether members of a jury would think that *maybe* he was the killer. If so, Davis would walk. The burden was on me to prove his guilt, not on Davis to prove his innocence, so any failure of proof worked against me, not him.

So I decided to talk with Marty Odem. I wanted to meet him face-to-face, to gauge not just what he might say, but also how he might say it. I wanted to see what kind of an impression he might make on the jury and the only way to do that was to sit across a table from him, to listen to him in his own words.

Two of the cold case members, Detectives Mark Gilchrest and Richard Faithful, had already spoken to him for a little while. They reported that he was out of prison, having served more than a decade of his thirty-year sentence, and now he had a job, a home, a wife and children. During that meeting he invoked his right to counsel, such as it exists, but then chatted away quite freely without the detectives asking questions, telling them about his life. To be safe, I decided to make the arrangements through Odem's lawyer, a young attorney named Adam Brown, whose offices were in downtown Houston. I called Adam and we got on well. He had spoken with his client and was happy to host an interview at his offices.

On Monday, March 29, 2010, Tom picked me up in his SUV and we headed south on I-35. En route, we listened to the first interview, which Detectives Gilchrest and Faithful taped. I didn't learn much, but it was interesting to hear Odem's voice, this man I had read so much about. And none of it good.

Juries are required to judge witnesses; it's in their job description. They weigh witnesses' words, demeanors and looks. As soon as I saw him, I wasn't sure that Marty Odem was someone I wanted testifying. He was earnest and forthright with us, animated when he spoke and he talked a lot. He was powerfully built, not the thin figure from photos of his youth, and his hair was buzzed short. There was a power to his body and an angular gauntness to his face that relayed much exercise and a difficult life. He was gentle in the conference room and exceedingly polite, but I got a vibe from him that was less tranquil. Not aggression, exactly, although I wondered if maybe I sensed aggression that had been dissipated with time. Prison couldn't have been easy, not for a sex offender, and life on the outside must also be a constant challenge for a convicted felon. But whatever I was sensing, I knew the jury would, too. And they might be less understanding.

Marty himself was in agreement with me: He didn't want to testify. He told us about his life outside Houston, the love for his wife and children who had become the center of his life. He didn't want to be paraded in front of a jury, maybe even in front of news cameras and accused of a crime he didn't commit.

One thing I was most interested in was whether or not he knew Natalie, because the accounts of that were not consistent. He didn't remember her, but he acknowledged that if he told Glen Sloan that he'd slept with her, it was a lie. Marty acknowledged it was possible he'd seen her around, perhaps in the laundry room, but he was sure he never slept with her and insisted he never had any animus toward her.

During the meeting Marty did most of the talking and occasionally I got the impression it was because he didn't want us asking questions. He told us over and over about his new life and I saw how tenuous that hold was for a man on the sex offender registry and on parole. When we left I was not sure he'd been frank, but I felt satisfied he had nothing to do with Natalie's death. And that was what mattered.

Back at the office, I started reviewing the law. I wondered if Wade had an unfettered right to present Odem or anyone else as an alternate suspect. As I read the case law I was encouraged, because the courts seemed to share a concern I had about this strategy: If the defense could present alternate suspects, did the trial become a mad scramble to prove that each of them was innocent? If so, the guilt or innocence of the defendant would become a sideshow as the defense presented possible suspect after possible suspect and I had to prove each one innocent, prove that each one didn't kill Natalie Antonetti. And proving a negative is very often an impossibility.

As I read on, I saw that courts have set a standard for when a defense lawyer can put an individual on the stand and call him a viable, alternative suspect. It was not enough that the victim and alternative suspect knew each other and it was not enough that the alternative suspect had a criminal past. It was possible Wade could prove the former and he could prove the latter. But it was not enough: Texas courts required that there be some nexus, some connection, between the alternative suspect and *the crime itself*.

And so I sat in my office pondering the law and my case, looking for connections between Marty Odem and the assault on Natalie

Antonetti. Odem had a bat and it was possible Natalie was killed with one. But then Davis also had a bat, as did flasher Stan Rivera. Chelli said that Odem resembled the man he'd seen outside the apartment that morning, but that was hardly definitive. Do you slander a man and call him a killer over "might"?

All the other connections I could think of fell under the "knew her" or "criminal" categories, but there was a possibility that the underwear found by the pool would have fit Marty Odem. And there was a way to test that theory.

Otherwise, I thought about the kind of criminal Marty Odem was. Forced entry into an apartment, followed by rape and theft. A stranger as the victim. It seemed to me that we were looking for a different kind of criminal altogether, because everything about Natalie's attack indicated to me that whoever assaulted her knew her and for those few moments that person was uncontrollably angry with her. No signs of sexual assault, nor theft.

I knew I was beginning to profile the murderer. My knowledge of behavioral science had trickled in over many years, through classes in college, books, films and many interviews with a former FBI profiler who lived in Austin. I considered myself knowledgeable on the subject, more so than most, but to know whether Marty Odem fit the profile of whoever killed Natalie, for that I needed an expert.

Chapter 12

BLINDSIDED

Serial killers are everywhere. At any given time, roughly two hundred are roaming America's highways, using the black ribbons of tarmac that bind the lower forty-eight states, hunting grounds where ruthless men locate, incapacitate and kill their victims. Roughly five hundred bodies, mostly belonging to women, have been found along our highways, their murders unsolved because the men who killed them are mobile, their whereabouts untraceable. Their victims are the weakest among us, prostitutes and drug addicts making their way (and sometimes their livings) on the nation's freeways, vulnerable because they have no choice but to trust strangers with their bodies and their lives. English television host Jeremy Clarkson got a lot of backlash for making a joke about lorry drivers being serial killers. He was partially right, he just had it the wrong way around: Serial killers are often lorry drivers.

Not exclusively; that's too simplistic. But the FBI is targeting these men, in some cases actually knows their names, and they are turning the tables by making the hunters watch their backs. Dozens have already been caught and more will be.

The notion of so many killers operating in America, killing in cold blood and almost at will, appeared on my radar screen when Tom invited me to a seminar put on by FBI profilers and highlighting their Highway Serial Killer Initiative.

The Initiative had been running for a few years, but at the time the top experts in the Behavioral Analysis Unit (BAU) were in Austin and there was no way I was going to miss that.

I sat amongst the rows of tin chairs alongside troopers, detectives and officers from every law enforcement agency in Texas, which meant a lot of hats, boots and drooping mustaches. With my British accent, buzz cut and suit, I didn't immediately fit in, but the thing about Texas is it's friendly. And the seminar was fascinating.

The presenters told us about the BAU's makeup: four profiler units, one for counterterrorism/threat assessment, one for crimes against adults, one for crimes against children and one for the Violent Criminal Apprehension Program, known as ViCAP. Serial killers are tracked down by the second unit, focused on crimes against adults, and it was their lead agent who held us rapt with stories about the men caught as a result of the program. At one point, he demonstrated how the BAU operated and how they approached a case by showing us crime scene photos and then explaining precisely how they correctly deduced the identity of the killer.

This particular story taught me a lesson. The crime scene the agent used as his example was a woman's house, the victim a suburban mother who was bludgeoned to death inside. Police had focused on a broken window in the bathroom as the point of entry. Not so, said the FBI agents. They thought the woman knew her killer. They were right and the busted window proved to be nothing more than a misleading coincidence. This gave me a measure of comfort, because the defense theory was based on Odem-related coincidences and this showed me that they do, indeed, happen.

At the end of the first day, I approached and introduced myself to an expert, Special Agent Bermingham. I asked if I could tell him about Natalie's murder. He leaned on the edge of a table, folded his arms and indicated to me to begin. I told him about Marty Odem, as many details as I could remember about the man and his crime: its random nature, the stranger as victim and sexual assault and theft his motives. Then I detailed Natalie's case, trying not to shade my telling in any way, because I wanted an objective opinion, nothing else. He listened closely and nodded.

"We don't give advisory opinions," he said when I finished, "and we like to look at full case files before we render any opinion."

It was a mandatory disclaimer. I knew he was letting me know this was an impromptu opinion and nothing on which I should base a legal decision.

"But if your description of the assault on and wounds to your murder victim is accurate," he continued, "these crimes were committed by two different people. Whoever attacked that woman knew her and was very angry. That crime was personal."

He offered me his business card and said to contact him in a week or so, suggesting maybe he could be of more help. I thanked him.

In the following days I considered the words of SA Bermingham as I prepared for the first courtroom encounter. I felt sure that Wade Russell would bring up Odem. I planned to follow up with the FBI to see if they would have someone review the case file and make sure we were on the right track, but for the time being I was happy knowing that Odem as Natalie's killer simply didn't fit.

The court date was to discuss logistics, to reassure the judge that Wade was happy with the discovery he'd received and possibly to talk about a trial date. I had a secret agenda, though, an idea that a colleague suggested partially as a joke. So on April 9, a few weeks before our court date, I took the elevator up to the eighth floor and sprang a surprise suggestion on Wade: We abandon the idea of a jury trial and try the case in front of the judge.

This held some advantages for me: I was positive that much of my evidence would not be admissible, either because I couldn't prove a chain of custody or because witnesses simply had forgotten things. I had evidence in the form of hearsay, too, which would never make it in front of a jury. But if a judge heard the case, he had to know the evidence before he could rule on it and if he knew the evidence, that had to weigh on his mind. Ultimately, this option was appealing to me, because I knew that Judge Lynch wouldn't play favorites, that he'd do the right thing and that if the evidence supported a guilty verdict, he would make the tough decision and say so.

There were disadvantages to this approach. Just as he'd know the strengths of my case, Judge Lynch would know its weaknesses too, and the strengths of Wade's defense. But more important, I had a genuine sense that on serious crimes, especially when the evidence might make it a close call, the community needed to decide whether someone was guilty or not. A jury was the judicial representation of a community and I felt that taking this matter away from them was somehow a disservice.

There was an element of fear in me, too. This was a very important case to me, especially because of Johnny. A jury trial was always a spectacle and I was worried about losing. I wasn't worried for my career; I was lucky enough to work in a place where winning and losing trials had no bearing on reputation and advancement. No, it was the idea of letting people down, people who had waited so long for justice. And I didn't want them or anyone saying, "Why did we let him handle this case? He's never even tried a regular murder case." So my motivations for exploring a bench trial were, in part, selfish and in the coming days and weeks I knew that I needed to parcel those feelings out and consider whether abandoning a jury was the best thing for gaining justice for Natalie and her family.

Wade listened to the idea with raised eyebrows but little comment. He told me he'd think about it and talk to his client about it and I knew that his friendship with Lynch reassured him that Davis would get a fair trial. But it would be highly unusual for a judge to try a murder case and, quite properly, Wade wanted time to consider the suggestion.

He had something else to tell me and it wasn't his theory that Odem was the real killer. In measured tones and his gentle southern accent he delivered a double blow more painful than any alternate perpetrator theory, a one-two punch that could prove utterly devastating to my case.

First, Wade told me that a significant witness was changing his story, blurring the timeline and potentially moving the defendant a safe distance away from Natalie on the night of the attack.

Second, he said as matter-of-factly as he could and with no hint of gloating or glee, was that my most important witness would not be testifying at all.

Chapter 13

FINDING CREDIBLE EVIDENCE

The woman who kicked off the whole investigation, the wife who turned in her husband, had switched sides. Rebecca and Dennis were the Davises once more and, as his loyal wife, she had instructed her husband's lawyer to inform us she wouldn't be testifying at our trial. At least, not for us.

In court, I represent the State of Texas and I can compel anyone to come and testify. All I have to do is draft a subpoena and have it properly served on the witness and if the person doesn't show up to trial or refuses to testify, he or she can be held in contempt by the judge. This can include a monetary fine or imprisonment in some cases.

But there are limits to my power and that of the judge.

Over the years, lawmakers have decided that some institutions require protection from meddling prosecutors. Institutions such as the church and marriage, which is why you are free to speak to your minister about your sins without fear of him relaying everything in a courtroom. Similarly, lawmakers wanted husbands and wives to be able to share their deepest and darkest secrets without the possibility that a prosecutor or defense lawyer could force one spouse into court to make him or her give up those secrets, thereby creating marital strife or retribution.

They are known as "privileges" and, when properly asserted they bar any lawyer, judge or court from making an individual testify, no matter how important the person's evidence might be. And Rebecca Davis was asserting the spousal privilege.

Losing her as a witness gutted my case in a number of ways. I saw her as a strong witness, perhaps even more so now that she'd realigned with Dennis Davis. Her testimony was powerful, because she was the person who knew him best. He told her a secret, something that had him weeping with remorse and shame and she carried that secret for twenty years, all the while his words eating at her conscience because to her, the fact that he had "sinned against God and man" had something to do with the murder of Natalie Antonetti. She knew it; she felt it; she believed it. And she called the police to let them know too. Even though she did so when she and Davis were separated, potentially allowing the defense to argue that she was spiteful or looking for revenge, I realized that Wade could no longer make that argument. Any claims that she was biased and out to get Dennis Davis had just gone up in smoke.

Relatedly and crucially, in my opinion, was the fact that Rebecca was not saying, "That confession didn't happen." She was saying, "I refuse to testify about it." This reassured me that it *did* happen and she wasn't prepared to go so far as to lie by saying she was wrong, misheard him or was making it up. So if I could make her take the stand and repeat the words Davis said to her, the truth about what he said, then my case would be stronger because she was not just a neutral witness; she would be hostile to me. I believed the jury would see that and they would understand that she was testifying against her will but that, even so, she would be giving damning testimony against the man she was trying to protect. And that made her evidence all the more credible and all the more believable.

More credible, too, because it struck me that no one had ever offered an explanation for Davis's words. If Rebecca, Wade or Dennis himself could think of and offer a reasonable alternative explanation for why Davis had said he "sinned against God and man," maybe the phrase would lose some of its impact. But no one had and no one seemed to be trying to. To their credit, the defense wasn't trying to change the evidence, merely block the jury's access to it.

And if they succeeded, what would I be left with? I would be left attempting to prove a twenty-five-year-old murder case with no DNA, no fingerprints, no confession, no eyewitnesses and no other direct evidence of Davis's guilt. All I still had was the testimony of one woman, Kellie Torres, a failed alibi and too many faded memories. That was it.

Very soon I realized that if I could make Rebecca testify, I must do so. The spousal privilege wasn't an issue I had dealt with before—this case presented many firsts for me—and so I intended to discover the boundaries of the privilege. It seemed entirely fair to me that if the defense was invoking a technical rule to suppress important evidence, I was entitled to make sure they had satisfied every one of the prerequisites for assertion of the privilege.

Before I hit the books, I chatted informally with Wade in an attempt to understand the basis for the assertion. He told me that Davis made the statement to Rebecca about four months after they met, before they were legally married but after they considered themselves to be common-law husband and wife. As he was talking, I had no idea if the privilege extended to common-law marriages, but he seemed to think it did. And he gave me no specifics to back up Davis's claim, leaving me in the dark as far as facts, with only the unknown law as my possible savior.

Back in my office, I made a note of what Wade told me and then put the issue aside while my mind turned to the other concern Wade presented, that of a witness changing his story.

Jimmy Rose, Davis's former roommate and best friend, talked to Wade about the case, including the argument he had witnessed between his friend and Natalie. According to Wade, Jimmy Rose was now far from sure when that argument took place. It could have been Friday night, Rose said, not Saturday night after all. If true, it was not the same blow that Rebecca's failure to testify would be, but it was a shadow of a doubt in a juror's mind, a thinning of my argument of motive. It meant I had no one to tell the jury that on the night Natalie was assaulted Dennis Davis was angry with her.

I pulled out the statement Rose gave to Tom Walsh, signed and sworn to by Jimmy Rose on October 17, 2007, to see if there was room for doubt or maybe some drafting error on Tom's part that lent ambiguity to what Rose told him. I saw no ambiguity:

The night before Natalie was beaten I was at the club Steamboat on Sixth Street in Austin. About 1 A.M. in the morning I witnessed a big argument between Dennis and Natalie at Steamboat. I knew Dennis to be a very jealous and very violent man. I believe the argument was because she was talking to another man. The argument was mostly verbal but was very emotional. I knew this because I was walking out of the club with them as they were arguing.

I reached for the phone and called Tom. He needed to know about both of the developments I learned from my visit with Wade. He listened while I told him first about Rebecca asserting the spousal privilege.

"Can you beat it?" he asked.

"I don't know yet. I'm going to look into it and I'll do my best."

"I know you will. And you'll beat it, don't worry." Tom the believer didn't sound worried. But when I told him about Jimmy Rose changing his story, he was annoyed. "He was real clear with me that it was Saturday night. Real clear."

"So is his statement."

We speculated as to Rose's change, but Tom cut the theorizing short, practical as ever. "We'll go see him. He's a friendly guy. We'll just go down to Houston and talk to him."

Tom said he would set it up and after we hung up, I called Johnny with a quick question.

"Is there any way you remember whether your mother went out on Friday night, the night before she was assaulted?"

A silence as he thought. "I'm sorry, I don't remember. It's possible, but I couldn't say one way or the other. Why?"

I didn't want to tell him a witness was revising his testimony. Johnny was already well aware of the weaknesses in the case and I had no intention of causing him more stress than I needed to. "Just trying to nail down our time line as much as possible." Which was absolutely true.

I also took this opportunity to fill Johnny in on other aspects of the case. I knew he was impatient, but he carried it well. He trusted that we were not just doing the right thing, but also doing it as fast as we could. When I told him about the chat with Marty Odem he listened intently, asking few questions, but it was clear to me his interest wasn't in accusing someone for his mother's murder; it was in accusing the right person. I hung up, hugely impressed with Johnny Goudie and as inspired as ever to do right by him.

Then I called Special Agent Bermingham and left a long message, reminding him of the case and asking if he could help. He called me back in minutes and we talked for a while. Once again he asserted that whoever killed Natalie almost certainly knew her and was almost certainly not Marty Odem. They were completely different MOs. But he was not hopeful he could help. The FBI worked on unsolved cases, he told me. There were too many of those keeping profilers busy to send agents to work on cases that had potentially been solved. He promised me that he would ask, but he was not optimistic. When we hung up I was disappointed, but because, like Johnny, I was interested in getting the right guy, not just any guy, I was also very encouraged that Agent Bermingham was so sure Odem wasn't our man. Encouraged and relieved.

On Friday, May 21, just a couple of days after we last talked, Tom called me at work.

"Ready to go to Houston and meet Jimmy Rose?"

"Sure. When?"

"Tomorrow."

Tom picked me up at nine on Saturday morning and we started the three-hour drive southeast to Houston, giving us plenty of time to talk about the profiling issue. Even though he'd invited me to go, Tom hadn't made it to the serial killer seminar, so I filled him in on some of the details. I asked what he thought about using a profiler and he was hesitant, resistant even. I got the feeling that Tom liked the evidence we had and didn't think that an outside opinion would add anything significant. But I emphasized that using a profiler would be more to exclude Marty Odem than inculpate Davis and we'd use a profiler to testify only if the defense put on evidence that Odem was the real killer.

"The idea," I explained, "is to show how the two crime scenes are different, the work of different men, rather than to say the Antonetti assault is consistent with Davis."

Put that way, Tom nodded. "I like it," he affirmed. "What does Efrain say?" A colleague of mine, Efrain De La Fuente, a highly-regarded prosecutor with a thoughtful and serious demeanor, was the court chief for the 167th District Court.

I smiled. "Exactly the same as you. A bad idea if we try to use a profiler to point the finger at Davis, assuming the profiler would even do that, but a possibility to rebut the defense theory it was Odem."

We wound through the back roads of north Houston, new developments appeared at more and more regular intervals and eventually we found Jimmy Rose's house. He was friendly and relaxed as we sat down together, eager to help but not eager to take sides.

"If he's guilty, he needs to serve time," Jimmy said. "If not, he needs to get out now."

We assured him that we agreed completely and I told Jimmy what I told every witness who was concerned about getting someone in trouble: My worst nightmare was convicting an innocent man.

Tom let me take the lead in the questioning, knowing that one of the reasons we were there was so I could evaluate Jimmy as a potential witness. We had copies of his statement, but I left them in a folder while we went over what he knew and what he remembered. The main thing I wanted to know was whether the argument he'd seen between Natalie and Dennis happened on Friday or Saturday night. Jimmy seemed genuinely confused and unhappy that he couldn't remember.

Suddenly I realized that perhaps I was asking the wrong question and that Wade Russell might have asked the wrong question, too.

"Forget Friday or Saturday night," I said. "The day of the week doesn't matter, so don't worry about it. Tell us this: When did you find out about the attack on Natalie in relation to the argument?"

He didn't hesitate in his response. "The very next day."

I smiled. That was one problem cleared up, but Jimmy gave an indication of other issues we might experience. He gave us his opinion of our other star witness, Kellie Torres, making it clear there was no love lost between the two of them. He told us about Kellie's relationship with Dennis Davis and how they constantly fought during the time Jimmy knew them. Kellie knew just how to set Davis off, Jimmy told us, perhaps even reveled in pushing Davis's buttons and making him mad. When they'd been drinking, which was most of the time, it was worse than usual and they fought "like cats and dogs," mostly verbal but with a lot of slammed doors.

Jimmy also said that Kellie used to be a liar and could be vindictive, maybe even vindictive enough to make up a lie about Davis killing Natalie. I doubted that, especially twenty-five years later when she was looking to move on with her life and forget about Dennis Davis. But I was pretty sure Wade would make that pitch about her to the jury, so I was not shocked to hear Jimmy say it. I just didn't look forward to hearing him say it on the stand.

As we talked, though, I saw him as an excellent witness for us. He was Dennis's best friend and, with no dispute or argument between them, had no reason to make up anything or lie about Dennis's actions. By virtue of once being Dennis's best friend, Jimmy had built-in credibility. He was not eager to see his former roommate go to prison. Quite the opposite; he was visibly struggling with the idea his friend could be guilty of murder. But whatever he believed now he also thought so back then and he admitted to us that on at least one occasion he considered calling the police because Dennis was acting so out of character, so crazy after Natalie's assault. Not crazy with grief but with something else; something Jimmy believed to be guilt. I think it fit with another story he told Tom, one that appeared in Jimmy's written statement:

When I lived with Dennis, I found a wooden baseball bat under my bed. The baseball bat was a souvenir type bat maybe eighteen inches long. I assumed that it belonged to Dennis. I thought that Dennis put the bat there. I later felt that Dennis put it there so I would find it. This was about a year after Natalie died and I thought of that incident and only from what I knew of the injuries that Natalie received, that she was beat in the head with something like this bat. This is when I really started believing that Dennis killed Natalie.

After I found this bat, my thoughts were that maybe this bat was the one that was used to kill Natalie. I moved out right after this and I put the bat between the mattress and box springs. I never knew what happened to the bat.

It was Davis's behavior more than anything else that led Jimmy to suspect his friend. He told us, just as he told Tom, that Dennis was violent and jealous and went into rages from which even Jimmy couldn't calm him.

Toward the end of our conversation he added something that hadn't made it into his statement: Even though Dennis had been the one to break up the relationship with Natalie Antonetti, he'd acted more jealous over Natalie than anyone else. Jimmy never saw the pair of them argue, he told us, but Dennis was so possessive with Natalie that she wasn't even allowed to *talk* to another man in Dennis's presence.

As we were leaving Jimmy told us he had once received a letter from Dennis Davis. He couldn't remember its contents in detail, nor was he able to find it, but he said one thing about the letter bothered him. Jimmy had written to Davis first, saying something along the lines of, "I don't know whether you did this or not." Nowhere in his friend's response, Jimmy told us, did Davis deny killing Natalie or otherwise assert his innocence.

Tom and I looked at each other and I saw by the twitch of Tom's eyebrow that he was thinking the same as I was: The lack of a denial wasn't so much strange as it was telling.

Chapter 14

A KILLER GOES FREE

The early summer passed with no trial date being set. Wade Russell told me in court that he'd considered having Mike Lynch try the case himself but ultimately rejected the idea. Wade was a decent man and I thought part of this was that Wade didn't want to put that kind of burden on his friend. But I saw it as a smart, strategic move on his part, too. From a defense perspective, Wade only had to raise the specter of reasonable doubt in one juror's mind. I, on the other hand, needed to surpass that highest of burdens with all twelve jurors, convince every single one of them beyond a reasonable doubt that Davis was guilty. When Wade told me his decision, I smiled like I didn't mind and expected that news, though I was disappointed I had allowed myself to get my hopes up. Truthfully, part of me was a little relieved.

Wade gave me additional news in court: He wanted his client out of jail. Dennis Davis, Wade told me, had been sick for some time. Heart problems and other health issues were exaggerated by the paucity of health care in a county jail. Wade set a bond reduction hearing for July 9 and I called Johnny and prepared him for the possibility that the man who might have killed his mother and lived free for two decades might walk free once more.

As ever, Natalie's son Johnny took the news calmly and rationally, asking if he'd be needed to testify. I told him no, because in a bond reduction hearing I was allowed to present what would otherwise be hearsay evidence—documents and reports—and usually didn't put witnesses on the stand. I explained that I didn't want a defense lawyer to get a "free shot" at my witnesses. Anytime a prosecution witness testifies in a pretrial hearing, the defense cross-examines him as thoroughly as possible and obtains a transcript for the trial. And at trial, the defense disputes even the most minor discrepancies in testimony to make the witness look not credible.

"Wow, I wouldn't have thought of something like that," Johnny said.

"Nothing's easy, I know, but don't forget he's trying to save his client's life," I replied, adding with a smile, "Don't worry, we're here to think of these things for you."

"Good thing, too." He hesitated. "Does this mean the trial won't be this summer?"

"Probably not; sorry." I hated disappointing him, but he needed to know the truth. "Here's how it works. If a defendant is out of jail, there's no hurry to get to his trial, but if someone's locked up then he's going to be putting heat on his lawyer to hurry up and try the case. The lawyer will also be getting heat from the judge, because every month stats come out ranking the courts on how many inmates they have in jail. The more your court has, the lower you are on the ranking. And judges don't like to be low on that list."

"Well, let's worry about that when it happens," Johnny responded. "Just do what you can."

And, of course, I would. But the case was moving very slowly. It was filled with hazy memories of a long-forgotten crime scene and many unknowns.

As July heated up we had our first hearing in the Davis case. On July 6, the courtroom was packed, because Dennis Davis was trying to get out of jail. His bond was set at one million dollars, which was high even for a murder case. Efrain De La Fuente had offered to sit with me, because Jim Young was tied up in another court. Behind us, Johnny sat with his cousins and aunts, his support group and mine, too.

Texas law requires a judge to consider certain factors in setting the amount of bond, also called bail. The bond needs to be high enough so the defendant doesn't abscond, so whether or not the defendant is a flight risk is highly relevant. The law also says that a bond shouldn't be so high it becomes "an instrument of oppression." Thus the ability to make bail is crucial and testimony at these hearings often revolves around an inmate's financial resources—the poorer he is, the lower the bond should be, goes his argument. The safety of the community is another factor, as is the nature of the offense for which the defendant is charged.

The hearing was the first time I really had a chance to look at Davis. He seemed nervous as he looked around. His family, or so I assumed, sat behind him and I wondered which one was Rebecca, his wife. I wondered, too, if she would testify, because if she did I'd get a chance to question her. Wade might try to stop me, because Rebecca's trial testimony wasn't really relevant to the bond hearing, but I wanted to document her story in case Davis was released, allowing the defense time to polish her account.

Wade started with the defendant's brother. His testimony was very brief, telling the court that his brother was not a danger to the community and that if released, Dennis could live at his home in Austin. On cross-examination I established that the brothers didn't have a close relationship and that Dennis's brother knew nothing about Dennis's financial situation. Dennis's nephew testified next and said pretty much the same thing, but on cross I discovered a dispute between the brothers over the will of their father and a property in Pennsylvania. Nothing that seemed important to either this hearing or my case, but I stored the information away for future use.

Next up was Mike Gonzales, the first of many musicians who would testify in this case. A longtime friend of Davis, he added little other than another opinion that Davis wouldn't flee and wasn't a danger to the community.

On cross, I threw out a line hoping he'd bite. "You testified that you didn't think Mr. Davis would be a danger to the community. Is that what you believe?"

"Yes, sir."

"Are you aware of Dennis Davis's temper?"

"No, sir."

"You don't think he has a bad temper?" I pressed.

"No, sir."

"Are you aware of any instances other than his conviction where he has assaulted women?"

"No, sir."

"Never heard anything like that?"

"No, sir," he responded.

"Do you know if Mr. Davis has a problem with alcohol?"

"No, sir."

"You don't know or he doesn't?" I asked.

"I don't know that he does. No, sir."

"Okay, thank you."

I glanced at Efrain who was sitting next to me and he just shrugged. *Worth a try,* I thought.

Gonzales was excused and my hopes soared as a woman made her way to stand in front of the judge to be sworn in. *Is that Rebecca?* I wondered.

It turned out the woman was Rebecca's sister. She made the same assurances about Davis and said he could live with her about three hours away, if he was released. I asked her whether she had ever seen or heard of any violence between her sister and Davis and, unsurprisingly, she said no.

We adjourned for lunch early, as Wade's next witnesses weren't available and when we returned at 2 P.M., he put Dennis's niece on the stand. She also offered her home as a place to live, but added nothing else of significance.

The next witness, however, changed the subject and in a direction I found interesting. Cliff Byers, a former FBI agent and now a private investigator, had a languid style. He settled in the witness stand and talked about Donn Chelli, the neighbor who gave a statement to police about a tall man carrying a bat and wearing a T-shirt from the band the Lotions loitering outside Natalie's apartment building the night of the assault.

He related to the judge the essence of Chelli's statement, so the Court could understand why the man's testimony was so important at trial. Then he talked about his effort to locate Chelli. "He's in Las Vegas," Byers said, "but he wasn't home when I went to his house and he hasn't responded to calls, hand-delivered notes or a certified letter."

"It is fair to say he has not been cooperating with you so far?"

"No, sir."

"It is also fair to say he is an essential witness for the defense?"

"Yes, sir."

And I didn't disagree. Dennis Davis didn't fit the description that Chelli gave. If I was defending the case, I'd also see him as an essential witness.

I had no questions for Byers and Wade stood to address the court. "There are no more witnesses for the defense, your Honor. Oh, I'm sorry. I do need to call…I'm sorry. I apologize. Call Becky Davis."

Rebecca Davis stood tall and walked resolutely to the stand. Red-haired and attractive, she was dressed like a working professional. She kept her eyes on Wade.

I paid close attention, because this woman could be my most important witness and also my most hostile.

She began by telling Judge Lynch about her relationship with Dennis: They married in May 2002, after being together over ten years, and divorced four or five years later. She denied enduring any physical violence at Dennis's hands and confirmed that she was currently in touch with him. Quickly Wade moved on to the money issue and Rebecca told the Court she could raise $10,000 through family and friends who supported Dennis. She denied Dennis was a flight risk and Wade ended his questioning.

I felt sure Rebecca expected me to come roaring out of the gate and I wanted to keep her off balance. I began with innocuous questions. We discussed the Pennsylvania home. I didn't care about it, but this got her talking, made her comfortable and while she was that way I asked her gently, "You are kind of the one who got this investigation started in the first place, isn't that true?" She confirmed it with a simple, "Yes" and I decided I wanted to hear the story for myself.

"How did that happen?"

"Well, I was visiting a Buddhist therapist and I was encouraged by my therapist to basically allow all of my worries and fears to be talked about and one of the things that had worried me was a statement that Dennis had made right after I met him."

"What was that statement?"

"That statement was that he had sinned against God and man. He made that statement after we first met."

"Did he explain that statement to you?"

"No and I never asked him to follow up."

"What did you think that it meant when he said it?"

"It concerned me that maybe there was an involvement somehow with a girl. I knew nothing about Natalie, but I knew that there was a girl."

As we continued with the cross-examination, Rebecca started to prevaricate a little, seeming to me like she was playing down Dennis's statement. Then she surprised me by playing the victim card. There she was trying to get something off her chest and the mean policeman started calling and asking questions. It seemed narcissistic that this woman had no understanding of why Tom Walsh might pursue the lead and that something larger than Rebecca Davis's peace of mind might be at stake.

I hesitated to ask my final question, because I was scared she might have an answer ready for me. But it was something I felt I needed to ask and the sooner I did it the better. I wanted it to become the linchpin of my argument to the jury when we finally went to trial.

"Do you know of anything else that Dennis Davis might have done that would fit into that category of sinning against God and man?"

"No. Other than maybe grief over his parents and his mother dying without him really getting to see her first."

Bingo, I thought. The woman who knew Dennis Davis better than anyone in the whole world couldn't think of a single thing, other than Natalie's murder, that would warrant his anguished statement. If there was an alternate explanation, she was the one to know it. And I was a little shocked that even now, this far into the legal process, Dennis hadn't corrected her initial assumption that this was about Natalie, hadn't given her an alternate explanation. Either way, he made the statement and she couldn't explain it away.

Which left me hoping that I could get her to testify at trial.

After she left the stand and took her seat it was clear Wade wasn't finished with the surprises.

"Call Dennis Davis."

I started to panic a little. The boundaries of a bond hearing were vague and this was my first one. I didn't know exactly how far I could go with my cross-examination of Davis or whether I could include facts relating to the murder itself. I whispered quick questions to Efrain and considered turning the cross-examination entirely over to him. But this was my case and I knew it better than anyone.

"Keep it short," Efrain whispered back to me. "The judge will shut you down if you get too close to the interesting stuff."

Wade began his examination by discussing the Pennsylvania house, an old stone place in the middle of nowhere, according to Davis. He and his brother owned it jointly, but there was a difference of opinion about selling it. I assumed that the brother with the job and the family didn't want to and the one in jail desperate for money did, but Davis didn't clarify. He admitted to his assault case in the 1980s but assured the Court that since he'd moved out of Austin he was a changed man. He revealed his health problems: an irregular heartbeat that wasn't being treated in jail, as well as some teeth that required medical attention.

Wade brought the conversation to Davis's career, I suspected to remind the judge that Davis once was somebody, that he was not an average street thug but a man with an impressive work history. Davis talked about working with country music stars Tim McGraw, Faith Hill and Jo Dee Messina. He said that he could still work as a sound engineer if he got out of jail and if anyone would hire him.

Then it was my turn. I started politely, bidding Dennis a good morning. I confirmed his lack of a job and asked if he had transportation. But after five questions like this I moved on.

"I want to ask you about that statement you made to Becky Davis about having sinned against God and man. Is it true that you said that to her?"

"Yes."

"Did you ever explain that to her?" I asked.

"No, not until just recently."

"Until after you were arrested?"

"Yes," he responded.

"Did that explanation have anything to do with Natalie Antonetti?"

"No. Would you like me to explain that?"

And here I made a mistake.

I let my pride, my ego, get ahead of me. So far I'd controlled the conversation and I'd heard just what I wanted to hear. There was no way that after Becky's testimony and the answers I just received that Dennis could later deny making that statement. All that was left was to explain it. I didn't believe that he told Becky the truth about it after he was arrested; it made no sense to me, particularly because she didn't seem to have an explanation for it, just some vague words about his mother dying. But here he was offering to give his version, his reason, for making the statement that led directly to him being investigated for and charged with murder. An explanation that, when he gave it, maybe we could investigate and disprove. Or at least have a chance to discuss. He was offering to reveal a part of himself, his strategy and even though I wouldn't believe a word of it, maybe I should find out what he was going to say, because he might say it again in trial and I wanted to be ready.

But I decided quickly and I didn't let him talk. I didn't want him lying on the stand, feeding some carefully thought-out explanation to the judge and to Johnny that we had to listen to with straight faces and pretend he wasn't committing perjury.

"No, thank you," I replied.

So I moved on, asking Davis about his assets as if the details of the hearing mattered greatly.

Wade closed his part of the hearing and turned it over to me. Normally I hesitated to put on a witness in a hearing like this, because it gave the defense a chance to examine him or her. I could tell the judge all he needed to know about the case from the PC Affidavit, which would be hearsay in a trial but was admissible in this kind of hearing. But this case was different and I wanted the judge and everyone in the room to know it was different, so I called Tom Walsh to the stand.

My interest in Tom's testimony wasn't the facts, but how he delivered them. Many of my witnesses for the trial would be lay witnesses, non-professionals testifying from memory. It would be their first time in a courtroom and they would be vulnerable to cross-examination. This meant I needed my professionals to be strong on the stand. I'd had numerous conversations with Tom and I knew how well he knew the case. But when we talked he had a tendency to meander, because his mind worked so quickly. He knew so much about the case that he could bamboozle me with details and make me forget the question I asked.

But he was perfect on the stand. In his quiet but firm voice he described for the judge the investigation, from the initial tip to disproving Davis's alibi and locating Kellie Torres. He turned his body to look at the judge when he talked; he was as precise and as spare with details as I wanted him to be. He answered our questions, mine and Wade's, carefully and thoughtfully and resisted any attempt to be led astray. I was hugely impressed and mightily relieved, because I knew he would be a good witness in front of the jury.

After Tom's testimony, Judge Lynch asked for brief arguments and I started by telling the Court, "The State's position is essentially that Mr. Davis has been out on bond or on the lam for twenty-five years. A million dollars is reasonable." I also appealed to the judge, because I suspected while he was likely to lower the bond, he was probably not keen about lowering it by much:

"This case is a year old. The State is essentially ready to go to trial. There is no delay on our part. The witness who has been testified about, Mr. Chelli, apparently has been sought since the turn of the year. There is no reason it should have taken this long. We think instead of any bond reduction, we should pick a trial date and try this case."

And then I sat down.

In his argument, Wade focused on Davis's peaceful history, his ties to the community and his cooperation with the investigation. He talked about Chelli, too, emphasizing that Chelli was crucial to the defense's case and that Davis couldn't get a fair trial without Chelli there. Wade told the Court that, in his opinion, $100,000 was a reasonable bond.

Judge Lynch took a few moments before speaking. Then he began by noting that the million-dollar bond was "extraordinary," adding that even if he didn't reduce it, an appeals court probably would. He continued, "I am going to reduce the bond to $250,000, together with the conditions of electronic monitor, surrender of the passport and the defendant must live in Texas and live with the closest relative available to Austin if he is released on bond. All of those conditions should be met prior to posting any kind of bond."

Just 10 percent of the bond amount. That's what Davis needed to walk out of jail and something told me he'd manage it.

Afterward, I talked with Johnny and his family and assured them that if Davis made the bond, he'd be instructed not to contact any of them. As usual, Johnny wasn't overly concerned about that. What he wanted to know was when we'd be trying the case. "It's clear to me from comments the judge made that we won't be going to trial until the Chelli issue is resolved and so far, the defense has failed to connect with him."

If I wanted this case to go to trial, I knew what I had to do: find Donn Chelli.

When Johnny had left and before we headed into the judge's chambers to discuss trial dates, I talked to Efrain about my idea. He was not on the case, but I trusted his opinion and he agreed with me.

"We'll help," I later told the judge. "The State will find Chelli and get him to trial."

"He's not great for your case," Lynch said with a little smile. "You sure you want him to testify?"

I smiled back. "Not really, but I want Davis to get a fair trial and I'd like that trial to be this century. I think Chelli's a loon, but I think I can show that to the jury through cross-examination."

"Great." Judge Lynch looked at Wade and then back at me. "Let's pick a date and try this case."

Chapter 15

SORTING THE EVIDENCE

If you think the government has the ability to track the major events in your life, you're only partially right. Take buying a car, for example. If you pay cash to a private individual, the only way to track the sale is through the title documents. But what if you buy a car and then wait a year, two years, before you send in the registration papers? This registration conundrum is similar to one we encountered in the Davis case.

And it was a conundrum made tougher by some incomplete police work in the original report. Natalie's neighbor Deanna Cooley had seen a gray/blue car outside the apartment complex that night, parked across multiple spaces. Finding Deanna was imperative, because Dennis Davis admitted in his six-hour interview that he owned such a car. My concern was if Deanna, like so many people, couldn't remember the details of what she'd seen, I would be out of luck.

There is a rule of evidence in Texas that allows a witness statement to be read to the jury if the witness herself cannot remember the facts contained in the statement but can verify that she did give the statement at the time of the crime. Unfortunately, a formal statement wasn't taken from Deanna at the time, just notes made in the offense report. With no written statement, a blank memory would mean a jury would never hear about the car and that seemed like a travesty. My only alternative was to rely on official documents to prove Davis owned the gray/blue car at the time of the assault, but so far we couldn't. We didn't have any identifying details on the vehicle and we couldn't very well ask Davis if he remembered the license plate or VIN.

It was a piece of evidence I was desperate to get in, because it added to the alibi-busting statements of Amparo Garcia-Crow and was even more helpful in putting Davis at the scene.

So I sat down with my investigator, Mike Henderson, with a to-do list and locating Deanna Cooley was at the top, right above finding Donn Chelli. Mike was one of the newer investigators but was a seasoned law-enforcement professional. He was of Mexican heritage, though he often joked about his Anglo-sounding name and since he shared my sense of humor, we got on well from the moment we met. It didn't hurt that he was hard-working and an absolute marvel at tracking down people. If someone could be found, Mike would find him, which in this case was very valuable.

On August 13 Tom Walsh and I met with Amparo Garcia-Crow. She didn't witness the crime, but she was happy to tell what she knew. Her face ageless, Ampie, as she was known, was charming and radiated energy. She was an artist, writer, musician, singer, director; she was the best of Austin personified and managed to transmit all of that without any effort at all. As a former University of Texas professor and the inaugural director for the opening of Austin's Mexican-American Cultural Center, she had impressive professional and community credentials.

She also seemed unfailingly honest. Much of what happened, she told us, she didn't remember. But when we talked about her diaries and the emotional connection she had to writing about her life, it was clear the entries were more than hurried-off notations, far more than recitations of events or people. Reading portions with her and listening to her talk about her diary entries, it was obvious the entries were essential to the way she saw and learned about herself. The important people and events weren't just described in her journals; they were analyzed as if by a therapist.

Which meant, she assured us, if Dennis Davis had been with her on the weekend of October 13, it would be recorded in her diary. She read us each mention of him—and there were several—and said confidently that every time she went on a date with him, she wrote about it. Yet nothing was recorded about him on October 12 or 13.

"And look at this," she said, turning to a page bearing the date October 15. I read the entry and it reflected a phone call from Davis to Amparo, telling her about the assault on Natalie. She had cut out a newspaper article about the attack and slipped it into the pages of her journal here. The entry and the article were significant, she told us, because if Davis had been with her when he was called to the scene that morning, as his alibi claimed, then this factual entry would have been more emotional. She would have had a more direct connection to the event and would have referenced his being with her when it happened.

But there was something more. Looking over her diary after all these years, she said, it reminded her that this was the weekend she got back together with her previous boyfriend. It was a honeymoon period for them, she recalled. "I remember that now."

She spoke confidently to Tom and me and she sounded sure of herself. But I had seen it happen before—a witness was sure as can be when sitting comfortably in a conference room or my office, but when the pressure of cross-examination came, that certainty disappeared.

"I need to know something," I said to her, "and I need you to be completely honest. I don't care what the answer is, I really don't; I just need to know the truth."

"Of course."

"I need to know how sure you are that Dennis Davis wasn't with you that weekend. I need to know. Is it sixty percent? Eighty? Ninety?"

She was already shaking her head. "No. One hundred percent. I'm a hundred percent sure he wasn't with me."

After Amparo left, Tom stayed to talk about the case. We talked about the gray/blue car, because Tom had tracked down the man who sold it to Dennis. He still lived near Austin and was happy to try to help, but he couldn't remember much, including when he sold the car. He didn't have the license plate or VIN either, so we couldn't get that information. We brooded about a possible dead-end. The only con-nection between Davis and the car was the man himself and in his in-terview with Tom, the man didn't specify the dates he owned the car.

And so far, Mike Henderson had not been able to find the only witness who could put Dennis Davis at the scene of the crime or at least put his car there: the elusive Deanna Cooley.

Someone else was proving elusive, too. Despite the best efforts of the Austin Police Department's cold case unit, my own investigator and the defense's former FBI agent investigator, Donn Chelli appeared to have disappeared entirely. We were pretty sure he was no longer in Las Vegas; we had tracked him from there to Los Angeles. But that was where the trail ran cold, dead-ending at a post office box stationed in a strip mall in downtown L.A. The law didn't allow us to serve a subpoena on Chelli by mail, certainly not to a post office box, so we needed to fig-ure out a way to find the man himself if we wanted him to come to trial.

Wade Russell, to his credit, wasn't willing to give up. He had a new strategy that made Chelli's absence a non-issue for him, an advantage even. It was a gutsy move and, from his perspective, the right one. His audacious, if inventive, plan was to have Chelli's writ-ten statement admitted into evidence. When he mentioned it in court I spluttered and the judge himself did a double take.

"You want to admit the statement, the written statement?"

"Yes," Wade said. "It's the only way my client gets a fair trial."

I knew that his argument had merit, because I also believed that Chelli's evidence should be heard by the jury. But not like this. Written statements are almost never allowed into evidence at a jury trial, because they are the epitome of legal hearsay.

The rule that bars hearsay governs every civil, criminal and fed-eral court in the land and the reason for its existence is simple. Each side in a trial is supposed to be allowed to test the evidence in front of the jury, to poke and probe and challenge so that the jury can make a reasoned, rational and informed decision. If hearsay were allowed, a person could testify in court, "Jake said that John told him that Michael said that Mary promised she'd kill Bob." How is a lawyer sup-posed to counter that kind of evidence, other than saying, "Nuh-uh, did not"? Likewise, if written statements were admissible, an expert, such as a medical examiner for example, could merely submit his report from the autopsy and not come to the trial. How does the defense challenge that ME's conclusions if he isn't there?

And how could I challenge Donn Chelli if all that came in was his written statement? I had plenty to ask him, enough that I felt sure I could destroy his credibility, but if he wasn't in court I couldn't even bid him good morning let alone quiz him on parts of his story that didn't add up and his possible motives for giving it, which were questionable. For example, the time line. As best I could deduce, it went something like this: Chelli went to the store and on the way back saw the man with the bat. He went inside his apartment and didn't mention it to Fran Alcozer for an hour or so, let alone call the cops. Then he went back outside an hour later where he found and talked to Johnny, who had already told us that Chelli invited him into his own apartment while asking questions, even offering him a soda. When Johnny left, because the ambulance had arrived for his mother, Chelli finally called 911. That seemed to be the time line and it smacked very much of a man who wanted to insert himself into a criminal investigation—he found out from Johnny roughly what happened and then let his imagination go to work, forming a story that would intrigue the police. It was a little far-fetched, admittedly, but given what I knew about Chelli it was far from impossible.

My impression of him as a man who wanted to be a part of a homicide investigation, on the good guys' side, was furthered by his subsequent call to police a couple of months after Natalie's attack to finger a homeless guy as looking like the intruder, some poor sap who was almost immediately discounted from the investigation.

I wanted to ask Chelli, too, about his own violent inclinations toward Fran Alcozer. And I most certainly wanted to ask him about the series of allegations he made in Las Vegas that revolved around elements of the mafia looking to whack him, drivers in bizarre vehicles stalking his home and even his police report claiming that his barber was passing on information to those out to get him.

Chelli appeared to have a tendency toward paranoia and an interest in plopping himself into police investigations, issues I thought the jury ought to hear about.

But I couldn't very well ask a piece of paper about them.

So I objected to Wade's idea. Not because I didn't want Davis to get a fair trial; I did. But from my viewpoint the cards were already dealt unfairly: The burden of proof was mine and so every forgetful or absent witness hurt my attempt to prove what Davis did. Letting Chelli's startling and, in my view, unreliable statement into evidence would be like letting Wade shuffle through the deck to choose his own aces.

The judge responded with what I was thinking, what we all knew: There was not a rule of evidence that would allow the statement into evidence. The hearsay within it ran several layers deep (the first layer was the statement itself, another was when the statement quoted words allegedly used by the mysterious bat-wielder). Wade was adamant, though, insisting that if the jury didn't get to hear about the man Chelli saw, his client wouldn't get a fair trial. Even though it wasn't legally sound, it was a good argument to make, because Judge Lynch was, above all else, a fair man. Wade didn't want Davis to stand trial for this most serious crime without his most important witness, perhaps his only witness.

Lynch looked at me and suggested I try even harder to find Chelli, track him down and serve him with a subpoena that compelled his presence at trial. Then he thought for a moment and told Wade to do some legal research, see if there was some authority that would permit the statement to come into evidence and put something in writing.

Which meant Judge Lynch was thinking about letting the statement into evidence, actually considering Wade's proposal. Which also meant I needed to add this to my own list of legal issues that needed researching.

Later, I found Jim Young in his office and I sat down, hoping that my anxiety at the upcoming conversation wasn't too obvious. I started by asking if he thought Davis was guilty and before he could answer I asked if he thought we could prove it. He gave me a "go on" look and I pointed out the practical difficulty of trying a big case without being able to chat frequently about the small stuff, to plan and strategize when ideas came to mind rather than at occasional meetings in the elevator. I asked him, flat out, if he'd rather someone else sat second chair with me and, typical of Jim, he smiled and nodded.

"I'm happy to try it with you; of course I am," he said. "But if there's someone in your court who can do it, who wants to do it, I'm fine with letting that person. I've not invested that much time yet, so we can do whatever you want."

There were two people in my court who could do it, I told him, one who very much wanted to, so we agreed he'd step aside. I was grateful to Jim, not just because he wanted to make sure I had someone capable next to me, but also because this was precisely the kind of frank and mature discourse professionals should be able to have.

I left Jim's office and went straight to see Efrain to let him know Jim was off the case and to talk about who would be sitting with me. I could feel the case gathering momentum and I knew that issues like the spousal privilege and Chelli's statement would soon take time from my schedule and require the input and energy of a second chair. I wanted to resolve that matter as quickly as possible. And I was pretty happy about the possibilities.

The first option was Kelsey MacKay. Like me, she had an international background, having lived on several continents and attended high school at the Jakarta International School in Indonesia. She graduated from the University of Texas School of Law and started working as an assistant county attorney in Austin, eventually serving as the chief of the family violence court. Hired at the Travis County District Attorney's Office in 2007, she was initially assigned to the Trial Court Division and between then and the time I met her, she'd filled positions including family violence grand jury prosecutor and family justice division prosecutor, dealing with both child abuse and domestic violence cases.

Tall and attractive, she was also incredibly energetic. She had one speed and that was "full on" and she had the volume to match. She was once told at a restaurant to keep her voice down and when she relayed the story to the office later, she was surprised that we all just laughed. Our only surprise was that it hadn't happened before. She and I hadn't tried a case together yet, but she was exceptionally bright and I'd seen her at work, channeling her energy into note-taking and list-making. For someone so energetic, she was also incredibly detail-oriented. And for a case as sprawling as *State v. Dennis Davis*, that energy and attention to detail would be invaluable.

On a personal level I was happy to work with her, too. I didn't have to be careful about what I said around her and as the stress of the trial built, I liked the idea I could be myself without watching the cuss words or reigning in the dark humor. I appreciated, too, that she was so into the case, that she knew enough to be totally on board with Tom and me in our belief that Davis was guilty. If Efrain decided Kelsey would sit with me, I knew that Tom would be delighted with her dedication and abilities.

The second option was Efrain himself. I would be just as happy to have him, though for different reasons. The chief one was his experience, something that, as he pointed out when we talked, Kelsey lacked: She had yet to try a murder case. His hesitation about taking the case was based on the fact that he was already helping me with another murder case and he was also working on a capital murder death penalty case that was keeping him extremely busy.

I left the decision with him, knowing I would be comfortable with either of my colleagues sitting beside me when the Davis case went to trial.

Chapter 16

GEARING UP FOR TRIAL

At the Travis County DA's Office, each prosecutor in the trial court division juggles roughly 150 cases at any one time, all of them felonies. After a big trial, praise and congratulations from colleagues is sincere and rewarding, but it's also fleeting, because each one of us has another big trial, case-killing suppression hearing or grand jury presentation looming on the horizon. Usually another trial.

I met with Wade Russell and the judge to decide one thing: The Dennis Davis case was set for the week starting Monday, April 11, 2011. The judge gave us a "preferential" jury setting and he made it clear he wanted all issues, legal, factual and witness-related, dealt with before then.

Six months seemed like a long time, but I had a full caseload to get back to and a slew of issues that needed resolving before *State v. Dennis Davis* kicked off. And many of those issues that were worrying the judge were still worrying me.

The first and perhaps easiest was the matter of who would sit beside me. I talked it over with Efrain and he told me that he wanted to do it. I had been hugely impressed with his organization and presentation skills, so I was pleased. Frankly, I would have been as pleased if he'd declined and put Kelsey on the case, so I was always going to be happy. Kelsey was disappointed. Efrain kept his placid and efficient self focused on the case.

Things were going smoothly. Mike Henderson, as I knew he would, had located the woman who saw a gray/blue car outside Natalie's apartment building. She didn't remember much and she was fearful of testifying, but we knew where she was and we knew she was coming to the trial.

I called Tom on October 13. It was my ninth wedding anniversary and also the anniversary of the attack on Natalie. We talked about the case a little, but not too much. For me, it was a matter of reaching out to someone else who recognized the importance of that date and together we hoped that it was the last anniversary that Natalie's killer lived free.

Two days later I woke up to the first cold morning of the year, at least cold for Texas. It was in the low fifties and the heater in my car blew out that burnt, dusty smell that comes with its first use in a while. At work I found a set of papers on my chair: "Defendant's First Motion in Limine and Motion to Dismiss."

A motion *in limine* is standard in all trials, criminal and civil. It lists factual issues that might come up at trial, matters the filing party believes are inadmissible and should not come into evidence. When a judge grants such a motion, he's not deciding that the evidence is inadmissible; rather he's saying, "You need to approach the bench before asking questions about it." For example, Wade's motion included Davis's criminal history and the assaultive past that Tom uncovered in the police reports. His legal argument was that these matters were not relevant to the case and even if relevant, they would have an unfairly prejudicial effect on the jury. As I read through most of the topics listed, I didn't plan on contesting the vast majority. After all, if I felt like they should come to attention at some point, I could just approach the bench and get a ruling from Judge Lynch. No big deal.

But a motion to dismiss?

This is the criminal law version of spotting a unicorn surfing on a rainbow. As I read through his motion, I was not even sure a district judge had the legal authority to dismiss a case. The only dismissals I'd ever seen or heard of happened because an ADA decided it was appropriate and filled out the paperwork.

The defense argument was essentially a rehash of the "we can't find Donn Chelli and we need him" position that they'd argued in court. This was a formalized version of that complaint and, after reading through it, I was impressed at the research and writing but less impressed with the conclusions. In several pages of argument there wasn't a single case that directly supported the proposition that a witness was so vital to a case it required the case be dismissed if that witness failed to appear or, in the alternative, that the witness's written statement be allowed into evidence in complete disregard of hearsay rules.

But Wade was being smart. He knew Judge Lynch would see this for what it was: a very clear signal that if Judge Lynch remained true to his ethos of giving all defendants fair trials, he had to at least consider letting the written statement in evidence. The dismissal aspect, I suspected, was not so much a realistic request as it was a chance for the judge to seem like he was "splitting the baby." He might grant an unprecedented motion (admitting Chelli's statement), but he also had a chance to deny part of that motion (dismissing the case). Another smart move on Wade's part.

In the interim, I needed to work on other cases, although I continued to ruminate on the Davis case while I had two jury trials in succession. Each night and whenever I had a moment free, I couldn't stop thinking about the Davis case.

Both of these other trials made it clear to me what I was up against in the Davis case, in terms of the jury. Everyone knew that Austin was a liberal city, one surrounded by counties that better fit the image of Texas, where justice was swift and harsh. And everyone knew that juries in Austin set the bar very high for prosecutors seeking convictions.

The run-up to Christmas was a flurry of long days and book work. With no trials before the New Year, I had time to work on a couple of the issues I knew would be pivotal in the Davis case.

In the peace and calm of my office I read through the case law, brushing the dust off my writing skills to put together a persuasive brief. And the issues were important, maybe even critical to the trial. One was, would I be able to use the comment Davis made to his wife, Becky, that he had "sinned against God and man"?

Not only had this remark gotten the case out of a filing cabinet in the first place, but also it was hugely telling. That a man's wife called the police, relayed the exact words and demeanor of a near-confession and associated those words with the murder of Natalie Antonetti would be huge from the jury's viewpoint. I was developing a trial theme in my mind, which was: "He committed a heinous act and he's been trying to confess ever since." This confession to his wife seemed to be crucial support for that theme, the one piece of evidence that gave credence to an otherwise fairly unlikely confession to Kellie Torres.

And it was on reinforcing Kellie's testimony, her credibility, that I concentrated in the latter part of the brief, because another issue I needed to address was her account of an attack that mirrored the one on Natalie: Kellie claimed that four years after Natalie's attack, Davis broke into her home a short while after they had ended their relationship and just hours after a screaming argument with her. She was attacked by Davis while she slept and beaten with a small base-ball bat.

While evidence of a defendant's other bad acts are expressly forbidden at trial, there are exceptions. One is known as the modus operandi exception. It allows the State to produce evidence of a previous crime committed by the defendant if there are enough similarities between the former crime and the one for which the defendant is on trial, such that it's almost certain the same person was responsible for both. I looked for cases with facts similar to mine and found some, though nothing identical.

I thought about how to argue this idea and scribbled on a piece of paper, coming up with a chart showing the "common characteristics" of Davis's attacks on Kellie and Natalie. When laid out, the similarities looked remarkable to me and I decided to put the chart itself into the brief.

Characteristics	Kellie Torres	Natalie Antonetti
Time	Late at night	Late at night
Relationship	Ex-girlfriend (recent breakup)	Ex-girlfriend (recent breakup)
Buildup	Argument in hours prior to attack	Argument in hours prior to attack
Motive	Jealousy	Jealousy
Victim's situation	Asleep when attack commenced	Asleep when attack commenced
Location	Victim's home	Victim's home
Access	Surreptitious but without damage	Surreptitious but without damage
Weapon	Small bat	Blunt object
Injuries	Multiple head injuries, spinal injuries, requiring hospitalization	Multiple head injuries requiring hospitalization

I felt strongly that the judge would view this kind of evidence as extremely prejudicial against the defendant and that he wouldn't want Davis to be convicted for killing Natalie based on his attack on Kellie. But, as ever, I knew Judge Lynch to be fair and I hoped that in this case fairness meant letting me include evidence of the attack on Kellie. Just to make sure I could prove the attack, I drew up a subpoena for medical records from the hospital that treated Kellie after the assault and asked Mike to acquire all documents relating to assaults committed by Davis.

As I was working, I was brought back to the issue of spousal privilege by an e-mail from Wade. A few weeks previously I had asked him the basis for the privilege, knowing that he couldn't and wouldn't raise the matter frivolously without some factual support. His e-mailed response relayed information from Rebecca Davis, stating when she and Dennis met, when they began living together and when they began referring to themselves as married in relation to when Dennis made the statement to Rebecca, approximately three months after allegedly moving in together and telling others they were married.

Certainly enough to raise the issue, but I wrote and told Wade it was not enough to convince me and, I suspected, not enough to convince Judge Lynch, either.

I looked over the e-mail again and an idea came to me. I drafted another subpoena and, hoping for the best, handed it to Mike to serve.

Then I set the spousal privilege matter for a hearing.

On December 15, the Davis case was set for a ruling on the Chelli issue—whether or not the judge would allow Chelli's written statement. Judge Lynch, as it happened, wasn't ready to rule. We talked informally at the bench and he told Wade that what Wade was asking for was outrageous and inconsistent with the rules of evidence. But it was, he said, consistent with the notion of a fair trial and while he was leaning toward allowing it, he told Wade he wouldn't until he was satisfied that every effort had been made to get Chelli himself to court.

And right now, Judge Lynch was not satisfied. The judge, astute as ever, wondered aloud whether it was in the defense's best interest to find the man, as they'd be better off without him there, with just his incontrovertible words on paper. Wade, a little sheepishly, admitted that his pretrial strategy might include this line of reasoning.

After the hearing, Efrain and I spoke privately. We both knew that Chelli's statement would hurt our case badly. The defense would use it to highlight the differences between the man described by Chelli and the height, weight and physique of the defendant. And while on the surface the discrepancies were concerning, we felt that Chelli was a hugely unreliable witness. If we couldn't persuade the jury of that through cross-examination, we might be sunk.

We decided to redouble our efforts to find Chelli and bring him to court. We met with Ron Lara, head of the cold case unit, to get his best men working on it. Detectives Richard Faithful and Jerry Bauzon set to it. I knew both men and would hate to have them on my trail; they were bright and dogged. If Chelli could be found, they would do so.

Then I decided to contact Tom Bevel, a leading expert on crime scene reconstruction and blood spatter evidence who had testified in hundreds of cases, for defense and prosecution, out of his home base in Oklahoma. We wanted him to look at the crime scene photos to see what the blood spatter patterns might have looked like. Specifically, we wanted to know whether the assailant would have been covered in blood or not. We already had a narrow window of time between the assault and when Jolene Wells called Davis to come to the apartment. If Bevel (or someone else) testified that Davis would have been covered in blood, that would close the window even tighter. When I called him, Bevel told me he'd worked with Efrain before and would be glad to help. He asked for a copy of the medical examiner's report and all the crime-scene and autopsy photos.

Before closing the office for Christmas, absolutely my family's favorite holiday of the year, I prepared a packet for Tom Bevel and mailed it to him in Oklahoma.

Chapter 17

A NEW YEAR

I could feel the momentum gathering. There was no doubt that the biggest trial of my career would take place in the coming year and when I returned to my office on January 3, that trial was just three months away.

I called the 167th's court reporter, asking whether she'd finished preparing a transcript of the bond-reduction hearing. She had. I asked her for a copy, because I was preparing for the spousal privilege hearing and in the back of my mind I had a sneaking feeling that, quite by luck, I had asked a question of Becky Davis that could prove crucial.

Racing up to the offices behind the 167th courtroom, I signed off on a request and authorization for payment, thanked the court reporter profusely and headed back to my office with the transcript.

My fear with hearings like this was that, put frankly, witnesses would lie. Becky Davis was smart; so was Dennis. They would realize the importance of her not testifying. I had worried over the Christmas break that she would lie about when they were married, say that they ran off and had a private ceremony somewhere. If so, I was in trouble, because the spousal privilege would have begun immediately. Her testimony would be out.

What I needed was for her to claim the privilege under the auspices of common-law marriage and my questions at the bond hearing seemed to settle the issue. I had asked Becky Davis: "Can you tell me again the dates of your marriage?" Her response: "May 18, 2002 and the divorce was October 31, 2007, I think." Additionally, she confirmed that Davis had "made that statement after we first met."

So common-law it was. For that to work, the Davises had to satisfy three factors set out by the family code that establish whether a couple is common-law married. First, the couple must have "agreed to be married." Second, they must have "held themselves out" as husband and wife; in other words, represented to others that they were married to each other. For example, the woman might have introduced her partner socially as "my husband" or they might have filed a joint income tax return. Third, they must have lived together in the state as husband and wife.

On the first and third, I lost. I would never be able to disprove an agreement between them to be married. All I could ever do was call her a liar and that would get me nowhere. Likewise, there was no question that they lived together in Texas; no possible way I could prove they didn't.

But did they hold themselves out to be married? Wade's e-mail suggested several ways in which they did, ways that Rebecca would no doubt testify to at the hearing. But I had timing on my side. Rebecca acknowledged that the "sinned against God and man" statement was made soon after they met. That militated against marriage just because of the timing. Sure, people meet and fall in love quickly, but when they get married so soon after meeting, they usually get married in a church. They don't reach a verbal agreement on the subject; they go all out. At least, that was what I'd be arguing.

But overall I was relieved, pleased even, with the bond hearing testimony. We still had a chance.

Also helpful was the news that came in from Tom Bevel, my blood spatter expert. On January 4, he e-mailed me his initial impressions as promised, saying:

> In looking at the scene photos and M.E. report, in a cursory manner, I offer the following observations.
> The photos show blood saturation, smears, passive drips, transfers and do not show actual spatter or cast-off from the blows to the victim.

I would not expect much in the way of spatter or cast-off onto the attacker if the wounds are inflicted with a baseball bat as the blood goes in the path of least resistance and in the direction of force which is away from the attacker.

Likewise unless the attacker handled the victim after blood loss I would expect little to no blood on the attacker.

All of the blood loss in the multiple rooms is consistent with movement by the victim after blood loss began in the form of drips, transfers, etc.

While I can establish movement by the victim after blood loss, I don't know how this information may or may not assist you in your case.

Donn Chelli, assuming he saw anyone at all, saw his mystery "Lotions man" forty-five minutes before Natalie was assaulted, so even if he was the killer I wouldn't expect him to be covered in blood at that time. But according to Bevel, who had no idea what I was thinking, Dennis Davis could have bludgeoned Natalie, returned home, cleaned and then returned to Natalie's without having to do much more than change his shirt and wash his hands. Which was precisely what we thought happened.

The second full week of January kept me hopping. Ron Lara and his cold case team had moved into high gear and were now sure Chelli was in Los Angeles. They also continued to uncover interesting background details about Chelli, information I planned to use once we found him and served our interstate subpoena. I planned to start with his longstanding claim that the mafia was out to get him for some unknown reason, a vendetta he asserted they'd been pursuing for decades (apparently without much success).

On Friday, January 14, I met Kellie Torres for the first time and she was nothing like I imagined. I had pictured her as aloof, disinterested and hard to get talking, but she was quite the opposite. As the memories came flooding back to her, the difficulty was keeping her focused, something we'd have to work on for trial.

I'd heard the stories that she was telling me before, either from police reports or from the taped interviews with Tom, but it was not the substance so much as the delivery that I was interested in. She came across as very credible indeed, an impression bolstered by the list of civic and community positions and involvement she related to me. This was a woman who had moved on and up from her life with Dennis Davis.

However, I spotted one potential problem with her description of the attack that Davis carried out on her while she was sleeping. It didn't match the account in the police report. That report made no mention of a bat being used, nor did it say he attacked her while she was sleeping. Rather, it said she left a party with him voluntarily, went to his studio where they argued, then went to her place where he as-saulted her. Kellie was emphatic that the report was wrong and that Davis attacked her with a bat as she slept. I watched her as she told that story, showing us how he held the bat over his shoulder, an image of Davis that seemed to have been burned into her memory forever. As for the discrepancy, she suggested something that had already oc-curred to me: Maybe she downplayed the police report so as not to get Davis in too much trouble, because she was still so afraid of him. It's a phenomenon we see every day in this business, wives and girlfriends letting their abusers off the hook. It usually comes in the form of refusing to file charges or testify at all, but an abused woman playing down her injuries and the circumstances of the assault is almost the rule rather than the exception.

We talked about Kellie's hospital visit, too, because my investiga-tor Mike Henderson had served subpoenas on Brackenridge Hospital where Kellie told us she went after the assault. They claimed to have no records of her visit. I asked if maybe it was one of the other hospi-tals in town and she frowned.

"I guess. But I'm sure it was Brackenridge. I really am."

Subpoenas cost me nothing, so I resolved to seek records from every hospital that was open in Austin at the time when Kellie said the assault happened. For now, I declined to think what would happen if no records existed at any of them.

The following week I progressed further in my trial preparation: more legal research and more asking Mike Henderson to find people and documents. He humored me and produced the goods and on

Monday afternoon he appeared in my doorway with a piece of paper in his hand.

"This is what we got back from Brackenridge. Not on Kellie; the other."

I looked at it. "One page?"

"One page." He handed it to me and I scanned it quickly. He asked, "Not much use?"

"On the contrary." I waved it, but gently. "This, my friend, is worth more than gold. Much more, so good work, Mikey."

He looked at me like I was crazy, the limey prosecutor grinning at a piece of paper, before he shrugged and headed back to his office with a, "Whatever, dude."

Very carefully I carried the sheet of paper to have my secretary file it in the court's file after making several copies. Precious indeed, but I decided to keep it to myself.

My mood declined the next day when my victim/witness coordinator Lynn Cragg forwarded an e-mail from Kellie Torres stating that "with great thought and not great memory" she no longer wanted to testify.

I swore and then picked up the phone. After a brief conference with Lynn, both she and I left phone messages for Kellie. Quite a few of them. I understood Kellie's reluctance, because I saw the emotions that were resuscitated when she started talking about her life with Dennis Davis. But this case was bigger than her and I was determined she was going to testify. My messages were understanding and polite, asking just for a return call so we could chat. Just in case, I asked a colleague to start on the paperwork for an interstate subpoena, a document that would take time and energy to prepare and serve, but one that would replace my gentle pleas for her to testify with the full force of the law.

A week went by and still Kellie had not responded. Trial was now six weeks away and I was irritated that I had to deal with this. She apparently didn't understand how important this was and that she didn't get to decide whether or not the jury heard some of the most damning evidence possible against Dennis Davis.

February 4 brought two unexpected events. The first was snow in Austin, Texas. Amid the excitement of my and the neighborhood kids'

throwing snowballs, I continued to work at home and that brought
the second event. I was trying to find anyone I could to verify Amparo
Garcia-Crow's story that she wasn't with Dennis Davis the weekend of
Natalie's attack. It wasn't that I didn't believe her—I absolutely did—
but if there was more evidence to support that she was telling the
truth, I wanted to know about it and share it with the jury.

She had given me the phone number for a former roommate and
assured me he had an almost genius memory for people, places and
events. His name was John Hawkes and very soon after speaking to
him I learned he'd be glamming it up at the Oscars, having been nom-
inated for his role in the movie *Winter's Bone*. When I placed the call
I had no clue he was such a star, because Ampie neglected to tell me
and I mentioned his name to my wife only after the call. Hawkes was
eager to help if he could, remembering Ampie fondly and assuring
me she was honest. And she was also right about his memory. When
I mentioned the dates I was interested in, twenty-five years earlier, he
thought for a couple of seconds and said, "Ah yes, I was out of town
that weekend. I was in a band and we were touring in Michigan, I
think it was."

I hung up and smiled to myself, unable to ignore the irony. The
only person connected to the case who had a photographic memory
had been out of town that weekend.

Three weeks passed and I was working on getting my other 150 cases in
order so I could focus my attention on Natalie's murder for the weeks
up to and during the Davis trial. Kelsey MacKay moved from our court
to the family justice division and her replacement was Jackie Wood.
Jackie was tough, a slender, dark-haired woman who'd been a prosecutor a lot longer than I had. She was a little like Kelsey in some ways: She
called it like she saw it and didn't care for office politics. Some found
her abrasive and she and easy-going Mike were having a tough time
seeing things the same way, but I liked her. Knowing where I stood with
someone saved me from watching what I said or playing guessing games
about his or her feelings. Jackie suited me perfectly on that score; she
often used colorful language and appeared impossible to offend.

with a plea for us to leave him alone. Next I scanned the medical records which, at first glance, seemed to support the cancer diagnosis.

When I finished reading I checked my watch and trotted over to Efrain's office. He was still seated behind his desk and raised an eyebrow when he saw me grinning.

"Whatcha got there?"

"Oh, a little missive. A note from a man a million miles away."

"Oh? The man on the moon?"

"No, someone much harder to find," I said.

Both eyebrows went up. "No way."

"Yep. A fax from Donn Chelli."

Quickly Efrain was out of his seat, taking the papers in his hand. He perched on the edge of his desk and I stood silently by while he read.

"What do you think?" he whispered when he was finished.

"I think we use that phone number and call him. Right now."

Efrain circled back behind his desk and sat down. His hand hovered over the phone and he looked up at me. "Here goes."

Chelli answered and Efrain took the lead, introducing us. Chelli was immediately defensive, not understanding why we were looking for him, why we couldn't just leave him alone. It was evident he was worried about getting involved in the case, as if the trial of Dennis Davis wasn't proof we believed we had the right man. But Efrain and I got him talking, making encouraging and sympathetic noises as he talked about his illness and treatment. When we got him on the topic of the case, though, he insisted his statement was correct and was what he'd say at trial. First getting his e-mail address, I asked if he'd seen his statement lately and if he'd mind looking it over so he was sure. Then we hung up.

Back at my computer, I sent Chelli a copy of his statement by e-mail then shifted focus from Donn Chelli to another key witness, someone else who didn't want to testify for the State of Texas: Becky Davis.

On Monday, March 7, the State and defense teams took our places in the 167th District Courtroom. Judge Mike Lynch called the case and

Despite her somewhat maverick attitude, I discovered that she was a team player. She covered for me in court while I worked on the Davis case, listened and responded when I wanted advice or an opinion and put her considerable legal researching skills to use when I needed her to. And never once did she mention the extra shifts she was putting in or ask for anything in return.

The same went for Geoffrey Puryear, the fourth and newest member of the court, and by far the most handsome. He had the jawline of a cartoon sheriff, the body of an athlete and George Clooney's charming, boyish smile. To compound all this, he was truly one of the nicest people and despite being new to the court, we'd readily handed responsibility to him, because he was a bright and top-notch lawyer. And he, too, had stepped up, covering my dockets in court and offering to do whatever he could to allow me to concentrate on the Davis trial. As much as I was alone standing and talking in front of a jury, there was no doubt that getting me there was a team effort and I continued to be delighted by my helpful and selfless team.

The team was absent, though, in the early evening of Friday, February 24, gone home for a well-deserved weekend break. I was working late but trying to wrap up for my own weekend and I headed down the hallway to the water fountain, as much to stretch my legs as anything, before the last push. I saw one of the secretaries still there, walking down the hallway with a puzzled look on her face and a piece of paper in her hand.

"Do you know anything about who this might belong to?" she asked, holding out the paper.

"What is it?"

"A fax. It's directed at one of our prosecutors, but it doesn't say who and I can't figure it out."

"Who is it from?" I took the fax cover sheet, but before I could scan to the end she gave me the sender's name and my mouth dropped open.

"Never heard of him," she said. "Some guy named Donn Chelli."

Chapter 18

RELUCTANT WITNESSES

The letter was two pages long and accompanied by four pages of medical records. On the top right-hand side of the page was an address, one I knew to be a post office box and not his home. Below it was a phone number. I devoured the words, not waiting to take the fax to my office to read. The letter began by stating he had been notified about our request to testify at trial and he correctly guessed it had to do with the report he filed after Natalie was attacked. Chelli stated, "I want to inform you at this time that due to my medical condition I am not able to travel the distance from Los Angeles to Austin to possibly testify and I may not be able to speak for any length of time if I were able to travel." He described his health concerns and included reproductions of his MRI and PET scans for us to review, explaining, "I try to live in a serene environment that is conducive to healing."

Donn Chelli went on to insist that the report he gave after Natalie's attack was the unadulterated truth and that he was thoroughly "questioned, scrutinized, investigated, evaluated, fingerprinted and my information was verified."

So far nothing surprised me and the next paragraph exhibited a flash of the paranoia I'd come to expect. He talked in detail about his work history and his reputation, building himself up as a man of the utmost integrity and honesty. His concerns seemed to flip-flop between being made to travel and testify and being believed. He ended clarified the issue he was being asked to decide. "We are going to hear evidence today concerning the defendant's claim of a certain privilege, right, some sort of spousal privilege?"

Wade Russell rose and replied: "Yes, your Honor. Becky Davis does not want to testify in this matter and the State is seeking to have her testify as to certain statements made within—during the course of the marriage which are confidential and she is seeking not to testify regarding those statements or any other matters."

Wade called his only witness, Rebecca Davis, and as she headed to the stand, her head held high, I wondered if this would be the only time she took this slow walk to the witness box, if this would be the last chance I had to get truthful answers from her.

Then Judge Lynch did something I'd never seen before: He warned the witness about perjury. It was as if he knew how important her testimony was to both sides and how easily she could be tempted to lie and take back what she'd said before. I knew Judge Lynch and I knew he did this not because he wanted her to repeat the same story she gave before, but because this was his courtroom and he wanted only the truth. He told her: "You understand you are under oath, subject to the rules of perjury and required to tell the truth. You understand that fully, correct?"

Her reply was a simple, "Yes, sir."

Quickly Wade moved through the preliminaries. He established what we already knew: that the Davises hadn't been formally married and they were claiming this privilege under the theory of common-law or informal marriage. And so he began laying the groundwork to clear the three hurdles that stood between Becky Davis and not having to testify: an agreement to be married, the Davises having "held themselves out" as husband and wife and that they lived together in this state as husband and wife. Listening to that very first element, I strongly felt she wasn't being truthful.

She told the Court that she had to have surgery in the last week of January, just over one month after she met Dennis at a Christmas party on December 10. She explained that before the surgery was when they agreed to be married. "Dennis and I agreed that we were married, but because we wanted to make sure that he could be mine in case of emergency and he could be with me at all times and there would never be a question about who he was, so we pretty much told the doctor and the surgery folks that we were a married couple then."

That answer also went some way to addressing the "holding themselves out" element, but on that she had more.

Wade Russell: "You told the doctor that you were married?"

"Yes."

"To Dennis Davis?"

"I did."

"What was the purpose of that?"

"In order for Dennis to be able to be my next of kin and be that in case of emergency contact and to be in the recovery room with me and if there was any complications he would be there to help make decisions, because since I am a nurse, I know you need to have some-body there with you, so I asked him to do it."

She went on, saying that they lived together in Texas (something I didn't plan to challenge) and she gave numerous examples of them holding themselves out to others as being married, including during a trip, to her coworkers and the time her mother "told the minister at the church when we went to Sunday service that Dennis was her new son-in-law, so we were married in their eyes."

She ended her testimony by placing the statement Dennis had made to her about sinning against God and man in context: "It was either in March or April."

"That was after you had held out to the general public, to doctors at the hospital, to a hotel owner in Llano, Texas, and your coworkers that you were husband and wife?"

"Yes, sir."

"Pass the witness."

I began my cross-examination by tossing her own words from the earlier bond hearing back at her. In that hearing she told the Court that she and Dennis had been married since May 2002. Now she was asking the Court to believe that she considered herself married to him since early 1991. Her response was classic evasiveness and I was confi-dent the judge would see it as such.

"When you talk to people these days and they say, 'How long have you and Dennis been married?' what do you tell them?"

"Over twenty."

"When somebody says to you, 'When did you get married?' what do you tell them?"

"That—no one really asks us. We say we had a big party in May of 2002."

"But if somebody were to ask you. 'When did you get married?' what would you tell them?"

"Well, that is a good question. I would say that we got married then, but that we had been together as a couple and as man and wife since the early 1990s, since we met."

"I ask because do you remember testifying in the bond reduction hearing here?"

"Yes."

"Mr. Russell asked you when did you get married and your response was, 'We got married in May of 2002.' Do you remember that?" As I asked the question I held in my hand a certified copy of the transcript of that hearing, the exact lines highlighted, just in case she disputed her own prior testimony.

"Yes, but this is a court of law. I can't, you know—"

"What do you mean by that?"

"Well, it is a legal question about a legal affair, so a legal answer is legally—because I didn't know anything about common-law at that point. Legally, we got married in May of 2002. Prior to that when we were married informally or whatever you want to call it, Dennis was my domestic partner through the City of Austin as long as that held out, which wasn't very long, they repealed it and we did lots of things as husband and wife, including living together in the same house and then moving over to Nashville."

"When did you take his last name?"

"2002."

"Why would you wait until 2002 if you were married in 1991?"

"Oh, he wanted me to."

"Why did you wait until then though?"

"He just said, 'I always wished that you would do that. Let's do that' and we went down and signed the forms. I said okay."

"Do you have a firm date in your mind that you consider yourself actually married to him?"

"Well," she responded, "I like to think of December 10 as our anniversary and that is really the date that we met at the Christmas party."

"Are you telling the judge that you were married to Dennis Davis from the first day you met him?"

"Well, you asked me is there a firm date in my mind."

I leaned toward her. "That you considered yourself married to him."

"I considered myself—yeah, together with him."

"Well, I am asking about marriage."

"A formal marriage?"

"I am asking when do you consider the first day that you were married to Dennis Davis?"

"I don't know that I specifically have a date. I think that when we got pregnant and when my girlfriend came over to make the honorable announcement in our presence, she wasn't a judge or anybody that could legally do it, but we certainly felt married."

"What date was that?"

"Well, that was in—I guess after February 18, so it was probably closer to the end of the month. I know that we drove out to Dripping Springs and had our rings made and I know that he sent me this necklace that spoke of our love or whatever until we could afford to get wedding rings, so I don't have a date. I am not real good with those."

I hoped that I'd shown her to be evasive and inconsistent on this issue, made my point at least, so I moved on.

I turned to what I hoped would be the end of the matter. She was smart enough to know that her testimony thus far had been defensive, incomplete and unspecific. I knew she was looking for sure ground, a place she could be definite and certain, impress the judge with how positive she was about the facts of her informal marriage to Dennis. What she didn't know was that the firm ground she sought was but quicksand.

I laid my predicate carefully, giving her easy questions that I knew the answers to, that I knew she'd agree with. I wanted to ensure that once she agreed, she wouldn't be able to backpedal. At some point she might figure out what I was doing, but I wanted that moment to come as late as possible.

"I think you just testified you were a nurse, is that right?"

"Yes."

"I wanted to ask you, can you tell the Court how information gets on a patient's records, information about that particular individual?"

"What do you mean?"

"Well, if you are looking at a patient's records and it has their name, date of birth, Social Security number, that information all comes from the patient themselves; is that correct?"

"Uh-huh."

"I'm sorry, you have to say yes or no for the court reporter."

"Yes. Not all of it. There is a medical record number, there is insurance codes, there is—"

"But the personal information comes from the patient themselves?" I continued.

"Yeah."

"And they give that to a nurse or admin person and that admin person puts that into the document?"

"That's right and it goes into the chart."

"How many times did you go to the hospital in the year after you met Dennis Davis?"

"Well, I went to Seton as an outpatient and then I went to Brackenridge after I had a miscarriage and had a hysterectomy."

"When was that?"

"It was in the first few months. That is right before we went to New Mexico. The reason that we went, we took some time off so I could recuperate. So it had to be in March or April."

"You are telling the judge," I said, "that on those occasions that you went to the hospital, you held out to the doctors and to the hospital staff that you were married to Dennis Davis?"

"Yes."

"If we could somehow magically go back in time and look at those records, they would reflect that presumably?"

"Somewhere. It is not on every page, but when you first sign in, they do ask the marital status."

"What would that say?"

"Married."

She nodded as she said it, leaning into the microphone, her first step onto solid ground. Slowly, so that everyone was watching me, I picked up two pieces of paper. The top one was a legal document that allowed the sheet under it into evidence, a necessary formality. And that second sheet was the paper that Mike Henderson had brought to my office a few weeks ago, my explosive piece of evidence that I'd kept to myself ever since.

I kept my voice casual. "Your Honor, may I approach the witness?"

"You may."

"Ma'am, show you what has been marked State's Exhibit No. 1. The first page you probably won't recognize. It is titled business records affidavit; is that correct?"

"Yes, that is correct."

"Would you mind turning to the second page, please? Do you recognize that document?"

"Yeah, it looks like a Brackenridge label on the top of it. There is my name, address, my employment."

"So that is a medical record that pertains to you?"

"Right."

"It pertains to a visit by you to Brackenridge Hospital in September of 1991, is that correct?"

"Uh-huh." She was wary now, sensing a trap.

"Is that yes?"

"Yes, that is correct."

"Can you tell the judge what it says under marital status?"

She read the paper and her mouth tightened. "Single."

"Can you tell the judge who you put down as an emergency contact in case you needed somebody?"

Her eyes went back to the page before looking back up at me. "My father."

"Thank you."

"May I say something?"

"Not right now, no." I took the paper from her hand and addressed the Court. I wanted this moment to settle in before she tried to drag herself from the quicksand. "Your Honor, I would offer State's Exhibit No. 1 into evidence."

And so State's Exhibit No. 1, our only exhibit of the hearing, became part of the Court's record. That one page showed Becky Davis was using her maiden name, was claiming to be single and used her father as her point of contact, the most important man in her life, if you like. And all that six months *after* Dennis Davis's crucial admission.

Walking slowly to my seat I turned my attention back to the witness, asking if she had any other documents or witnesses prepared to testify that she was married to Dennis Davis in 1991 or whether the Court had to rely on her word alone.

She admitted she didn't and, seeming desperate to explain away my exhibit, started talking, remembering another hospital visit she'd had but never thought to mention to Wade, me or anyone else before.

"That document was for an outpatient mammogram. That was not a surgery procedure, so I might have said something different about my ICE, in case of emergency, and I might have said something different about my marital status because of insurance. I don't know."

"Wait. You are prepared to lie about insurance?"

"Yeah, I would have."

"And you wouldn't be prepared to lie to protect him today?"

"No, I am just sworn on the Bible that I wouldn't."

"Pass the witness."

Wade tried damage limitation and his witness repeated her explanation for the document, but as far as I was concerned the damage was done. I hoped the judge saw it that way, too. When the evidence closed, Judge Lynch told us his plan was to take the matter under advisement, read the brief I'd submitted to him on the issue and consider the facts from the hearing and the case law. But he asked us to summarize our positions, essentially give closing arguments. I nodded and began:

"Judge, just to kind of focus in, there has been some testimony about whether they are married recently or what happened in the late nineties. Really the only important part is the spring of 1991, which is just four months after they met.

"That is my first point, is that it is unbelievable and it is not credible that two people would consider themselves to be married just four months after they met. I know they were living together, but that is not the standard. If it was, a lot of people in this courtroom would have a lot more marriages.

"Second of all, despite Ms. Davis's testimony about all these friends, all his family members to whom they held themselves out to be married, not a single other person has come forward.

"You will see the case law, Judge. It is fairly clear that the Court is to scrutinize these claims very carefully. I cited a case to you in which the testimony of just the one witness, the person claiming the privilege, was insufficient to establish that privilege.

"Your Honor, this witness has basically admitted that she is prepared to lie about her marital status if it is in her interest. In fact, on State's Exhibit No. 1, before I showed it to her, I asked what it would say, I asked whether it would demonstrate that she was married and she said the information on this document would come from her and then when I showed it to her and it showed that she was single, then she had a story and an explanation.

"This is the only piece of verifiable, independent evidence and it demonstrates very clearly that she says she was holding herself out to be single, that she wasn't even putting Mr. Davis as her emergency contact and that is when they were living together still, so that is a very strong indication right there that they were not holding themselves out to be married.

"In the domestic partners issue, she talked about that. Where is the paperwork from that? There is no other corroborating evidence to substantiate the claim of spousal privilege.

"Your Honor, I think common sense, the law and the evidence that has come from the witness stand today make it very clear that the spousal privilege does not apply in this case. Thank you."

Then Wade Russell made his pitch:

"May it please the Court. Your Honor, I think we have completely proven up the three criteria for being married. We are talking about a common-law marriage. We are not talking about legal marriage at the courthouse. We are talking about the issue of did they consider themselves married, were they generally holding themselves out to be married, were they living together as husband and wife in a domestic situation.

"I think we have clearly covered all of that. They discussed marriage from the first few dates in December of 1990. When Ms. Davis returned from Europe in January of 1991, she moved in with Mr. Davis, he moved in with her, they began holding themselves out to people as being husband and wife.

"Sometime in I believe February, she stated they had a spiritual marriage of some sort. There were problems. She had a miscarriage. She had surgery. There were issues, money issues that prevented them from having a legal marriage, yet they continued, according to her testimony, to tell others around her that they were married.

"I think it is perfectly logical for a person to, in their mind, bifurcate these. An intelligent person like her will know that there is a difference between a legal marriage on paper and holding yourself out to be married.

"What we are talking about is a common-law marriage. We are not talking about a legal marriage. There could have been times when for certain forms, like this form, this medical form in State's Exhibit No. A, where she may have stated for legal or whatever reasons that no, I am not legally married, so she may have in her mind believed that it is appropriate to let them know we are not legally married.

"Nonetheless, that doesn't take away from her overall intent with Mr. Davis to be husband and wife. The record is replete with her discussions of how she considered herself to be married. I don't think it takes independent outside witnesses. It is the assertion of this by her that is the foremost focus of this.

"If the Court would like to put this on hold, I can seek to find persons who she related this to, hearsay statements, if the Court will entertain hearsay statements from others that they consider themselves to be married, but I think we have met our burden.

"The privilege continues past the divorce. It is an ongoing privilege and I think we have met the test for the exclusion of her testimony from March of 1991 under the spousal privilege rule of the Texas Rules of Evidence."

And with that, the Court declared a recess on the case, promising a ruling on the spousal privilege issue on or before March 21, at the last pretrial hearing.

Chapter 19

FINAL COUNTDOWN

As Efrain and I continued to prepare for trial, everything else ceased to matter. The decisions had mostly been made and we found ourselves busier with the mechanics: which witnesses to call, whom to leave in the lineup and whom to drop. Meanwhile, our colleagues Jackie Wood and Geoffrey Puryear handled the daily docket, the churning of cases in the 167th, making a few executive decisions on my other cases. They checked in frequently, sounding boards for the trial theories that were taking shape, those slowly forming silhouettes in the pre-dawn we were living in, and I hoped that those theories kept their shape once the bright light of trial shone on them.

One of those theories related to Donn Chelli. The second time we spoke to him, I felt it became glaringly obvious that it wasn't just his health that was preventing him from coming. It was his paranoia. Then it clicked: Chelli's fear was that all this was a ruse, an elaborate trap to lure him to Austin where we'd clap him in irons and frame him for Natalie's murder. We tried hard, Efrain and I, to persuade him that that was nonsense, we had the killer already and didn't need to frame him. We even offered to provide him with a lawyer when he arrived in Austin, free of charge, someone who could advise him every step of the way. He liked the idea of coming armed with counsel and he seemed to like the idea that we wanted him here so badly. On several occasions, he wondered aloud how we could possibly try the case without such an important witness as himself.

He also told us something interesting: There were a couple of mistakes in his statement. He was now sure that the man he saw was six feet three inches, because he himself was six feet and the man "towered" over him. He was also adamant that he never spoke to Johnny that morning, even though his statement to police seemed clear:

> Me and my girlfriend then went outside and saw John (L.N.U., approximately 17or 18 years old). John is the son of the lady who was beaten. He told us that his mother was bleeding and he was looking for the emergency van. He told us that somebody had beat her.

He didn't tell us, "I don't recall talking to Johnny" or "I don't think I talked to him, but I'm not sure." He was adamant that he had no conversation with Johnny at all that morning and, in fact, *never even saw him.* On their own, the retractions didn't carry great significance, but they were further indicators to me of Chelli's reliability or lack of it. He'd added three inches to the height of the man he claimed to have seen and the insistence of never having seen Johnny, let alone having talked to him, was directly contradicted by Johnny and by his own statement.

Then Chelli faded from view. Our calls started going to voicemail, our entreaties to come, to talk with us some more, to just answer the phone, all fell unheeded into the electronic void. After we'd essentially given up hope of his cooperation, we received a call from an experienced Los Angeles attorney who confirmed what we had guessed: Donn Chelli would not be coming to Austin.

And that meant Judge Lynch would have to make a decision. Would he allow Chelli's statement to be brought in as evidence or deny the defense what they saw as vital exculpatory evidence? I was pretty sure I knew the answer even though Efrain, a man of rules, thought the judge wouldn't do it.

As we talked about the problem, a new idea began to seep its way into our minds. We'd always assumed Chelli to have been lying, to have made up his story based on what Johnny and others had said to him that morning. But what if he wasn't lying?

What if he was just *wrong*?

Just because Chelli was paranoid and wanted to be a part of the in-vestigation and, in some ways, the trial, didn't automatically invalidate his having seen something, seen *someone*, outside Natalie's apartment building the morning she was murdered. But similarly, just because he gave a detailed statement to police didn't make every detail in the state-ment correct. Time and again, we'd seen it in the criminal justice arena. Not just in our own cases, but also in those splashed over the front pages of the newspapers, in documentary after documentary that set out to prove that some police force or prosecutor somewhere had convicted the wrong man. And in every single case, how had this happened?

With faulty, untrustworthy, inherently unreliable, mistaken eye-witness testimony.

Innocent men have been wrongly convicted, because eyewit-nesses were wrong and here we were faced with a murderer hoping to get off the hook by using eyewitness testimony we'd *always* believed to be faulty. It had just taken us a while to figure out that not only was the man less than reliable, but also his honestly-given statement might be plain wrong.

This was usually the purview of defense attorneys: attacking the prosecution's case by bringing on board an expert to point out the many ways an eyewitness might make mistakes, might truly think he saw a particular person when he did not.

For us though, as prosecutors, this was uncharted territory. It was like pointing out some flaw in DNA testing or fingerprint analysis. Was it a door we wanted to open? The more we talked, the more we decided it was. But to adopt such an unusual strategy in such a high-profile case called for some good backup. We'd need approval from the higher-ups to hire an expert, so we asked for permission to do so and requested the money to pay for it.

And this was the brilliance of that quiet, honest, forthright law-yer Efrain De La Fuente, because not only was it his idea to challenge Chelli's statement with an eyewitness expert, but also he came up with the man to do it.

On March 16, less than a month before trial, I dialed the phone number for Charles Weaver, a professor of psychology and neuroscience at Baylor University in Waco, Texas. He was a well-known expert on the subject of memory and eyewitness identification and, as his university Web page said, he'd testified in numerous civil and criminal trials on those subjects (though never for the prosecution, I was willing to bet). I had his university profile on the computer screen in front of me as I dialed (if possible, and these days it usually is, I prefer to have an accurate picture of someone when I talk to him or her on the phone, not just his or her background but also his or her physical appearance). I scrutinized his image. He looked like a cross between travel writer Rick Steves and Microsoft founder Bill Gates. When Weaver answered, I identified myself as a prosecutor in Austin and he was friendly, if a little cautious at first. I was amused, because Dr. Weaver didn't seem used to an ADA asking questions about his area of expertise in a respectful, even friendly way, something he readily admitted a little later in the conversation.

We talked for a while and I gave him a rundown of my case and the specifics of Chelli's statement. After just a few minutes I knew we were doing the right thing. After he and I spoke about the facts of the case and the parameters of his potential testimony, we discussed travel arrangements and his fee. I was pleased that his interest in the case was so strong; he was almost eager to testify, saying he'd make the two-and-a-half hour drive from Waco whenever we needed him.

After we hung up I went next door to Efrain's office and gave him the good news: Weaver was our man and was willing to testify. It was my opinion that he'd be a good witness. Not because he'd say what we wanted him to, but because his explanations of how memory works and how and why witnesses can make mistakes were sound, honest and logical. I really thought he'd make sense of Chelli's statement, his testimony, even to the point of making it work in our favor.

As I was talking to Efrain I heard my phone ring. I ran back to my office to answer and found Dr. Weaver on the line. His tone was hesitant, seeming embarrassed, and I almost laughed aloud when he told me why he was calling. He'd never heard of prosecutors using an eyewitness testimony expert, let alone testified for them, so he was worried Efrain and I might get in trouble for doing so now.

With a smile in my voice, I reassured him that we had permission and that we were not opening a prosecutorial Pandora's box. As Efrain and I had told others in the last few days, one can hardly argue that there *aren't* problems with eyewitness identification; there have simply been too many exonerations for that line of thinking to hold. I said goodbye with a tongue-in-cheek promise that if we did meet on opposite sides of the courtroom in the future, I'd be as ferocious as possible.

With every two steps forward, we always seemed to get knocked back one. With the Chelli problem almost solved, I had several others nagging at me. The most significant was Kellie Torres. She was still ignoring our calls and the district attorney's office in her town hadn't responded either. I needed the DA to serve our interstate subpoena. Without Kellie's cooperation and without the district attorney's help, I lost her completely as a witness. And that meant, almost certainly, I lost my case.

I made several, probably desperate-sounding, calls to Kellie and the DA and left messages. Then I turned my mind to other things, because I was powerless to do more. I didn't want to sit around and torture myself with the idea that the presence or absence of the two women so important in this case, Kellie and Rebecca, rested in the hands of others.

But I stayed close to Kellie by working with Mike on getting her medical records. I subpoenaed every hospital in Austin for records reflecting her beating by Davis over twenty years earlier. Mike had done more than serve the subpoenas, too; he spoke to the people behind the closed doors who responded to (and sometimes ignored) them.

Two weeks before trial he plopped down in a chair opposite me. "I've got bad news and...I suppose, not-so-bad news," he said.

"Can I just have the not-so-bad news?"

"Nope."

"Okay then. Spill it."

"She was right. I believe Kellie did go to Brackenridge Hospital."

I sat forward, excited. "You have the records?"

"Negative. They don't exist."

"They don't?" I felt my world shrink horribly. "Don't tell me she was lying, please."

"I won't. That's the not-so-bad news. They destroy records after twenty years so even if she'd had major heart surgery we wouldn't be able to prove it."

"Twenty years?"

"Those records got shredded three years ago," Mike confirmed.

"Dammit." I sat back. "If only we'd known."

Mike shrugged, got up and left me to my thoughts, which turned back to Chelli. I wondered if there was more we could do with his statement than just use Dr. Weaver as a witness. I went back over Chelli's words and Balagia's encounters with him as captured in the official police report.

Suddenly it hit me. I read over the brief entry in the OR, dated November 2, made a note on my pad of the details I needed and then called cold case, speaking to Sergeant Ron Lara directly. I told him my request.

"You bet, we can get that for you," he replied. "Might be a day or two, if that's okay."

"Fine with me."

In fact, the next day, Detective Jerry Bauzon stopped by my office with a packet of information.

"There's no photo from that incident," he told me. "But I pulled his picture from other involvement and there's all the info you'd need on him from back then."

"Any clue where he is now?"

"We looked, but he's fallen off the grid. Given his condition so many years ago, he's probably fallen all the way, if you know what I mean."

I understood. Jerry left me with my packet of information and I opened the file, suddenly nervous to test my hunch. But there it was: three different information sheets telling me exactly the same thing about the man identified by Donn Chelli as "looking like" the mystery "Lotions man" lurking outside Natalie's apartment building, the homeless man whom rookie officer Kenneth Cannaday arrested after Chelli had called police and said, essentially, "He's the guy I saw." That lookalike for Chelli's hulking six-foot thug with the baseball bat was the shiftless Seth Pickett. And at that time, Seth Pickett was five feet six inches tall and weighed 160 pounds.

Maybe not a match for the mystery "Lotions man," but most certainly a perfect match for Dennis Davis.

Immediately I sent Mike to track down Kenneth Cannaday, because I wanted him on my witness list. I knew from the fact that Cannaday didn't write a supplement to the police report that I might have some hearsay issues come up at trial, but I was hopeful that if Judge Lynch let Chelli's statement into evidence, he would give me a little leeway to counter it with my own otherwise inadmissible evidence.

I let Efrain know my find and I felt a little like I used to as a child, when my dad was impressed with something I'd done, because Efrain's eyes lit up as he recognized the importance. Not only did it cast doubt on some of the damaging specifics of Chelli's statement, but also it reinforced our theory and the expected testimony of Dr. Weaver that Chelli's observations were faulty. That, it seemed to me, was as solid as any fact we had in the case: From Chelli's statement (six feet) to our conversation on the phone (six feet three inches) to this discovery (five feet six inches), we had a huge variance in the mystery man's height. That, I intended to tell the jury, was the definition of unreliable.

On Thursday, March 17, Efrain and I went over the witness list. I was taking my family camping, a final getaway before the stress of trial, and I wanted to have our playlist reasonably settled in my mind. We ended up with sixteen witnesses and divided them according to theme. We'd start with Johnny and Jolene to set the scene, then use the rest of the first day painting a full picture of the apartment and the circumstances surrounding Natalie's death. Days two, three and (if necessary) four would be spent tying Davis to the bloody murder scene. We estimated that our case would take about three full days to present, which meant in reality it'd be four. But even so, twenty-five years of waiting for Johnny and his family and in less than a week it'd be done, over.

The week of March 21 began with our final pretrial hearing. First Judge Lynch denied the motion for husband-wife privilege. Rebbeca Davis would be testifying.

Then Judge Lynch let both sides make their arguments on the Chelli issue. I had the law on my side, we all knew that, but everyone also

knew that Wade had that intangible thing called fairness on his. I didn't
over-argue my case, because I didn't expect to win. I wasn't even sure I
wanted to anymore, but I did want the judge to appreciate the difficult
position he was putting us in. I knew he'd see that and so I was confident
that what I was saying wouldn't keep Chelli's statement out, but it would
buy me some legal leeway when the time came to challenge it.

Judge Lynch didn't rule immediately, which surprised me. When
he did, it was through a written order, but before releasing it he called
me to ask me to come to his chambers to pick up my copy. I was
grateful for this professional courtesy. I was hardly the most senior
lawyer in the office and wouldn't necessarily expect him to do that, so
when he handed me the order I thanked him for telling me himself
and made it clear I was neither surprised nor offended by his ruling.

On March 23, Mike received word about Kellie. The holdup had
been, in part, respectful courtesy; in their small town, the DA's office
hadn't wanted just to show up with a subpoena. Once contact was
made, though, she'd accepted it with good grace and waived a hearing
on the matter. Bottom line: Kellie Torres would be testifying.

Another witness came forth, too. When I returned from my
camping trip I listened to a voicemail from someone named Kent. I
didn't recognize the name and when I spoke to him he said he called
because Dennis Davis, apparently, had called him and Kent didn't
know what to do. I asked why Dennis would have called, what Kent's
connection to the case might be, and Kent told me it had something
to do with the car seen at the murder scene.

My heart beat a little faster hearing this, because the car was a big
issue for me. In my opinion, it was key that a car similar to the one
owned by Davis was seen near the crime scene right about the time
of the attack and I thought the jury would also be impressed by that
evidence. But as things stood, it was not great evidence. First, Deanna
Cooley, who saw the car that morning, had a poor memory of the details and she never gave a statement, so I couldn't use that to guide her
through her testimony. Second, proving the car belonged to Davis on
that date had proved problematic. Through his license history Mike
found documentation for the car, but the documents showed that
Davis filled out the registration papers, transferring it to his ownership,

after the murder. I had turned that information over to the defense, but while it was technically exculpatory, I didn't think those papers fully answered the question of when Davis actually had possession of the vehicle. People buy and sell cars all the time and leave the paperwork for later and I imagined that was especially true back in those booze and dope-filled days. In the interview with Tom Walsh, Davis himself admitted owning the car, but no time frame was ever established.

Kent, however, provided my answer. His friend Dale Streiker (aka Dale Hopkins), Kent told me, was the one with the good memory and a tendency to hang on to ancient paperwork. When I called Dale he immediately remembered giving the car to Davis in exchange for studio time. He and his friends were in a Christian rock band, he told me, all long hair and scary makeup, and they used Davis's studio to produce an album. And he remembered when.

"It was for the album we put out in early 1986," he says. "So we would have given him the car back in 1985. Maybe even 1984. I don't recall the exact date."

The one thing he *was* sure about? The car was in Davis's possession by the night Natalie was assaulted.

I hadn't been to court much lately, working almost full-time on the Davis case. But on the odd occasion I was needed there, people noticed a change in me. I was quieter, more reserved. I didn't linger in the courtroom to chat like I normally did but flitted in and out. Even when I had moments of spare time I was less social and several people asked if I was alright. I was, but I was tired. I'd never lost sleep over a case before, not in such a literal way. I lay in bed at night wondering what else I should be doing, what more I needed to take care of. And like a monster under the bed, scratching at the mattress, I heard whispers in my mind suggesting that I was out of my depth and not only was I destined to lose the case, something I was not afraid of, but also I'd lose it because I was not ready, not prepared, not smart enough. And I'd lose it with the whole country watching the English prosecutor strutting his stuff in cowboy boots while a killer walked free.

Chapter 20

SELECTING OUR JURY

Everyone has a theory, but no one knows for sure. Imagine ten doctors standing around a patient who has appendicitis. They agree the appendix needs to come out, but the first doctor wants to use two scalpels and a socket wrench. The second doctor wants to use a Swiss Army knife and a monkey wrench. The third doctor wants to go into the patient's body through his belly button. And so forth.

That's the science of picking a jury: We all want the "right" one, we all have a few ideas on how to get it, but none of us has a clue which method works best. There's nothing as ugly and sometimes agonizing as jury selection.

The process, called a *voir dire*, is straightforward. A large group of people from the community file into the courtroom and sit in the benches where the public sits during trials. The judge explains to them that they're there to be chosen for a twelve-person jury and he makes them take oaths to tell the truth when questioned by the lawyers. He explains a few legal concepts relating to a defendant's right not to testify, the presumption of innocence and the burden of proof being on the State. Then he turns the questioning over to the lawyers.

Because the burden is mine as the prosecutor, I would go first and Wade, the attorney for the defendant, would go after me. Judge Lynch liked to be done by six or soon thereafter and since we began after lunch I was looking at an hour of talking, maybe a little more, maybe a little less.

Before I began, I had an idea of whom I'd be talking to, because every juror had to fill out a questionnaire giving details about him or herself, such as name, age, education, family status, criminal history. I'd read and reread this packet and didn't plan to reference it during the *voir dire* itself, so when I rose to speak I had two things in my left hand. One was a chart showing the name of each juror and where he or she was sitting, so that I could call on that juror by name if I wanted to. All panelists had a paddle with a number on it, but I preferred to ask a question of "Ms. Johnson" rather than "number thirty-two."

The other thing I held was the script for my *voir dire*. It wasn't word-for-word; it was a list of prompts to keep me on topic, keep me flowing. My own theory was that the only way to make sure to get a "good" jury was to talk to as many people as possible. One couldn't tell, in my experience, from the questionnaires who would be State-oriented and who would be defense-oriented. In a few cases maybe, but for the most part people are far more complex than that. I also liked to believe that if I had a good case, then even a defense-oriented juror who took an oath to do the job would find the defendant guilty. That belief was born out by the trials that I'd done; in every case, I'd been impressed by how seriously jurors take that oath, how hard they work to find the right verdict, be it guilty or not.

My plan, then, was to let the jurors know a little about me, make them understand the law that applied to the case. In some cases, the law can be pretty complex. For example, proving a DWI requires an explanation of the concept that someone can "lose the normal use of their physical or mental" capacities. In this case, though, the law was simple: Did Dennis Davis intentionally or knowingly kill Natalie Antonetti? In other words, did he intend to kill her or did he know that by bashing her skull she might die? Not difficult concepts, legally or morally, in my mind. I wanted to make sure that whoever moved from the gallery to the jury box would give me and the defense a fair hearing.

I started with a joke. I knew that the majority of these people had never been in a criminal courtroom; the closest they'd come was seeing one on television. I imagined they had been waiting to take their seats for a while and I knew they'd taken time out of their lives to respond to the summons, time which inevitably included a painful circling of the courthouse and the nearby streets for a parking spot. They were slightly in awe of all the formality, slightly nervous about being called on, slightly bored by the waiting and more than a little grumpy about all of it.

So when I stood and after making sure no one there knew me or Efrain personally, I told them that I liked *voir dire*, because it was the only part of the trial when we could talk to each other, when they could ask questions, because the eventual twelve-person jury would have to sit and listen, no questions allowed. I told them that the first question I usually got was about my accent:

"I know from some of the information sheets we have people who have traveled a bit, who have lived in a number of places, so I am sure somebody by now has figured out that I am from…Alabama."

I had used that in every trial I'd ever done and it never failed to get a laugh, to loosen them up and, hopefully, make them think, *Maybe this won't be so painful after all.*

Then I told them that the case involved a murder and not just any murder: It was a cold case. When questioned, several prospective jurors admitted they'd read about it, but they didn't recall details and, wanting to make sure they weren't disqualified, I verified that they still had open minds. They all agreed that they could be "fair and impartial," the phrase I used and so I moved on.

My first real challenge came when I asked a juror about "reasonable doubt." Everyone in America knows the phrase, but because so few people have to apply it, when it comes time to do so it can be problematic. What does it mean exactly? How much doubt creates reasonable doubt? I couldn't really answer these questions; all I could do was give the jurors a general idea and then emphasize what reasonable doubt was not.

I picked a juror candidate at random: "What do you think reasonable doubt means, beyond a reasonable doubt?"

"I think the facts would show that there would be no other choice in the case," he replied, "so there is no—there is no doubt that the event occurred the way it was described."

"No doubt at all?"

"No doubt."

"In your mind do we have to prove the case beyond any doubt whatsoever?"

"Yes."

I didn't like to pick on jurors or make them feel bad, but I much preferred it when they got the answers right. So I moved on to another panelist to make my point, having her imagine driving past a hypothetical car accident. Without much difficulty, I got her to admit that the best way to know the accident happened, that *anything* had happened, was to see it herself. Then I pointed out that *seeing* the accident made her a witness and that if she were to sit in the witness box, she couldn't very well sit in the jury box, too. Heads nodded as I took the prospective jurors through this explanation and I was comfortable that I'd made my point clear: We didn't have to prove our case beyond all doubt; that wasn't the legal standard, because it wouldn't make sense for it to be the legal standard.

We started to go over the kinds of evidence a jury might expect in a cold case and I was struck by how engaged and intelligent this panel was. Often, getting answers was difficult and more often than not there was someone who wanted to spend the afternoon haranguing either me or the defense lawyer over irrelevancies. But this afternoon people were interested and responsive.

Then we hit the subject of DNA.

I expected this, because the whole world seemed to know that cold cases and DNA go together. I knew that my panel would want to see DNA. After all, they knew nothing about the case and DNA was how most cold cases were solved, in their opinions.

But the question wasn't whether they *wanted* to see DNA; it was whether they would *require* me to present DNA evidence. Several said they did and I let Efrain get their names, because it indicated to me they would hold my case to a higher standard than the law put on me. If so, they would be disqualified as jurors, but even if not, they might be people we wanted to strike. In a felony case like this, each side would get ten peremptory strikes. That meant that we could exclude ten people for any reason at all. The only limits were constitutional, which meant we could not strike someone solely because of his or her gender, color or religious beliefs.

After letting people talk about the importance of DNA, I explained that the law merely required I prove my case beyond a reasonable doubt and did *not* insist I have a certain type of evidence (in this case DNA), which meant that no juror may acquit a defendant just because that juror doesn't get to see that type of evidence. I saw eyebrows go up as I explained that and it seemed to make sense to most people. But not everyone.

One candidate remained adamant about wanting DNA and I heard the judge behind me shifting in his seat, uncomfortable with the woman's position. As Judge Lynch did sometimes, he stepped in and, because he was the judge, he was a little more confrontational. "Before we go further on this," he said, "I want you to understand what you are saying. You are saying if the State brought you video— an old video was uncovered of the murder clearly showing who did it and you uncovered some eyewitnesses and you had some fingerprints, that would still be not enough for you unless there was DNA. That is what you are telling the district attorney. I want to make sure that is what you are telling the DA."

"I feel being a cold case—"

"Hold on. I will let you get all this on the record in a minute. When you are saying you would have to have DNA, you are saying no other evidence would work, no other evidence could have risen to the level of beyond a reasonable doubt, no matter what it was, unless there was DNA."

Her answer was, "Yes." Even if we had actual video of the crime itself she'd require us to produce DNA before finding Davis guilty. I'd known it would be an issue, but until that answer, I had no idea how inculcated some people were with the popular fictions that associated themselves with criminal justice.

Interestingly, one of the panelists took up for me. As he put it, "On the whole DNA thing, thank you for the clarification, but if I were on trial and say I was a meticulous person that committed crimes and didn't leave any DNA anywhere, in those scenarios where they say they had to have DNA, if I had a jury of those types of people, if

I never left DNA, then I would be clicking my heels all the time I am sure...Wore gloves, cleaned up with bleach, whatever."

I welcomed his comments and pointed out to the panel that our meticulous criminal would not only be found not guilty, but also might even escape having a trial altogether.

By lingering on the DNA issue, I'd done more than ensure the final jury would follow the law. I'd made them aware I didn't have DNA. This was good, because their expectations were lowered and their curiosity was raised. I also suspected that Wade would hammer me for not having DNA and I wanted the twelve people to be sitting in the jury box to be thinking, *Well, the law says he doesn't have to have DNA. The prosecutor said so and the judge agreed.*

That issue settled, or so I hoped, I moved on to what the jurors would discover to be another problem with my case: old age. I asked several panelists whether they could identify possible problems with bringing a cold case to trial and they were happy to play along. Deteriorated evidence, dead witnesses, changes in technology—all these answers had people thinking about the problems I'd faced and with which the final twelve would likely have to deal. I covered the topic briefly.

Next was the issue that defense lawyers normally revel in bringing up: eyewitness identification. It's their chance to undermine the prosecution's case before opening statements, but today it was my secret weapon. One panelist told me he questioned the validity of eyewitness testimony, because maybe the situation was influenced by the witness's own personal feelings, by background information being fed to them or by sheer adrenaline and excitement. It was as if the potential juror knew my case and Donn Chelli; I nodded along encouragingly.

Another panelist didn't mince words: "I believe eyewitness testimony or eyewitness is the worst possible evidence; that it usually is the most inaccurate."

I covered my tie with my hands and asked a prospective juror what color it was. She answered wrong.

A woman in the third row co-opted the very hypothetical I was planning to use, telling us, "I actually viewed an accident and was with a group of people that evening and when we actually got into the car and were trying to tell the driver we were with, who was not at the accident scene, the story, we had six different stories." As each candidate spoke, paddles waved all over the courtroom, people eager to share their opinions or experiences with faulty eyewitness identification. I even had a psychologist, someone who taught Psychology 100, reinforce the point with an anecdote.

Point well and truly made. The next time I would raise the issue would be in closing arguments, when I planned to talk about Donn Chelli's statement, the testimony of my expert Dr. Weaver and the panelists' comments today.

I was near the end, but the energy from the prospective jury was good. They were still fully engaged and I had one more important topic to discuss. I asked them about domestic abuse, whether any of them had experience with it, either themselves or someone they knew. The two categories of responses I got were past or present victims of domestic abuse and friends/relatives of victims. I'd never had someone admit to being an abuser.

As before, and as is common with this subject, the paddles flew up. I got the panel talking about the cycle of abuse and about why victims might keep quiet. My purpose was twofold: I wanted people to understand why Kellie Torres minimized Davis's attack on her to the police and I wanted them to understand why she never called the cops when he confessed to killing Natalie.

Several panelists fed me every answer I could hope for: avoidance, coming to terms with the issue, denial, stability from the partner, fear of retaliation, hassle of filing charges, shame.

I heard similarly good answers when I asked why they thought someone might be given immunity from prosecution. My thoughts were to dull the eventual attack on Jolene Wells when she testified, to arm the jury with several (hopefully non-nefarious) reasons why someone might get immunity. People's responses evolved nicely, with very little guidance from me.

And that was it. I thanked them for their attention and turned the floor over to Wade Russell.

His style was relaxed, folksy, like the man himself. I knew the jurors would instantly like him, but then I'd always known that. He began by pointing out that the age of the case was a problem for the defense as well as the State, which was true, and he told me he was planning to call one or more witnesses himself. He then identified the panel members who were connected to law enforcement, starting with the wife of a DA investigator. Each one promised they could be fair and impartial, but I knew he'd strike them anyway. He moved on to those who had been the victims of violent crime, assuming that they were going to be less forgiving, less open-minded than others.

Most of his *voir dire* was directed at the constitutional protections afforded his client: the presumption of innocence, the burden being on the State to prove the case and the standard of reasonable doubt. He managed to find a juror who was given a speeding ticket after an accident, even though he claimed he wasn't speeding. "You didn't get the benefit of the doubt," he told the man.

He also tried to lay some groundwork for Becky's statement. I'd been wondering if he would and how. He linked it to my discussion of faulty eyewitness testimony, asking, "Has anybody ever thought they heard a family member or a loved one say something, later to find out that that is not what they said? Anybody had that experience?" No one spoke up, but just about everyone nodded and smiled. He didn't belabor the point.

Wade got a little hung up on a topic defense lawyers usually raise in *voir dire*. What they want is to find people who will not be unduly swayed by other jurors when it comes to deliberation. That's because in most trials where there are hung juries, in other words where the jurors can't reach an agreement on the verdict, it's because one or two defense-oriented jurors stick to their guns and refuse to convict. In my experience, those jurors may latch onto something irrelevant to the case and for whatever reason just don't want to vote "guilty."

Wade, like any good defense lawyer, not only wanted to identify those jurors (although in doing so he ran the risk we would strike them), but also he wanted to get that notion across to the whole panel. He wanted people to know that it was okay to be the lone hold-out, to stick to your principles even if they run counter to the position being taken by the other eleven jurors. Unfortunately for Wade, the panelists he talked to emphasized the importance of continued dialogue and consensus. Finally one juror accepted his position, but it took some time. Even though no jurors spoke up to help out Wade, I thought he made his point. He'd talked on the subject long enough for him to be able to bring it up again in closing and have them remember what he was saying.

Finally, Wade thanked the prospective jurors and sat down. The next step was for each side to tell the judge which candidates for the jury they believed should be struck for cause. Efrain and I had six candidates, two relating to criminal convictions of panelists which automatically excluded them from serving. The other four indicated that, in one way or another, they wouldn't be able to follow the law, to follow the judge's instructions. The lady who insisted on wanting DNA evidence despite video footage of the crime was one of them. To his credit, Wade recognized her failing (and perhaps the judge's attitude toward her) and did not object.

In total, we needed to talk to thirteen jurors to firm up their positions on certain issues. I could tell Judge Lynch was irritated; it was certainly more than we usually had. It took us another twenty minutes to finalize the list of those struck for cause, at which point the judge excused all the jurors for a break and sent us our separate ways to consider our peremptory strikes.

We retired to the jury room, leaving Wade and the defense team in the courtroom. We knew we wanted people who would see the big picture, who would look at our presentation and feel comfortable, compelled even, to make that hard journey to a guilty verdict. But how to know who those people were? Engineers, we suspected, would parcel out each piece of evidence and analyze it to death, focusing too closely without remembering to see the bigger picture. We threw out names of potential jurors and evaluated their personalities and deliberation styles without knowing much about them at all. We deselected on our gut instincts as much as anything, recalling the way a juror responded to us or to Wade, more than age, marital status or even job. Some folks that other prosecutors would automatically strike we left alone: a doctor and a psychologist. This process took us about twenty minutes and then I headed back into the courtroom and handed in our list to the clerk. The defense team finished soon after us and as the panelists filed back in, I got a flash of nerves. Or maybe it was excitement.

Finally, we were there. The preliminaries were over and the final participants in the trial were about to be revealed.

One by one, as their names were called, the jurors chosen walked from the gallery to the jury box and took their seats, the twelve people who would decide the fate of Dennis Davis.

Well, twelve plus one. The judge and I had discussed earlier, with wry smiles, the need for an alternate juror and Wade had agreed.

Because you never know what will happen in a jury trial.

Chapter 21

DAY ONE FOR THE PROSECUTION

The courtroom was packed. What I noticed first was the huge television camera manned by a broadcast network crewman. It was beside the jury box and pointed at the two counsel tables, forbidden from capturing jurors but free to memorialize every nod, smile, grimace and twitch of the lawyers. And the defendant.

After the initial jolt of knowing national TV was watching, I found myself too busy to worry about it. Johnny and his family were there as well as several members of his band. As ever, I was impressed by the loyalty he inspired and I was touched that so many people were taking time out of their lives to be there for him.

I exited into the hallway. I wasn't really looking for anyone in particular, but I didn't feel like standing still in the courtroom or sitting. After a few minutes I headed back inside and noticed a flash of red hair sitting opposite the courtroom doors. When I looked over, Becky Davis spoke to me.

"Excuse me, Mr. Pryor."

I hesitated, wondering whether I should panic. "Yes?"

"Can you tell me when I'll be testifying, please?" Her voice was quiet, polite.

"Probably Thursday. If it's before, I'll be sure and let Wade Russell know."

"Thank you." She paused then surprised me by saying, "Good luck."

"Thanks."

She spoke again as I started to move off. "I just want the truth to come out," she said and I thought I heard a note of desperation in her voice.

All I said in return was the truth. "Me too."

The courtroom soon quieted and Judge Lynch walked in. We talked over a few preliminary matters, batters taking their practice swings, nothing important. When we were ready, Tony Casarez, the court's bailiff and one of my favorite people in the world, opened the door to the jury room and the jurors filed in, the center of attention, taking their seats and looking expectantly at the judge. He had them stand and swore them in and after they sat down he explained about the television camera.

The formalities began when Efrain stood and read the indictment, his voice firm as he stood before the jury and recited the charges. When he was done, Judge Lynch asked, "To which indictment, how does the defendant plead?"

"Not guilty, your Honor. Not guilty."

Lawyers disagree on which part of the trial is the most important. Some say *voir dire*, some say closing arguments, but for me it's the opening statement. When a prosecutor rises to give his opening, the jury is stretched taut with anticipation, especially in an important case like this, with the courtroom filled to capacity, a watchful camera and the defendant facing the most serious crime we can charge. It's as if a vacuum lives inside the jury box, created by a hunger for the answer to one single question: What is this case about?

I like to structure my openings to answer this question, using pretty much the same format for each case: I give a snapshot that summarizes our theme, one that satisfies that initial thirst for knowledge, but leaves jurors thinking, *But how did this happen?* To answer that question I tell them a story.

Story-telling is an age-old tradition, one that we've all grown up with and experienced all of our lives. I've seen lawyers deliver opening statements by listing their witnesses or their evidence, but none of that means anything to jurors if they don't have the framework of a coherent narrative. Names, places and objects all fall away if they can't nestle themselves comfortably within a clear and consistent story. That's how we see and understand the world and I know that if I can present jurors with a believable narrative, the defense will have a hard time shaking it from the jurors' minds.

I have to be careful, though, to promise only what I can deliver. I can't make grandiose claims or oversell my case, because jurors hold prosecutors to our promises (and defense lawyers are even quicker to point out our failures in that regard).

So I laid out my twin themes: The case was about a man who descended into a jealous rage and took out his anger on a beautiful woman as she lay sleeping on her couch. And Dennis Davis, a man not a monster, could not help giving himself up, even though it took twenty-five years. As I put it: "This man, Dennis Davis, left a trail of breadcrumbs, small mistakes, that eventually, after two decades, led the police to his door."

Then I told the story of that fateful day, how Natalie went out to Sixth Street and came home in the early hours. How she changed clothes and went for a walk by the pool, how she fell asleep on the couch as Jolene went upstairs to the room she shared with Johnny. I dropped in snippets that I knew would get their minds racing, like the fact that Jolene Wells pushed the front door closed but never checked that it was locked.

I didn't use notes; I carried nothing in my hands. I didn't use pictures, either. I walked slowly up and down in front of the jury box, moderating my voice, speaking clearly and deliberately.

Jolene heard banging sounds and came downstairs to find Natalie sitting upright on the couch, covered in blood, I told them. I stopped pacing and my voice quickened as I tried to channel the panic that Jolene must have felt, transferring some of that desperation to the jurors. They sat entranced as they pictured poor Natalie moving about the apartment, her son pleading with her to sit and wait for the ambulance. I felt sure they were guessing at what Natalie was trying to say as they imagined the horror Johnny and Jolene endured.

I told them Davis came to the scene and I told them a little, just a tiny bit, about Donn Chelli's presence. But I did tell them the truth, that Chelli wouldn't be at the trial for them to judge his credibility as a witness: "He has absented himself from this proceeding." I hoped they could see past the words and understand what I meant, what I was really saying: "His testimony is unreliable."

Next I talked about the case going cold, about Rebecca Davis's phone call and about Dennis Davis's alibi falling through. I promised the jurors an hour with Davis himself, fifty-seven minutes of the interview he gave Detective Walsh, and I let them know about Kellie Torres, to whom Dennis Davis finally admitted the truth: He killed Natalie.

The final part of my opening was a run-through of the other witnesses from whom the jurors would hear. It was all very well hearing a story, but they wanted to know which of the participants would be appearing in court. They knew about Kellie and Davis himself, so I added the other main participants: Johnny, Jolene and Rebecca Davis.

I paused, because I was about to finish. "Ladies and gentlemen, that is the evidence the State expects to put on for you this week and at the end of it, I will stand before you again and I am going to ask you to find this man, Dennis Davis, guilty of the murder of Natalie Antonetti. Thank you very much."

Wade began his opening statement by asking the jurors to hold me to mine. He went on to tell them what they wouldn't be seeing, focusing on the State's lack of forensic evidence. I wasn't worried; I had covered this issue in *voir dire* and if there was any residual doubt, I could point out in my closing argument that finding Davis's DNA or fingerprints at his ex-girlfriend's house told us nothing conclusive.

Defense lawyers aren't there to tell a story; in many cases they don't call any witnesses. That makes opening statements very tricky and usually all they can do is remind the jurors of the high burden of proof and other constitutional protections. Picking holes in a story that has not yet unfolded is pretty much impossible.

Wade did give them a small story, the one told by Donn Chelli, and the jury listened carefully but, other than the description Chelli gave, Wade's story didn't conflict with mine.

He touched on Becky's testimony and on Kellie's, calling both "false," and as he wrapped up, he tried to reduce the State's case to just two people: "In order to convict Mr. Davis of this crime, you have to do these two things: Discount what Mr. Chelli said and believe Kellie one hundred percent and that is a steep burden for the State. There is a reason that we have the rule 'beyond a reasonable doubt' and I challenge you to stick with your conclusions. If you don't buy that theory of the case, you need to stick by the facts as you see them and render a true and fair verdict for Dennis Davis. That is all I am asking you to do. Thank you."

As soon as Wade sat down, Judge Lynch looked at Efrain and me and told us to call our first witness.

Efrain responded: "State calls Johnny Goudie."

Over the past year or so, I'd talked to Johnny about this case and his testimony a dozen times. We met just once to prepare formally, in a large conference room and with Efrain at the helm. I usually like my second chair to handle the first witness; otherwise I end up doing the *voir dire*, the opening statement and the first witness questioning, which not only is a lot to prepare for all at once, but also can leave the jury wondering who the other person with me is. I also wanted Efrain to handle Johnny's testimony, because I knew Johnny, an exceptionally bright, open and honest man, was going to be a great witness for us. I knew he'd tell it the way he remembered it and if there were any discrepancies, any inconsistencies for the defense to pick at, I knew he'd handle those with the same open, honest manner. With some professional witnesses, good at their jobs and at testifying, we talk about putting them on the stand and "pressing the play button." I'd always felt it would be like that with Johnny.

The moment Johnny walked in and sat down, we were in good shape.

Efrain introduced Johnny to the jury the usual way: name, age, where he lived. He asked Johnny about his music—how long he'd been playing and the names of his bands. Soon he went back, though and asked when Johnny first moved to Austin.

"In the summer of 1984 I moved here with my mom."

"What was your mom's name?"

"My mom's name was Natalie Antonetti."

I felt the room crackle as he said her name, but in the witness box Johnny was still, unmoving and his voice remained soft and uninflected. I felt sure the jurors wanted to reach out and hug him, tell him it would be okay, because I wanted to as well. He was a musician, yes, but right now he was the stoic son. He wasn't letting himself feel the pressure of the moment and he was also blocking out the pain from the past. He had become emotional once with me, during our trial preparation session, and he wasn't going to let that happen here. He had a story to tell.

It was the story of his mother. He told the jury how she moved to the United States with her family when Fidel Castro took over Cuba, how she married her high school sweetheart, Johnny's father, but just he and his mom moved to Austin when he was fifteen. He told them how she worked hard at her landscaping business and how she loved the "outdoorsy-ness" of Austin and its lively music scene. Like everyone else in the packed courtroom, I was riveted.

"She was a very gregarious person. She always liked to have a good time. She liked to dance. She enjoyed other things, like reading and doing artistic projects and craft things. She crocheted hats and made earrings and stuff. Just a very creative person."

"Was she a very sociable person?"

"Very sociable person. Had a lot of friends and was active in her friends' lives. A lot of friends."

"At the time that she died, can you describe her physically as to hair and what have you?"

"She had long brown hair, bangs, very physically fit. She ran and ate right, took care of her health."

Efrain introduced a picture of Natalie into evidence, the one that had been on the news, the one that made up the cover of the first binder I put together on the case. Her hair flowed down her back and her smile dominated the picture, a smile that was even brighter because of her tanned skin. Her eyes looked right at you and when you looked back you knew you were seeing a woman who was beautiful.

Johnny told the jury that the photo was taken a month or two before his mother died, imbuing it with even more power. That power was recognized by the defense and Wade asked to approach the bench. He told the judge he didn't object to the photo being in evidence, but added, "I object to it being displayed to the jury the entire trial."

Efrain passed the photo to the jury and gave them a moment to look. Then he moved on, taking Johnny through the time he met Dennis Davis. "It would have been very early in January of 1985. I guess my mom had met him when I was away visiting my father over the Christmas holiday. I don't remember meeting him, exactly when I met him, but I do remember that that was the time that I met him."

He described Davis and his mother's relationship as "on again, off again" and Efrain took a moment to have Johnny look at and identify Davis in the courtroom. This can sometimes be a moment of high tension, but it passed quickly with Efrain's methodical and matter-of-fact manner and Johnny's obvious self-control. Efrain asked about Johnny's relationship with Davis.

"It was friendly. He had—obviously, I was very interested in music and recording and anything like that and he had kind of, I guess, invited me to come by whenever to his studio and see what was going on, watch sessions or whatever, like that, watch recording sessions."

"Outside the studio, did you socialize with him?"

"Not like I would call him on the phone and go get lunch or anything like that, but when I saw him, yes, I did socialize with him."

"In relation to where your apartment was, where was the studio located?"

"I imagine if you went through the neighborhoods, it would be about a mile."

"Suffice it to say it was close to your apartment?"

"Very close."

Johnny described the layout of Studio D and did the same for the townhouse he shared with Natalie. And he told the jury about Jolene Wells. Though he admitted he didn't recall how they met, he described their friendship, how at some point they started dating and how she was the one who took him home after he'd been drinking the night of the attack on his mother.

"When you got home to the apartment, what happened then?" Efrain asked.

"I went up and laid down and my exact recollection, what I can actually still remember, is my mom came into my room and rubbed my back some and put a garbage can under there and I think she said that she was going out or something."

He told the jury that he then fell asleep, essentially passing out.

"When do you recall waking up?"

"I recall waking up when Jolene woke me to tell me that my mom was downstairs and something had happened to her."

Efrain paused for a moment, preparing to elicit Johnny's description of finding his mother, battered and bloody, on the couch downstairs. Suddenly, Judge Lynch jumped in and called time out, sending the jurors to their room for the first break of the day.

The break was longer than we'd all anticipated, but when the jurors filed back in I felt the air slowly tighten as people remembered where we left off.

"You were talking about Jolene waking you up, so why don't you start from there and tell us what happened?"

"She woke me up and was yelling that my mom—something happened and my mom was lying in a pool of blood downstairs and so I jumped up and went down there immediately."

"Can you tell us what is it that you observed once you made it downstairs?"

"My mother was on the couch. She was not unconscious. She was conscious and she was obviously in shock. She couldn't talk, form words. She was covered in a substantial amount of blood. You could tell it was coming from her head and I can't remember if she was sitting or lying on the couch. I do believe, though, that she was sitting on the couch when I got down there."

"At that point in time, do you recall what she was wearing?"

"What appeared to be like running clothes, like shorts and a shirt that she had brought me from a recent trip to California."

"She was sitting there on the couch?"

"Yes."

"Did you talk to her?"

"Yes. I asked her repeatedly what had happened and who had done this to her, if she could tell me what happened and she couldn't respond verbally."

"All right. Then what happened at that point?"

"At that point she was kind of moaning and she got up and was walking around, obviously in shock. She was walking around and went to the bathroom and tried to wipe some of the blood off of her with toilet paper and then she wanted to go upstairs and I accompanied her upstairs."

"How was she able to get to the bathroom?"

"Well, with my assistance she was able to walk."

"How did you know that she wanted to go to the bathroom?"

"I was just kind of following where she was moving. She was walking in that direction and I just kind of helped her."

"Again, there was no verbal communication between you and her?"

"No, she wasn't able to say anything."

Johnny and Efrain were still talking in quiet tones, Efrain the more animated of the two, Johnny still reciting the events with a calm and seemingly dispassionate tone. With anyone else I might have worried, as I usually encourage my victim witnesses to emote freely but genuinely on the stand. Even though a victim or witness may have told his or her story a hundred times to cops, prosecutors, even friends, jurors are placed in the position of having to judge credibility and when doing so they can easily forget they're not the first to hear the account. But with Johnny I wasn't worried. The jurors knew twenty-five years had gone by and they knew Johnny's somewhat flat affect was just that, an affect. He had battened down his emotions to make it through testifying and while I knew that his tears would be powerful testimony, I was far more interested in preserving Johnny's psyche than putting on a show.

The jurors hung on his words as Johnny continued telling how he helped his mother up the stairs toward her bedroom.

"Again, Johnny, how did she indicate she wanted to go upstairs?"

"I just basically went the direction that she was walking and assisted her in that way. She didn't say. I don't remember her pointing anywhere."

"Was she supporting herself with any of the walls?"

"She was, yes, yeah. She was supporting herself between me and the wall. I was on one side of her."

"All right. Did she go upstairs?"

"Yes, into her bedroom."

"What happened when you all went upstairs?"

"She briefly sat on the edge of the bed and I remember her looking in the mirror a couple of times, maybe even in the downstairs bathroom, but in her bedroom when she sat on the edge of the bed she did and then she…she reached over for a drawer, one of her drawers in the chest of drawers that was across from her bed and got a nightie out of there and then she got up and I helped her in her bathroom where she pushed the door shut and I believe at that point that she changed from the clothes that she was wearing into that."

I saw several jurors shake their heads in wonder, eyes glued to Johnny, and he went on to say that it was around this time he asked Jolene to watch over his mother while he went to see where the ambulance was, frustrated that it was taking so long. Which was when he ran into Donn Chelli.

"You said you encountered a neighbor?"

"I think so. I mean—yeah, I mean a neighbor, somebody stopped and talked to me and in my statement it says that I talked to somebody who told me he had seen someone walking around with a bat. I don't really remember that conversation as much as I just kind of remember someone trying to talk to me when my mind was obviously somewhere else, on making sure that the EMS got in there all right."

Here we ran into a problem we knew would hamper us: memory. Johnny also testified that he remembered someone stopping him from going back into the apartment and acknowledged that his statement, given at the time, identified Dennis Davis as that person. But sitting in the courtroom at trial, he couldn't picture Davis being that person.

We were ready, though, to use Texas Rule of Evidence 803 (5). This is an exception to the hearsay rule, which normally prevents a written statement from being entered into evidence, either in written form or by being read to the jury. The idea behind the exception is that if someone made a statement at the time of the relevant events and is in court to testify that the statement is the one he or she made and also that he or she is unable to remember the events, the parts the witness can't remember can be read to the jury. The judge granted our request over Wade's objection.

Johnny read: "Dennis Davis, the man that Jolene called, pulled up. He was dating my mom at the time. I spoke to him about it. He was trying to hold me back from going back inside and then a neighbor who was just getting home, I can't remember what his position was." Efrain then confirmed with Johnny that he didn't remember Davis ever going into the apartment to check on Natalie. Maybe he did go inside, maybe he didn't.

And then came a touching moment. His voice quiet but firm, Johnny described his last exchange with his mother in the ambulance on the way to the hospital: "My mom was able to put two words together and I guess the straps on her—around her ankles were too tight, because she kept on saying, she said 'put foot' a couple of times and then she did not say anything. When we arrived at the hospital and she was going into the emergency room, I asked her for a kiss and she gave me a kiss and that was it. She didn't regain consciousness again."

There was silence no one dared fill for a few moments before Efrain asked him about the eighteen days in hospital before life support was removed. In response to a direct question, Johnny said he didn't remember seeing Davis visit his mother, nor did he remember seeing Davis at the funeral in Houston.

Efrain asked to approach and presented Johnny with a stack of sixty photographs, all taken by the police at the apartment the morning of the attack. Once entered into evidence, Efrain placed them on the projector so the jury could see them. He didn't use them all— Efrain knew not to bore the jurors—but every one he used to make a point. The bloody couch showed the horror Johnny confronted that morning; the keys, bicycle, guitar and briefcase in the background all indicated this hadn't been a robbery and the furniture in the correct places showed there was no struggle. Each photo helped rule out the possible alternate explanations and, in their controlled, reasoned back-and-forth, prosecutor and witness made it abundantly clear that Natalie was the intended target of this attack and surprise was the second deadliest weapon used by her killer.

Before Efrain sat down, he asked Johnny about an odd conversation Johnny had with Dennis Davis long after the murder. Johnny had come to Austin with his band and visited Davis at his studio. Someone in the band asked how the two knew each other and Davis's response was to say that at one time he'd almost become Johnny's dad. Surprised, Johnny responded that that wasn't true and that was the last time they talked.

Then it was time to break for lunch and the lawyers approached the bench to talk about scheduling, because we needed to go out of order. We needed to interrupt Johnny's testimony and put on the medical examiner who conducted the autopsy on Natalie, because he was leaving town on vacation. This brought up the discussion of which autopsy photos we intended to use: We had a total of fourteen from the autopsy but didn't plan to show them all and Wade (as every defense lawyer does) tried to limit the number as much as possible to reduce the emotional impact on the jury, afraid that the jurors would be so horrified by the wounds they would be too quick to hold his client accountable. The judge settled on the four we wanted to show and Wade did not object.

Dr. Roberto Bayardo was a character. Always had been, if you believed the stories. He was a large, ruggedly attractive man, originally from Mexico, and he spoke with a thick accent that had remained undiluted despite his half-century living and working in the United States. Like many who work with the dead, his sense of humor was dark and his tolerance for the squeamish was high.

"Dr. Bayardo, what do you do for a living?" Efrain began.

With a smile and in his thick accent he replied, "Right now I am retired, so I don't have to do anything for a living."

As the jurors and the court reporter strained to listen, Dr. Bayardo rattled off his impressive qualifications, which included thirty years as the chief medical examiner in Travis County and more than 15,000 autopsies. He explained what that meant: "An autopsy is the examination of a deceased person. In doing the autopsy, we examine the outside of the body first and usually we make a description as we go along, a dictation typed in the report. After the external examination then we go ahead and open up the body cavities, including the head, the chest, the abdomen, remove all of the internal organs. All of these organs are carefully examined and dissected and described. We look for the presence of any injury and also for the presence of any diseases that might have caused the person's death.

"At the end of the examination, we make a list of our findings. That is what we call the diagnosis. The last thing to do is determine cause and manner of death."

Efrain inquired about Natalie's autopsy and Dr. Bayardo told the jury it was done on November 1. He described Natalie's body as it came to him, the only signs of violence being to the head, the rest of her body unmarked and unharmed (apart from signs of medical treatment). Efrain showed the four photographs and Dr. Bayardo confirmed they were from Natalie's autopsy. They were entered into evidence and Efrain showed them to the jury, the courtroom silent as Bayardo's deep voice explained what they were seeing on State's Exhibits 68 through 71.

"You can see a big defect on the scalp. That portion of the scalp had been surgically removed because it had been crushed by multiple blows that caused the tissue to become dead, so it had to be removed and then on the side you can see two other healing wounds, also the result of blunt trauma to the head."

"How many wounds do you note on State's Exhibit No. 69?"

"Well, we can see only three wounds, but as I said before, the larger wound was a result of multiple blows. How many I cannot tell, but it would have been more than two."

"The injuries that you see on State's Exhibit No. 69, would that be consistent with the instrument being a bat that inflicted those injuries?"

"Yes. That is very much so a difference from a wound caused by a sharp instrument and these wounds have crushed margins that tend to be so by blows with a blunt instrument."

"That being a bat?"

"Any instrument that has a round surface could do that. A bat could have done that, yes."

The matter of a bat would become relevant later on, so Efrain had done a nice job of making clear that a bat could have been the murder weapon.

He continued: "How much force, Doctor, based on your training and experience, does it take to inflict an injury like that, especially the one that is much bigger than the others?"

"It takes a lot of force. Because of the other injuries, just looking at that main injury, I would have thought that she had fallen from a height against a hard pavement."

"Someone of my build, Doctor, would someone of my build, would I be able to inflict those injuries if in fact I was doing that with a bat?"

"I believe so, yes."

Efrain turned to the largest of the fractures visible in the photographs. "That fracture, how far does it run as it relates to the front of the head?"

"One of the fractures starts at the top of the head and then goes across the other side around the outside of the right eye and into the roof of the right orbit and you can see multiple fractures all over the left side of her head." He'd already explained that the "panda eyes" evident in the photo came from this head injury, not from her being assaulted directly in the face.

Efrain then asked two questions that made me glad Johnny wasn't in the room. To the untrained ear they might have sounded unnecessary or grotesque.

"At the time that you performed your autopsy as it relates to the brain, was there an aroma that one can smell emitting or coming from the brain?"

"Yes, a foul smell, like a sewer-like smell that was coming from the brain. This brain had been dead for many days."

"I would like to draw on your training and experience as well, Doctor, in talking about individuals who are comatose or in a coma. Can you share with the jurors what exactly occurs with a person when they are in a coma?"

"When they are in a coma, you lose consciousness, so you cannot see, you cannot talk and she could not breathe, so she had—a tube had to be put into her airway, so there is loss of whatever is going on around that person."

There was a reason Efrain asked Dr. Bayardo both these questions: We wanted to make it clear that Natalie's death, for all intents and purposes, occurred on the night she was assaulted. She didn't die of an unrelated infection or from heart failure or anything else, but

Natalie Antonetti and toddler son Johnny

Clockwise from far left: Natalie Antonetti, Natalie's sister Olga Antonetti, their mother, also named Olga Antonetti, and Johnny Goudie

Natalie and Johnny shortly before her death

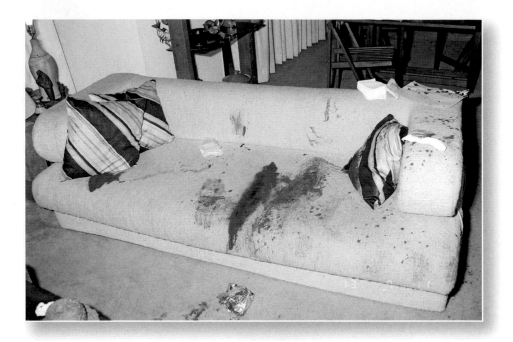

Crime scene photos show the bloodstained couch and hallway inside Natalie's townhouse

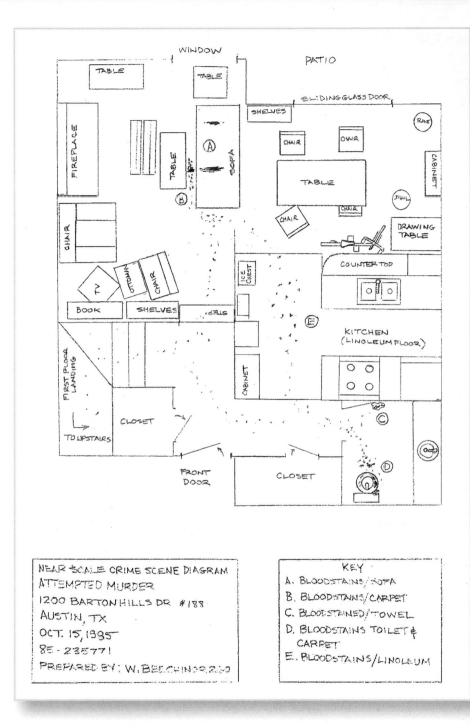

William Beechinor's precise, detailed sketch of Apartment 188 after the assault

Natalie's grave marker at Forest Park Westheimer Cemetery in Houston

The note that Dennis Davis left on Natalie's door

Marty Odem, convicted of raping a woman in 1986, is the man the defense alleged was the real murderer

Amparo Garcia-Crow's journal entry from October 15, 1985, mentions the assault on Natalie and contradicts Dennis Davis' alibi

Austin Detective Tom Walsh reopened Natalie's cold case

JUDGE MIKE LYNCH

Judge Mike
Lynch presides
over the trial

Johnny
Goudie,
the victim's
son and the
prosecution's
first witness,
testifies

Becky Davis on the
witness stand

Dennis Davis
listens to
testimony

Wade Russell, lead
defense counsel for
Dennis Davis

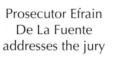

Prosecutor Efrain
De La Fuente
addresses the jury

Lead prosecutor
Mark Pryor makes
his closing argument

from the savage beating that began as she lay curled up asleep on her couch.

Efrain passed the witness to the defense and immediately I wondered whether Wade would try to challenge this witness, because Bayardo's testimony didn't necessarily implicate his client and seemed medically correct. But Wade had a strategy and it was not to attack this witness; it was to lay the groundwork for an attack on Kellie Torres, the woman who claimed that not only did Davis confess the murder to her, but also he attacked her in very much the same way.

Wade had Dr. Bayardo detail the bruises, cuts and broken bones that would result from a beating with a baseball bat. Wade knew, because he'd seen all our evidence, that we had no documents to prove any such injuries to Kellie Torres. He also established that Natalie was not pregnant, which would prove to be a discrepancy with what Torres said Davis told her: that Natalie was pregnant with Davis's baby. They were small points and if they were to go to the defense it would be later, but I saw Wade was prepared. He did ask one question that I thought Efrain would have asked: whether Natalie's body showed signs of sexual assault. Dr. Bayardo said no and from my perspective that was more good evidence for the prosecution: Whoever killed Natalie had no intention of raping or robbing her. Whoever assaulted her that morning did so for one reason: He wanted her dead. Why would a stranger take the great risk of sneaking in and killing someone? The answer, it seemed to me, was that he wouldn't. Only someone who knew Natalie would do this, someone who had an explosive temper and a specific desire to do her harm.

And Efrain and I would spend the rest of the trial demonstrating that only one man fit that description: Dennis Davis.

Johnny Goudie retook the stand midafternoon and the conversation between him and Wade was the opposite of what one might expect between the State's first witness and a dogged defense lawyer. There were no histrionics, no pointed fingers, no raised voices. In fact, early on Judge Lynch asked both men to adjust their microphones to be heard. It wasn't Wade's personality to be an attack dog and, even if it had been, he was smart enough to know this was one witness to treat carefully.

One of the first things Wade established was that Studio D had no bedroom and no shower or anywhere people could bathe. He'd use that evidence later to argue that when Jolene called Davis, it had to have been at his home, not his studio, putting him farther away from the crime scene.

Then Wade's questioning hopped around, two questions on how often Johnny went to Steamboat, a couple about his mother's relationship with Davis, a few about Johnny's drinking at Studio D. Wade took Johnny back over the events of that morning and Johnny confirmed what was in his statement: He was with his mother and can remember Jolene on the phone with someone, though he didn't know who at the time. The cross-examination continued like this, Wade asking questions in his soft voice, Johnny responding calmly, his memory the main impediment to his answers. Johnny was there to set the scene and talk about his mother, not necessarily to connect Dennis Davis to the crime.

Our next witness was in much the same vein, only Jolene Wells was a dozen times more fragile.

This had always concerned me, but I'd worked hard with her, starting the moment she signed the immunity agreement months before trial, when her attorney David Botsford allowed us to talk to her directly. He never believed she had anything to hide and I knew he didn't want to charge her money just to sit there, so I was able to meet with her several times prior to trial, just the two of us. And she warmed up. After the way she was treated in the 1980s, her distrust of law enforcement festered to make her nervous, anxious, resentful. But I was careful to treat her gently, to make it clear that she and I were on the same side. Part of her reticence was the shock of discovering that her former friend and boss, Dennis Davis, had killed her best friend; that much I could understand. She felt, I think, a little like she was in a movie, a fog of unreality descending every time she thought about or had to deal with the murder case.

One thing I did with Jolene was to show her the courtroom prior to trial. I showed her where the judge sat, where she would sit, where the jury would be and where the defendant would sit. Letting her walk around the empty room (when it's empty, the courtroom loses much of its power, the aura of formality and tension that fills it at trial) and sit in each place, see everything without people watching her, made a huge difference.

She started well, answering my preliminary questions, but I didn't want to keep her on the witness stand long; I had promised her I wouldn't. I moved on to the month of the attack on Natalie. Immediately Jolene tensed and I feared the worst. In our discussions her memory had not always been good and I worried that the stress of the moment would make her even more unsure.

I did have a backup plan, but first I tried to loosen her up by having her talk about Austin more generally, to remember the good things.

"What was Austin like back then as opposed to what it is like now?"

"It was a little different than it is now. It was more laid back. Sixth Street wasn't like it is now. It was kind of a—it was a friendly musical community. Everybody knew each other. It was kind of a great place to live, still is, but it was a little different, little divey bars, everybody knew each other. It was great."

I saw her shoulders relax a little, so I had her talk about Natalie and their friendship and then how she knew Dennis Davis.

I actually managed to get a smile out of her in what's a usually tense moment. "Let me ask you, the person we are referring to as Dennis Davis, do you see him in the courtroom today?"

"Yes."

"Can you describe an item of clothing he is wearing and where he is seated?"

Her eyes flicked to the defense table. "He is wearing glasses and he has a tie and a suit."

I paused then smiled at her. "That describes the defense lawyer too. Do you mean the gentleman at the end with the green shirt?"

She smiled, too. "Yes."

Jolene described Natalie some more for the jury, saying Natalie didn't date a lot of men and didn't party excessively but did have a penchant for champagne. As we closed in on October 12, the day before the attack, Jolene's memory failed her, as I knew it would. She recalled nothing of Johnny drinking at Studio D, bringing him home and helping put him to bed.

"Well, talking about the early morning hours of October 13, why don't you tell the jury what is the first thing that you do remember when Natalie came home?"

"I don't remember her coming home and I don't remember what happened that night. I remember—I mean the events that led up to the incident. I remember hugging her good night and I remember saying good night to her and she said I love you and I said I love you and I went to bed and then I woke up because I heard noises."

"You remember that?"

"Yes."

"Can you describe to the jury the noises you heard?"

"I heard—I am not sure what order it was in. I heard thumping noises. I heard moaning. It wasn't like normal crying and I heard—then I think I heard—I'm sorry, I'm sorry." She stopped talking and reached for a tissue, her hand shaking.

"That's okay. Take your time, Jolene."

"I heard a door shut, open or shut, I am not sure which and I thought it was very unusual noises, so—so I was kind of half asleep and I remember it was very late or early in the morning, however you want to put it and I decided to go down and investigate because—I just heard weird noises."

From there her memory came in dribs and drabs, as she put it. She saw scenes from that night but not a flowing narrative. I asked to approach the bench and requested permission to have Jolene read to the jurors the statement she gave on the day of the assault, using the same rule of evidence Efrain used earlier. The judge allowed it and in her quiet voice Jolene started reading the words she provided to the police twenty-five years ago.

"On Sunday, October 13, at approximately 2:30 A.M., Natalie came back to the apartment from Sixth Street. She had been to Toulouse and Steamboat. I asked her if she had fun and what she had done and she said she saw some friends on Sixth Street and ran into

Davey Kane, another friend. She didn't tell me the names of the other friends she had run into. Then she ran upstairs and changed into jogging shorts and a T-shirt and said she was going to go for a walk by the pool in the apartment complex. She didn't appear to be drunk. If she drank at all, it would have been only a couple of drinks. I told her to be careful when she went for a walk and she said okay.

"She came back about ten minutes later. I don't recall if she locked the door or not. I was watching TV in the living room when she came back in, then she lay down on the couch and started falling asleep. She didn't say anything to me after she came back from her walk. I watched TV for a few more minutes after she started dozing off. I told her that I was going to watch TV for a few more minutes and then go to sleep. I turned off the TV and went upstairs and got into bed. Just before I went upstairs, I pushed on the front door to make sure it was shut but didn't check to see if it was locked. I asked her if she had locked the door and she just kind of grunted so I took this as yes. Sometimes the door sticks and it is hard to tell if it is locked or just jammed."

She paused and looked up.

"Keep reading, please, Jolene. Keep reading the whole statement, please."

"I woke around 4:30 A.M. to get a glass of water. When I went downstairs, I noticed that she was sleeping peacefully on the couch. I tried not to wake her up. On Sunday, October 13, at approximately 5:15 A.M. I heard moaning and some thumping noises from downstairs. This is a townhouse and the bedrooms are upstairs and the living room is downstairs. I also heard a door shut. I thought this was strange because I still heard someone down there, the moaning noise, even after the door shut. The people who live at this address are John Goudie, Natalie Antonetti and myself. John is her son. I then got up and went downstairs." She looked up again. "Keep reading?"

"Yes, ma'am."

"When I went downstairs, I saw Natalie sitting on the couch and she—and she was covered in blood from head to foot. The couch was also all bloody. I went over to her and tried to find out what happened but she couldn't…she couldn't talk even though…she couldn't talk even though she tried. I then called the police and the ambulance. I went back over to her and tried to talk to her again. Then I went back to the phone and called a mutual friend of ours, Dennis Davis. I wanted someone I knew to be there and I didn't know who else to call. After this I went back upstairs to wake John up. We both ran back downstairs and tried to help Natalie. She started to get up and tried to walk around. She walked—she walked to the kitchen and then into the bathroom downstairs and then walked up the stairs and went into her upstairs bathroom. She then closed the door and wouldn't let us in. She was trying to take off the clothes that she was wearing when she was attacked. She had on dark blue jogging shorts, no underwear and a pink T-shirt. We tried to stop her from doing this because it might be evidence. She went ahead and took…took this off and put on white baby doll type pajamas. She then threw her shorts on the floor and her shirt on the bed and sat down on the bed.

"During this time, she was still moaning and trying to talk but it just came out garbled sounding. She was bleeding pretty badly, especially from her head and nose. We got some towels and tried to apply pressure to her head, but she wouldn't let us, kept fighting us off. The whole time—the whole time she was walking around and we kept trying to restrain her and keep her from moving around. She then went back downstairs and sat on the couch while John ran outside to find the ambulance. Just before John ran outside, the ambulance had called stating that they couldn't find the apartment. EMS then came in and tried to treat her. While they were doing this, she kept pointing to her feet, but I don't know why. She also kept trying to talk."

"I am going to stop you there, Jolene." I had a point I needed to make. "You mention in your statement about calling Dennis Davis, right, you just read that to the jury?"

"Yes."

"Do you have any recollection of where he was when you phoned him?"

"No."

"In other words, is it possible you phoned him at his house in Onion Creek?"

"It is possible."

"Is it possible you phoned him at his studio on South Lamar?"

"It is possible."

Point made, I moved on to the timing of the call. Johnny had testified to hearing it, so she must have called Davis *after* getting Johnny out of bed. But her statement said she called Davis first. "Even when you gave the statement, is it fair to say you were pretty traumatized?"

"Yes."

"Is it possible that some of these events occurred in a different sequence than you have in your statement?"

"Yes, sir," she replied.

"If somebody else were to testify that you woke Johnny before calling Dennis Davis, is that possible?"

"I suppose it is possible."

Next was a piece of evidence I knew would be powerful. We'd be hearing Jolene's voice, the very person on the stand right now, from twenty-five years ago: her 911 call.

The recording was scratchy, the operator on the other end calm, but Jolene was panicked, begging, crying for help, swallowing words in her terror but pleading for someone to come and come fast. The operator tried to find out what happened and this was when Jolene's terrified mind provided the only explanation that made sense: that Natalie had been outside and was hit by a car.

When the tape ended we all sat for a moment or two, our thoughts, senses and emotions leaving the past and skipping forward two decades back to the courtroom.

I needed to tie off that loose end. "Jolene, you said on that phone call that Natalie had just come in from outside. Do you know why you said that?"

"No, I don't."

"Does that confuse you now hearing that?"

"Yes."

"Do you have any reason to believe she had just come in from outside?"

"No, I don't believe. I think I was trying to process what I was seeing and I think I remember thinking that she was hit by a car or something. I just didn't know. I don't know why I said that. I don't know."

I wanted the jury to hear about two things Davis said to Jolene, one at the hospital and one at his home, and inquired about them. Wade objected before Jolene could answer my question and we approached the bench. We argued back and forth and the judge decided to prohibit Davis's comment about Natalie's wrinkles at the hospital and allow the second callous statement. I went straight to it.

"Was there an incident at his home that happened between just the two of you when you were attempting to talk to him about what had happened?"

"Yes."

"Would you please tell the jury what happened?"

"I was upset and I was trying to talk to him about Natalie. I was very upset and he—he put on a porno tape and said look at that, look at that and I didn't understand, it was so out of the blue and out of character for him, I didn't understand what—why he did that. When he saw that I was—when he saw that I was upset, he turned it off."

Jolene would be one of many witnesses to testify about Davis's odd and out-of-character responses to Natalie's death. People react strangely to tragedy so these were not the strongest threads to tie him to the crime. Stronger ones would come with my next questions.

"Did you know Dennis Davis to own or possess a child's small baseball bat?"

"I saw a bat at his house. I don't know what size it was."

"Do you know whose that was?"

"No."

"You don't know whose bat it was?" I asked.

"No."

"Whereabouts in his house did you see it?"

"It was in a room. I don't know which room."

Her poor memory again, but having gotten that much was a start. I touched briefly on the immunity we'd given her, making it clear to the jury that despite the agreement she had never changed her story, not once in twenty-five years.

On cross-examination, Wade jumped on the immunity issue, making sure the jury didn't forget what it meant: Jolene could not be prosecuted for anything she said at trial.

Then he probed her memory of events, distinguishing between what she could recall and what she knew from her statement. I wasn't sure that he was aiming for any major points and I sensed Jolene was confused and a little frustrated by his questions. He homed in a little on the timing of when Jolene found Natalie, pushing for it to be closer to 5:30 that morning. They ended up agreeing that all times were approximate; precision wasn't possible any more.

Wade got some good information for the defense when he asked about Jolene's impression of the relationship between Natalie and Dennis.

"She—Natalie wanted—I believe she wanted an exclusive relationship with Dennis and I think he kind of broke her heart."

"By dating other women?"

"Yes."

"Did you believe that perhaps—I mean there is no other way to put it—that she may have been in love with him, but he really wasn't in love with her? Isn't that what you told investigators?"

"I would say that that was my assumption, yes."

"Didn't you tell investigators that you asked her about why she continued to have these feelings despite the fact that he was dating other women around this period of time?" Wade asked.

"I believe so."

The question then being, why would Davis murder a woman out of jealousy when he wanted to break up with her? A good question in any other case, but I knew we had good responses to it. Davis himself would undo this defense theory.

Jolene stayed steady through Wade's next line of questioning. "You stated that you saw a bat one time, in Mr. Davis's house was it?"

"Yes."

"Have you ever seen any other people who have bats in their houses?"

"Not recently, no."

"I mean, are other people known to use bats for self-defense or to play softball perhaps?"

"I don't know. Honestly, I don't have any friends who have bats in their house."

I had no questions for Jolene on redirect. She had done fine and for her sake I wanted to get her off the stand. Her relief was clear as the judge turned to her and said, "Thank you very much, ma'am. You are excused."

William Beechinor was my next witness. He was part of the team that would feed information to the jurors about the crime scene. He was a tall, distinguished-looking man in his fifties. At the time of Natalie's death he was a patrol officer with a gift for drawing, a talent that was put to use by the Austin Police Department by making him an accident investigator. In that role, he was called on to sketch accident sites and crime scenes. As he explained to the jury with a wry smile, "This was well before the time of laser levels and other forensics. It was all rulers, tape measures and pens and pencils." In his deep but gentle voice he explained how he went about working with detectives to make a precise sketch of Natalie's apartment after the assault, measuring, noting, detailing. I entered the sketch as an exhibit then turned him over to Wade.

Wade and I knew from the offense report that Beechinor did something else in this case, the following day. He sat down with Donn Chelli at APD headquarters and together the two men assembled a drawing of the mystery "Lotions man." Wade and I also knew that Beechinor had no recollection of making that sketch and that the drawing itself had since been lost. But Wade asked Beechinor about it anyway, to make his point that there was too much doubt surrounding Chelli's sighting to pin the murder on Davis. Once Beechinor confirmed his lack of memory, Wade sat down and we moved on.

Efrain handled our next witness, Tom Bevel, who introduced his expertise: "I am the owner of a forensic education and consulting company. It is called Bevel, Gardner and Associates, Incorporated. About half of our work is in education, teaching seven different forty-hour courses in forensic science disciplines and then the other half is taking case analysis, such as this case."

I would have called him a blood spatter analyst. He also did crime-scene reconstruction, but we were using him for one limited purpose: to show that the assailant would not have been covered with blood. This would allow us to argue that Davis would not have attracted undue attention had anyone seen him that night and also that even if he'd gone back to his Onion Creek home, he wouldn't have had to shower or even change clothes before heading back to Natalie's apartment after Jolene called him.

Efrain began by asking Bevel to explain the various terms related to blood spatter. "Can you tell us what cast-off blood is?"

"Yes, sir. Cast-off is a term where you have blood that is still wet and it is on an object that is subsequently in motion. For example, if I had blood on the end of my fingers, if there wasn't a sufficient amount, it wouldn't even drip because of the surface tension, but if I start moving my hand, then that can certainly overcome the surface tension and cast blood in the direction that the hand is being swung."

"What is drip blood?"

"Drip blood, frequently referred to as passive. If I use my hand again and the blood source is contributing blood, once the blood volume is sufficient enough to overcome the surface tension helping hold it to the finger, then gravity will pull it downward. Drip blood is usually very large in size, depending on what it is falling from. From my finger it would be very large. If it was from the tip end of a knife, it would be very small."

"What about back spatter?"

"Back spatter is a term specifically applied usually with gunshots. An example of that would be if I held my hand up and if it were to be shot with a projectile, the blood that goes back in the direction from where the projectile was being fired from would be back spatter."

"What other bloodstains are there that we haven't covered, Mr. Bevel?"

"Well, actually a number of different categories. Pooling blood is blood that is coalescing where there is a large volume. That would sit on top of a podium such as this. If we have something on the carpet, the same volume, it will be absorbed in and that changes it to what is referred to as saturation. Any alterations of bloodstains such as smearing, wiping, swiping. There are a number of different terms that we could get into."

Efrain guided him through a series of crime scene photos and Bevel applied his terms to the pictures. Drops on the floor, handprints on the wall. But soon Efrain brought Bevel to what we wanted the jurors to know. Bevel pointed out that to have blood flow at all, the weapon used on Natalie would have had to be applied to an area of broken skin. In other words, no blood spatter at all for the first blow and only spatter when the bat landed on an open wound. He added, "If there is anything such as a person was wearing a baseball cap or a hat or a, unlike myself, a full, thick head of hair, that will kind of block the spatter from actually escaping. It kind of catches it and holds it."

As for direction of travel, he told the jury, "The blood tends to go in the direction of least resistance, which is going to be typically away from me and to the side. Can some of it come back toward me? It certainly can. With a full head of hair, it is less likely to. That helps to block it. If I am hitting with my, for example, my fist, certainly I would expect something to be on my hand. May or may not be spatter going back in the direction that I am swinging the blow from, so if the example were, for example, my hand, where the blood would end up going is typically about 180 degree radius, the majority of it out away and to the side."

Efrain followed up, just to be sure, and asked Bevel for his assessment of how much blood he would expect to see on the assailant in a case like this.

"I would expect little to none."

Chapter 22

REPLAYING THE PAST

This was going to be a major day. We had six important witnesses scheduled to testify. They all brought Dennis Davis into the picture and, I felt, strongly tied him to the crime in some fashion.

I arrived at the courtroom fifteen minutes before nine and Tony the bailiff opened the main doors. Several members of the media filed in and took seats at the back of the room and the benches right behind me filled rapidly with Johnny's friends and family. Johnny was allowed in now, too, because Wade had been kind enough to agree to excuse him from the rule that prevents witnesses from watching the trial. It's known as "The Rule" and is in place to prevent a witness from inadvertently or intentionally shading his testimony based upon what others say. But Johnny was done testifying and wasn't expected to be called back to the stand. Wade was doing the decent thing, recognizing that this was no ordinary trial but something Johnny had been living with, waiting for, for two decades.

We had no preliminary matters and so once the jury was settled I called my first witness. "State calls Tom Walsh."

We began with his law enforcement career, letting the jurors know where he worked and what he'd accomplished before retiring three months previously.

"I worked for the Austin Police Department for twenty-three years, seven months. During the course of my career, I worked patrol for probably about nine years. About a year and a half of that I was an undercover street narcotics officer. From there I became an FBI-certified bomb technician and I was a full-time bomb technician serving Central Texas for six years. In that time I was an operator on the SWAT team. After that I went to vehicular homicide and I was an accident reconstructionist. From there I worked sex crimes and from there I went to homicide cold case and my last duty assignment that I had I was assigned to the FBI violent crime task force and I worked out of the FBI office here in Austin."

He related this information calmly, quietly, looking at the jurors instead of me, making a connection.

Next I had him tell about some of the challenges associated with working a cold case. He talked about different evidence-handling techniques, before DNA was recognized as an issue, the loss of witnesses and memories, the way suspects and witnesses are handled. He was echoing many of the things the jurors came up with themselves in *voir dire* and at various times I saw several of them nodding along.

One of the issues, themes if you like, that I knew Wade would present to the jury was the idea that Tom fixated on Davis as a suspect, decided he was guilty and ignored all evidence to the contrary. So I asked Tom to talk about his approach to working a cold case.

Then we started to discuss Natalie's case and every time I asked Tom a question he gave me his full attention then turned his body slightly so he could provide the answer directly to the jury. As well as being a great detective, it turned out that he was excellent on the witness stand. The jury probably wouldn't recognize this, but I did: He testified from memory. Tom knew this case thoroughly, dates, names, places, events.

He told the jury about the spate of homicides in the days before and after Natalie was assaulted and that the police were stretched too thin. "From what I have been told, there were six homicide detectives and if you go back and you read these reports and you look in the case files, especially going back to the 1970s, the detectives were writing memos to their chain of command to see—or justify in making a long distance phone call to Houston. Everything had to be justified, the overtime, and I think there is a lot more leeway now with the department as far as letting you go with the case and investigate it and not have to justify every step that you take."

We turned to specifics, so I asked him: "On this case involving Natalie Antonetti, did APD receive at some point an anonymous tip regarding this defendant?"

"Yes."

"When did that tip come in?"

"That was called in to the homicide tip line June 6. Excuse me, July 7, 2006."

"Who took that phone call?"

"At the time—he is now retired—it was Detective Manuel Fuentes."

"Is that a tip line that is advertised generally for all homicides or is it specific to cold cases?"

"No, that is for all homicides."

"Who was the first person to follow up on that tip?"

"I was."

"Did you yourself speak to the person who called in the tip?"

"I did."

"Who was that person?"

"Rebecca Davis."

Although I told the jury in opening statements that Becky Davis flipped back to her husband's side, I couldn't go the next step and tell them she went so far as to invoke the spousal privilege so she would not have to testify against her husband. To bring this out, I had Tom discuss the interviews with her, the willing one and the ones where she told us she didn't know where Dennis was and claimed she had no way to contact him and didn't even know the names of any of his friends. As Tom said, "I thought that was kind of odd, that this woman had been with this man for, I don't know how many years, fourteen to seventeen years." And Tom told how Rebecca eventually admitted to lying to him, because she and Dennis Davis were reconciling.

I wanted the jury to know something that I'd always seen as crucial. "Did she ever, in any of your conversations, retract her initial tip?"

"Never."

With my gentle leading, Tom went over the challenges he encountered in the case, the death of witnesses like Eddie Balagia and the blank memories of some. I didn't linger on the point, because the jury had seen that firsthand, the clouded recollections of Jolene Wells.

We moved on to discuss the crime scene and Tom looked over thirteen photos I took of what used to be Natalie's apartment, front and back, and they were entered into evidence. Also into evidence went the clothes Natalie was wearing when she was assaulted, the jogging shorts and pink T-shirt. Tom stepped away from the witness stand to inspect these, donning latex gloves and holding them out to the jurors who stared, mesmerized by the clothes that were now stiff with age and Natalie's decayed, dried blood.

I turned the conversation to the cornerstone of my case, the piece of evidence that Dennis Davis offered to police in 1985 to exculpate himself, the same evidence that I felt strongly would show him to be a liar: his statement. Normally, as with witnesses like Donn Chelli, written statements are not admissible, but there is an exception for statements made by defendants. The theory behind keeping out hearsay is that the side against whom it is offered doesn't have a chance to test the evidence. As with Chelli, we didn't have the opportunity to cross-examine him and find out if what he said was true. Not so with a defendant's statement; the defendant is there in the courtroom and the defense has a chance to cross-examine the witness offering it.

Once Davis's statement was admitted, I had Tom read the entire statement to the jury. I wanted it to be clear I was not showing what I wanted to show and hiding the rest. But when he was done, I went over a few specific points that I hoped the jury would remember.

"A couple of things I just want to mention, ask you about. The time that he says he last saw Natalie Antonetti, when does he say, according to his statement, that he last saw her?"

"When he dropped her off at Fourth and Trinity at her van Saturday afternoon and they got up for breakfast at 2:00, so anywhere I am thinking three to 4:00 in the afternoon."

"Does this statement anywhere mention an argument with Natalie Antonetti?"

"No," Tom replied.

"Does this statement anywhere mention a note left on her door?"

"No, it does not."

There were more details, but I moved on, laying the ground-work for the most important piece of evidence Tom would introduce: his interview with Davis. I showed him the blue card that contained the Miranda warnings officers read to suspects. He confirmed his and Davis's signatures on the card, the date, the fact he read it and I even had Tom read the constitutional warnings to the jury. The little blue card went into evidence and to the jurors.

"I am going to show you what has been marked State's Exhibit No. 95. Would you please have a look at that? Do you recognize that?"

"I do."

"What is it?"

"I initialed this and dated it last week on April seventh. It is the Davis interview clips."

"How long was the initial interview, I'm sorry, the complete interview?"

"Probably about five and a half hours."

"Your understanding is that these clips are ones that have been worked out by the State and the defense and the Court as admis-sible clips?"

"That is what you told me. They are excerpts from the whole interview."

"As far as the clips that are on the tape themselves, this disk, have they in any way been altered other than obviously been shortened, put one after the other? Have they been tampered with in any way?"

"No."

"They accurately reflect the conversations you had with Dennis Davis?"

"Yes."

I turned to the judge. "State would offer State's Exhibit 95 into evidence."

Wade stood. "No objection."

I took a few minutes because rather than use the large screen on the wall, to the jurors' left, I wheeled in an equally large television that I planted right in front of the jury box. I believed that this next hour would be as crucial to my case as any and I wanted every member of this jury to be focused on the interview, not distracted by movement in the courtroom or stiff necks from craning to look to the left. This setup brought them closer to the interview, made them almost a part of it.

Except the disk didn't work. It played for a few minutes then stopped, sound and picture disappearing.

The tension dissipated and the moment of high drama dissolved into courtroom comedy as I poked buttons and prodded the connections. Efrain walked over to help, but he knew less about electronics than I did. The smooth professionalism of our presentation was threatening to come apart, Pryor and De La Fuente transmogrifying into a slapstick comedy duo. When I'd poked and prodded and made enough faces, I cut my losses.

"Judge, I would like to get one of the IT people down here. I don't know how else to do it."

The judge was kind enough not to laugh at me or be irritated and I adjusted as quickly as I could, moving on with my questions to Tom while we waited for the technician. In truth, I was rattled. I had a plan for Tom's testimony and now I was off my stride. I was worried, too, that the professionalism of the prosecution might become an issue—if we couldn't work a TV/DVD, could we be trusted to prove a man guilty of murder? But moments like this (if not as serious as this) happen in every trial and any decent trial lawyer will roll with the bumps.

I turned to what would become one of Davis's untruths. "During the interview, the interrogation you had with him, did you ask him whether he owned a baseball bat, a small baseball bat?"

"Yes, I did. I believe I did."

"Did he say that he did or did not own one?"

"I believe he denied it."

I liked that Tom underplayed this, whether he did it on purpose or not. When the jury heard Davis's response to Tom's question, there would be no doubt in their minds about what he said.

Then I approached the witness stand and handed Tom State's exhibit 96. "What is that?"

"This is a note left on her door."

"You read the contents of this to him in the interrogation?" I questioned.

"I had a copy and I let him read it and then I read it to him."

"Did he acknowledge that he was the person who had written that note?"

"Exactly. He said, 'That is me all right.'"

I offered the note into evidence, confident that the judge would admit it, but Wade wasn't happy because, as we both knew, we had no clue how the note came into the police's possession. It was one of the mysteries of this case and if Davis himself hadn't admitted writing it, then we'd have been stuck. For every piece of evidence there had to be a trail back to its originator and here we didn't have one until Davis claimed it as his own.

Wade asked for permission to question Tom now about the note's origin and the judge let him.

"Did you find this originally in the case file?" Wade asked Tom.

"Yes."

"When you found it, did you know what it was or come to realize right away—"

"Not immediately. I think when I was going through the case jacket I was just looking at everything and just taking it all in, so when I first found it, no. After a while it kind of started to fall into place."

"Your only knowledge about when this note would have been left would be either through Mr. Davis or through anything you may have read in the police report?"

"Just through Mr. Davis."

"You didn't see anything?"

"There was nothing in the report."

"Nothing that told you anything about how this appeared in the case jacket, when it appeared or who collected it; is that correct?"

"No, I just found it in there."

The note was then entered into evidence and the jury handled it with care in its plastic evidence bag, reading the scrawled words for themselves:

Natalie—you can go to hell, + take Andy with you...If you don't have the brains + the self respect to see thru his bullshit then "fuck you"

The note was signed "D.D."

While the note made its rounds, I turned to a potential avenue of escape for Davis, hoping to shut it off.

"How far was Studio D from Natalie's apartment?"

"I would say between a mile and a mile and a half."

"Have you done the drive from Natalie's apartment to Dennis Davis's former home in Onion Creek?"

"I drove from the home in Onion Creek to Natalie's apartment."

"What time of day did you make that drive?"

"It was between 12:45 and 1:00 on a weekday."

"You did that in recent years?"

"I did it in 2007."

"Having been in Austin for a while, is it your testimony traffic would be heavier now than on a Sunday morning twenty-five years ago?"

"Yes."

"Roughly how long did that drive take you?"

"It was somewhere in the neighborhood of between fifteen and twenty minutes."

We showed the route on a map, which also went into evidence for the jury to examine later. I then ended Tom's testimony; I needed the jury to watch the video before I could go on. I handed the floor to Efrain and his witness, who we both knew would not be as friendly as Tom. In his own way, though, he'd be just as helpful.

Jimmy Rose.

Efrain asked a few introductory questions but he didn't waste time getting to the point. "At the time that you were living here in Austin, did you know an individual by the name of Dennis Davis?"

"Yes, I did."

"Can you tell the jurors how it is that you came to meet Dennis Davis?"

"I met Dennis at Steamboat Springs. It was a nightclub on Sixth Street."

"Do you recall when that was in relation to when you were living here?"

"Well, '83."

"How would you characterize your relationship with Dennis Davis from the point that you met him until you, I guess, left Austin?"

"Dennis and I became very close friends from the time I met him. We became very close friends."

"At any given point after you met Dennis Davis, did you all live together?"

"Yes."

"Can you tell us when that was and where?"

"We lived briefly—I spent a summer with him at his parents' house in Onion Creek. I also lived with him in a house that I believe belonged to Perry Alston and then we also lived in a condominium. I believe it was in the Enfield area."

"On three different occasions you were roommates with Dennis?"

"Correct."

"Did you ever get to meet a lady by the name of Natalie Antonetti?"

"Yes."

"Can you tell the jurors the circumstances surrounding how you came to meet her?"

"I met her through friends, Davey Kane and people from the studios and then from Dennis, who was dating her for a time."

"How would you characterize your relationship with Natalie?"

"My relationship with Natalie was—I mean, we weren't real close, but I remember on several occasions I would go to her house and she would cut my hair and also cook Cuban food for me, kind of a special thing that she did…'Come over, I will cut your hair and feed you dinner.' That kind of thing."

"Was this during the time that Natalie and Dennis were dating?"

"Yes." Now the jury knew two things for certain: that Natalie was the kind of person who'd cook for you and cut your hair, even if you weren't close friends. Also, from what Rose had said and from his one-word answers, that Jimmy Rose was still a friend of Dennis Davis. That meant anything bad he had to say, any evidence he gave against Davis, should be believed, because the only way he would shade his testimony would be in favor of his friend, not against him. It was that built-in credibility that an anti-prosecution witness has. It might be tough to get him or her to testify, but once he or she does, his or her words can be devastating to the defense.

Efrain continued: "Do you recall a place named Studio D here in Austin at that time?"

"Yes."

"Can you tell us about Studio D?"

"Studio D was a recording studio that Dennis built. I helped in the construction of it. I spent a lot of time there, recorded two albums there. I spent a lot of time there."

"Would you see Natalie on occasion over at Studio D as well?"

"Briefly, yeah, sometimes."

"You know, Mr. Rose, that Natalie was assaulted in the morning hours of October 13?"

"Yes."

"In relation to that, do you recall witnessing an argument between Natalie and the defendant, Dennis Davis?"

"I remember an argument that they had at Steamboat, but I am not sure which date it was on."

He was starting to squirm; he didn't want to bring his friend down, so he was pushing back a little. But we also believed Rose to be an honest man and had no doubt that, when pressed, he'd tell the truth. For now, Efrain played it cool. "Okay," he said.

"I don't know if it was Friday or Saturday."

"When you say Friday or Saturday, are you talking about the Saturday or Friday before she was assaulted?"

"That is correct."

"You have given a statement to authorities, have you not?"

"Yes, I have."

"You were specifically asked about that argument that you witnessed?"

"Yes."

"Do you recall what date you gave them as to when you recall that argument between Natalie and Dennis Davis occurring?"

"I believe I said it was on Saturday night."

"The night before she was assaulted?"

"Yes. I don't know, because I never knew—I didn't know after she had been assaulted when she had been assaulted, because I hadn't heard anything."

"All right."

"I mean, it is not like the night that she was assaulted, the next day I found out. I didn't find out for a few days after that, so—"

"But as you sit there today, Mr. Rose, you believe it was either a Friday night or Saturday night when this argument took place?"

"Correct."

Now for the details. "First of all, where did this argument take place?"

"It took place in the club at Steamboat."

"What were you doing there at that club?"

"Listening to music."

"At that point in time, do you know whether or not they were seeing each other, dating one another?"

"I don't know if they were still together at that point. I believe they were or they had just recently maybe started separating. But they were still having a relationship."

"What time back then did the club close?"

"Club usually would close at 2:00 A.M."

"2:00 A.M.?"

"They would start last call at 1:30, so people would start leaving shortly after that."

"Where in relation to the club did this argument take place?"

"I do not remember."

"All right. Can you tell us about the argument itself?"

"I just remember it being quite emotional, more verbal, not physical."

"Was there any yelling that took place?"

"Yes, I believe so."

"Was there any screaming that took place?"

"Not that I remember."

"Do you recall who was doing the yelling?"

"I believe both of them were yelling."

"Do you recall whether or not Dennis Davis ever put his hands on her?"

"I don't remember. I mean maybe he might have touched her arm or something, but that is kind of speculation on my part."

"What time would you say the argument took place?"

"I would say at 12:00, maybe 12:30."

"At the point that this argument took place, what were you doing?"

"I was just in the club."

"Did you in any way intervene?"

"No."

"What made the argument stop?"

"I believe the reason it stopped is because the club had closed and we were pretty much told to leave the club."

"It is your testimony you think it was closer to the time the club was closing that this argument took place?"

"I am not sure, but I believe the argument went on for a while until the club was closed or maybe it was resolved and we left. I remember leaving the club with Dennis."

"Once the argument was over, where did Natalie go?"

"I have no idea."

"Did Natalie and Dennis go together?"

"No."

"After the club somewhere?"

"No."

"How did you get to the club that day?"

"In my vehicle."

"Do you know how Dennis got there?"

"No, I don't."

"But I think you testified that you and Dennis, after the argument, you both went your way?"

"I believe he went to his car."

"Do you know where Dennis went after that?"

"No, I don't."

"At the time that this argument took place, were you roommates with Mr. Davis?"

"No, I wasn't."

"Did you ever see him again that morning?"

"No."

The argument established, there was another vital piece of information Efrain needed to get from Rose.

"During the times that you did live with the defendant, did you ever locate a bat in that particular place that you lived with him?"

"I found a small souvenir bat underneath the bed I was sleeping on. The bed that was in there belonged I think to Dennis or Kellie. The bat was a small souvenir bat that I found underneath the bed."

"How long was the bat?"

"Maybe eighteen to twenty inches."

"What was it made out of?"

"Wood."

"How long after Natalie's assault did you locate this bat?"

"Year and a half."

"You said that you found it underneath your bed?"

"Under the bed I was sleeping in. It belonged to Dennis or Kellie, I am not sure."

"The furniture in the house at that time—"

"None of it was mine. All my stuff was in storage."

"What was underneath the bed that you were sleeping in?"

"Just stuff that belonged to Dennis."

"There were items other than the bat underneath the bed you were sleeping in that belonged to the defendant?"

"Correct, correct."

"Do you recall what, if anything, you did with the bat?"

"Not—I am not certain what I did with it."

"Did you ever confront the defendant about that bat?"

"No, I did not."

On cross-examination, Wade had Rose talk about Sixth Street in the 1980s and it took a moment for me to catch on to his strategy. As Rose talked about the bands, the ease of parking, the safe nature of downtown Austin, I saw Wade's point: Natalie would have been happy to go downtown by herself, walk around alone and maybe find herself the subject of unwanted attention. Maybe run across a stranger with murder on his mind.

He also established that Rose knew Kellie and knew her well, having lived with her and Dennis Davis for about eight months.

Then Wade sat down, letting the Court know he would likely recall Rose when he put on his own case.

On redirect, Efrain was almost done, but he addressed something we wanted the jury to be thinking about the whole trial: motive.

"I may have asked you this, but I want to make sure. Do you know why they were arguing that night that you saw them argue?" Efrain asked Jimmy Rose.

"Not specifically, no. I mean they—I believe it was because Natalie was talking to another man."

"That is what you stated in your statement that you gave to Detective Walsh in 2007?"

"I believe that is what I said."

"That night at Steamboat when you witnessed that argument, had you gone out with the defendant here or did you just meet up there, if you recall?"

"I believe we met there, because I—I was living in a house with my wife. I wouldn't have gone and met Davis and—Dennis—and then gone to the club. I would have gone directly to the club."

I took a deep, more relaxed breath. This put Davis on his own, traveling under his own steam before and after their evening at Steamboat. And it raised the specter of the green-eyed monster that Dennis Davis could become. With that image in the juror's minds, or so we hoped, the judge told us we were breaking for lunch.

I worked through the lunch hour, nibbling on a sandwich as the IT people inspected the television and DVD player. After just twenty minutes it was working and Davis's voice echoed over the empty jury box. I watched for a minute and when I looked up I saw one of the technicians entranced.

"Pretty interesting, huh?" I said to her.

"For sure. I might just stay and watch it," she said.

I hovered around the equipment and gave Efrain a nod when he appeared. The man was unflappable and he gave me a little smile in reply. *We shall see.*

When the jury came back in, Tom took his place on the witness stand again, but we started with the video. I played it from start to finish, beginning with Tom reading Davis his rights. The jury watched as Davis signed the little blue card I had put into evidence.

For an hour they sat and watched, but it seemed like five minutes to me. Each clip contained a nugget and sometimes I watched the jurors instead of the screen, imagining that I could see the wheels turning in their minds. A few times I saw visible reactions, like when Davis claimed he never had owned a baseball bat. Jolene Wells and Jimmy Rose, his close friend, had both exposed that lie already and other witnesses would also do so.

The information fell from Davis like puzzle pieces: yes, he knew of Natalie's tendency to leave her front door unlocked; yes, he wrote the angry note; yes, sometime around then he owned a gray/blue sedan. Some of the pieces didn't fit, though, not unless they were untruths. And that meant not only were the facts against Davis, but also that he was a liar. The best two examples were his ownership of the bat and his insistence that he was with Amparo Garcia-Crow all night.

When it was finished, there were a few moments of silence. I brought Tom down from the witness box to help me hammer home a few points. It was a fine line: I didn't want to treat the jury like idiots, but I did want them to listen to Tom and think, *Yes, I noticed that* or *That's not true; other witnesses and evidence show that the defendant was lying.* Like the bat.

I played a portion of the tape and turned to Tom. "Detective, testimony about her not locking her front door, why is that significant?"

"When the officers arrive on the scene and the detectives, one of the things that you do when you go on a crime scene, any crime that happens inside a residence, you look to see if there is any forced entry and there was no forced entry in that apartment and obviously Dennis Davis knew that she left her door unlocked."

I played another segment, in which Davis told Tom the reason he broke up with Amparo Garcia-Crow. "The question I have is how many times did the defendant tell you that Amparo Garcia ended the relationship because she was scared?"

"Twice."

"Once in the interview, in the interrogation?"

"Once in the first phone conversation on August 30, 2007."

I left it there; the other half would come when Amparo testi-fied that this was simply untrue. I had to trust the jury to remember Davis's words, but I also knew I could remind them in my closing arguments if I needed to.

The next portion of the tape I replayed showed Davis citing details about the assault, specifically the number of times Natalie was struck.

I turned to Tom again. "Do you know whether in the investiga-tion it was ever determined exactly how many blows were delivered?"

"In the body of the report, the initial investigator, Detective Eddie Balagia, says that Dr. Bayardo said—told him that she had been hit seven times on the head with a blunt instrument."

"Do you know whether Jolene Wells's statement gives a number?"

"No."

"It does not give a number?"

"No."

"In fact, if the ME's report doesn't give a number either—"

"I didn't see it in there."

"You don't really know where that number comes from?" I asked.

"Just in the report."

"And the interrogation?"

"Right there. That is the first time I heard it since the report."

"Are copies of offense reports given to members of the public?"

"Only if it is a closed case and it becomes public record. When it is an ongoing investigation, it is private information."

"This particular offense report with that information in it, would that have been released to the public?"

"No," he replied.

"In fact, is it even possible for regular officers now to get access to that report, do you know?"

"I believe it is locked. I believe most of the cold cases are locked, if not all of them."

It wasn't definitive proof, because details of an investigation can be leaked. But why was Davis the only one to seemingly know the number of times Natalie was struck? Who would have told him that detail and why? At that time there was no Internet where people in law enforcement could disseminate confidential information quickly and anonymously. Which meant there was probably only one plausible explanation for Dennis Davis's knowing how many times Natalie had been struck on the head: He was there.

The last section of the tape that I played contained three statements from Davis. First, the admission that he told Becky, his wife, that he'd "sinned against God and man." Second, his agreeing with Tom that he used to go into rages. This was an admission that surprised me when I first watched the interview and I suspect it surprised Tom. What Davis said, right there in the interview room, was that not only did he used to go into rages, but also they were "controlled" rages. Blind anger that he was able to direct and, to some degree, control. That admission always seemed, to me and I hoped to the jury, to fit the facts of this case perfectly. Third, his claim that Natalie yelled and grabbed at him.

I began with what Davis said to his wife and I wanted this statement front and center in the jurors' minds throughout the trial.

"Why is that term significant?"

"That is the term that was used in the original call to the homicide tip line and that is what Rebecca Davis told me."

"That is a phrase she had remembered for sixteen years?"

"Yes."

That's all I asked, because I just wanted to make sure the jury knew he said it. If Becky backtracked somehow, it was on the record: Davis admitted he said that to her. I moved on.

I asked Tom, "What is significant about that answer that he gives about going into rages back then?"

"When he did come up on the radar and became a suspect—"

Wade jumped to his feet and interrupted. "Judge, may we approach for a second?"

Judge Lynch replied, "All right."

At the bench, Wade leaned forward and whispered, "I'm just trying to be careful of not going into particular instances of jealous outbursts or rage with other individuals." This was an issue we'd batted around

before. We wanted the jury to know what a jealous man Dennis Davis
was and how angry he got when jealous. But that kind of evidence
fell under the category of "character evidence," which the law forbids.
The idea is that just because someone has a character trait or usually
acts in a certain way, it doesn't mean he or she acted that way this
time. It's the prosecution's burden to prove that the person did so on
the occasion with which the person has been charged, but if character
evidence makes its way into court, the jury might be unduly influenced into thinking, *Well, he usually acts that way, so he probably did
this time.*

Efrain and I had argued in response that, at the very least, we
should be able to show that Davis was jealous of Natalie, that whenever
she talked to another man he got mad. That was our theory of motive, the reason he killed her and the judge, without expressly ruling,
seemed inclined to give us some leeway.

"I'm just trying to tie the injuries sustained in this particular incident," I responded.

Judge Lynch looked at me: "Preface it."

"Maybe I can do it with leading questions?" I suggested.

Wade agreed, knowing that I could contain Tom better if I led
him.

We returned to our seats and I continued questioning Tom. "On
that issue, you have investigated a number of violent crimes in your
career; is that correct?"

"That is correct."

"Some of those have been coldly premeditated and some have
been more—"

"Crimes of passion."

"Yes, crimes of passion."

"Yes."

"The question that you had and the response you got in this tape
about rage, did you ask that because in your experience the injuries
sustained by Natalie Antonetti were born of rage?"

"That is what I believed, yes."

Job done. I turned to the third comment from that part of the
tape, something that made my blood boil when I first heard it. "Had

you heard that testimony that Natalie was getting grabby and starting to yell at him? Is that anything that Davis had ever said to you before?"

"Never."

"Anybody else ever said to you before?"

"No, no." *Of course not*, I thought, *because it isn't true*. Men who abuse women, in my experience, deflect blame, usually onto the victim. But since no one throughout this investigation had ever suggested Natalie being "grabby" or abusive to Dennis, I was confident the jury would see those words for what they were.

"My last question, Detective. It is about Jimmy Rose. How many times did you meet with him?"

"I called him on the phone, I spoke to him on the phone, drove to his house that day in Houston. I took a statement from him. That was in 2007 in October and then I met with him a second time when I took you to introduce him to you."

"Those times that you met with him, did you speak to him about the timing of the argument between Dennis Davis and Natalie?"

"I most certainly did."

"When did he tell you those arguments took place?"

"To be very specific and to clarify it, I specifically said, 'Did this happen four hours before Natalie was assaulted; was it the same night?' and he said yes. It was on two different occasions."

"He was sure about that?"

"Yes."

I looked at Efrain and he nodded. All done. "You honor, I pass the witness."

The judge gave the jury their afternoon break and at a little past three we reconvened.

Wade started his cross-examination of Tom Walsh by introducing Defendant's Exhibit No. 1, a map of the apartment complex and surrounding area. He had Tom point out Natalie's apartment, the convenience store behind it and the fence between them. He also had Tom point out Donn Chelli's apartment. I was waiting to object to any questions about what Chelli saw or said. None came.

Wade moved on to Davis's interview: "There has been some testimony about how many times Mr. Davis said that Natalie Antonetti was struck with a bat or a weapon and he said seven times. You know from reviewing the offense report from when Eddie Balagia was working on this case, you knew that Dennis Davis was in contact with Detective Balagia regarding this case, right?"

Tom nodded. "Oh, yes, yes."

"You know there were communications between the two of them about some of the facts of this case, right?"

"Yes."

"That is kind of obvious from the notes, the telephone notes left in the file. Dennis Davis called, left a message for Detective Balagia. You know there was communication between them for some period of time anyway?"

"That is correct."

I scratched a note on my yellow pad to ask Tom a question about this. I suspected the jury knew the answer, but I wanted to be sure.

Wade continued. "You know that Mr. Davis had—well, it appeared that he was trying to assist Detective Balagia in some way in figuring out who did this; is that correct? I mean, that is the appearance?"

"Yes, on the outside that was the appearance."

"But you, in fact, don't know what his motive was at that time, do you?"

"Whose motive?"

"Mr. Davis's. You don't know for sure now what his motive was at that point when he was trying to assist Detective Balagia?"

"No, no."

I was impressed with Tom. It would have been easy and, I was sure, tempting for Tom to fight with Wade and tell him, "I know exactly what Davis's motive was: to get away with murder." He didn't, though, and by refraining I thought Tom reaffirmed his stature as an independent investigator, not someone out to pin this on Davis but to uncover facts and testify to them. I also knew that if I was thinking about Davis's real motivation for keeping in contact with Balagia, so were the jurors.

Then Wade asked to approach the witness stand and he showed Tom a piece of paper, asking him to identify it for the jury. I hadn't seen it and didn't know what it was, so I asked to approach the bench. I didn't want Tom's niceness and cooperation to allow into evidence something that was inadmissible. At the bench I discovered the paper was a printout from the Internet, the Austin Police Department's information about this case. Wade told the judge it contained a mistake about the facts, specifically the time Chelli claimed to have seen an intruder, but I didn't understand the relevance and I objected. Wade backed down and said he'd just have Tom identify it now and maybe go into details later. But Tom quickly told Wade it wasn't something he wrote and was probably done before he was even assigned to cold case. Which made that piece of evidence irrelevant, as Wade, the judge and I knew.

The big surprise for me was what Wade said next. "Judge, those are all the questions I have right now. I would like to have him remain on recall until a later time."

"I have just a few questions," I told Judge Lynch before starting my redirect. I looked down at my legal pad and turned to Tom. "Typically in this kind of investigation, which way does information go when there is a communication?"

"I think as a good investigator, you pretty much want to hold your cards close to your chest and you are not giving out much information and you are trying to elicit as much information as you can. Sometimes you have to use different tactics with other people."

"Would you say the number of blows to a victim's head in a murder case would be a significant detail?"

"I would think so."

"Something an investigator would probably keep to himself?"

"I would think so." Despite the words themselves, his understated response sounded like, *Of course.*

Tom left the stand. It was late afternoon, nudging toward my four o'clock tea time and I was tired from concentrating so hard on Tom's testimony. But the next witness was critical and I had to stay focused.

"The State calls Amparo Garcia-Crow."

She seemed to float across the courtroom to take her seat, bringing that sense of peace and trustworthiness that she exuded wherever she went. She settled in her chair and looked directly at me, as calm and relaxed as if she were in her own living room.

"Good afternoon," I began. I had Amparo establish her residence and occupation. Then I had her discuss her background, professorships and family so jurors would have confidence she was telling the truth. Then I stifled a smile. As well as facing Amparo's incredibly strong personality, it seemed to me that cross-examining her would be like cross-examining the very best of Austin itself and I didn't envy the defense.

We discussed the year Natalie died and Amparo told the jury she was a graduate student then, recently out of a seven-year marriage. I asked Amparo to describe Austin and then moved to the topic at hand.

"Did you know Dennis Davis?"

"Yes."

"How did you meet him?"

"I came into the studio twice, once with my quirky band, which was called The Early Humans. We did a demo there. Then I came back soon after to lay down a track. I had written lyrics for a song with a friend of mine who had been hired to write a wedding song, so I came in to record. Both times Dennis was the sound engineer."

"At some point did you develop a relationship with him?"

"Yes."

"Do you remember when that was?"

Amparo nodded, her face thoughtful. "Yes, I do. I keep journals and that is really why I am very specific with what I do remember. We met about mid-September. According to my journal, it seems like it was…I came into the studio about September 16 and I think we started going out about September 21 or something like that."

I asked her about how long she had written in journals and elicited how she still keeps them.

Narrowing the timespan, I handed her a spiral-bound notebook with a blue cover. It was thick with use and in good condition, considering it was twenty-five years old. "Do you recognize that?" I asked.

"Yes."

"Is that one of your journals?"

"Yes."

"Was the last entry in that journal written more than twenty years ago?"

"Yes."

"Where was that particular journal stored?" I asked.

"This was found in the attic. I have boxes and they are all just stacked in there."

"Found by you?"

"Yes."

After asking questions about her retrieval of this journal, I turned to the judge. "Your Honor, I would offer State's Exhibit 98 under the ancient document exception to hearsay."

The court went quiet.

For a while I didn't think I could get the journal itself into evidence. I wanted to, very badly, because there was a big difference between Amparo telling jurors, "I wasn't with him, because it's not in my journal" and the jurors looking at the journal itself. If they got to do so, they would see the kinds of details she put in her entries and they would see the references to Davis. In context, with the testimony and her specific writings, it would be even clearer that there was no way Davis stayed with her that night, then abandoned her at his house when he got a call about Natalie being attacked.

I kept asking myself, *How do I get it into evidence?* Written statements are hearsay and that includes journals. There are twenty-four exceptions to the hearsay rule, but when trial lawyers try to think their way past hearsay, they tend to rely on the half dozen exceptions that come up the most, the ones that occur to them almost automatically. None applied to the journal and it took a lot of research to come up with this exception: Texas Rule of Evidence 803 (16): "Statements in Ancient Documents. Statements in a document in existence twenty years or more the authenticity of which is established."

Beautiful in its simplicity. All I had to do was establish that Amparo wrote down the information herself more than twenty years ago and that it was true when she wrote it.

I'd informed the judge and Wade during the lunch break that I intended to use this exception, one that neither of them in their combined decades of practicing law had ever seen raised in court. I didn't want to delay proceedings or seem like I was pulling a fast one and I wanted to give them time to look it up for themselves. They appreciated that courtesy, but it didn't prevent them from poking fun at me for using it and in court Wade couldn't resist an amiable jab in front of the jury.

"Can you cite ancient documents?" he asked with a smile.

"803 (16), I think," I mumbled, trying not to sound like a know-it-all.

Wade had looked over the statute and didn't object to its admissibility and once the judge let the journal into evidence, I returned to my questions. "This journal covers a period of your life, September, October of 1985; is that correct?"

"Yes. It seems to end on November 12." Amparo seemed comfortable with her ability to recall the information I needed and with my questions.

"In this journal, did you write about your relationships?"

"Yes."

"Did you write about your relationship with the defendant, Dennis Davis?"

"Yes."

"I would like to go through with you, if I may, some of those entries. Is it your impression as of right now that every interaction you had with him is recorded in that journal?"

"Yes, because we knew each other in a very short period of time. This is pretty much a capsule of that and from reading through it, it seems like every interaction, because we weren't in daily communication, but it is logged in."

"You don't recall any interaction with the defendant that, in your mind, doesn't appear in the diary, is that true?"

"Right or at least referenced, yes."

"Right."

"Because it was such a short period. It seems like every time we spoke or went out, it was in here."

"I want to very briefly, if I can, just give the jury an idea of some of the references you have to the defendant."

She nodded. "There is September 24. I write about a dream and I note that it is at Dennis's, because I do remember going to his home two times and this seems to document the second time that I was there or rather the first one, because it says I attended a party and I remember that is when I met Natalie and her son at this party."

"So first you have independent recollection of going to his home in Onion Creek twice; is that correct?"

"Yes."

"Tell the jurors about when you met Natalie."

"I met her at a party that was given. It was a lot of people and I remember being introduced to her and her son and we had a sweet conversation and I got the impression that they had a good relationship. I just remember being struck by how pretty she was and her very sweet, charming son. It was just a sweet interaction."

"Is that the only time you ever met her?"

"Yes."

"What about the second tab?"

"The second time we were already dating and we—I had gone there to spend the night."

"The subsequent entry, this page. What does that address?"

"Let's see. I went out with Dennis Saturday night, officially three dates old, so this is October 1 and I had just moved. I had a new location. I was living near campus at that point because I note that and basically speak about a conversation that we are having and that it seems to be the beginning of a potentially sweet relationship."

"Down to the next tab, if you don't mind."

"I think this is one. This is three—I am still being reflective, because even though the entry is October 1, I say, 'three days later,' so I am referring to previous time. I started—I wasn't dating just Dennis. I was seeing a man I had started dating that summer and he had come back into my life, according to this entry here."

I continued on with my questions about that period in her life and Dennis's reaction. "I just want to give the jury an idea of what is going on in your life."

"What is going on here seems like because I have started seeing the other man, the status of my relationship seems to be frustrating to Dennis, is what I am saying here or it is frustrating him and—the language I use, I say, 'conversation on the phone proved borderline volatile.' He was pressing me about being too busy, too philosophical, too cold, all of which I felt came as weak attacks for being consumed by what I am doing with and for myself."

"Do you have any independent recollection of his attitude toward you changing in those two weeks?"

"Yes, it seemed like—I wouldn't have remembered this without reading it, but yeah, definitely so. This was kind of like the climax of the relationship, because it didn't last very long, so the conversation seems to imply that I am even questioning that. I am saying how long have we known each other. It was very…it had a quality to it that was very emotional and kind of demanding and it just…that is what I am writing. I am saying how long have I known you? Two weeks."

I moved to the period of Natalie's violent beating. "Let's look at the next tab if we can, please?"

"The next one is October 15."

"What is that entry about?"

"This is saying that Natalie, Dennis's friend, was brutally assaulted this weekend and I had written this. This I do remember when I wrote it, because Dennis had called to tell me this had happened."

"You are talking now about an independent recollection above and apart from this?"

"Separate from this, yes."

"You remember that conversation with him?"

"Yes."

"What did he say in that conversation?"

"He had called, it seemed like it was a couple of days after what I write happened here, and he said that the police were thinking that someone had followed her from Sixth Street and maybe it was somebody she knew because it wasn't, like, a forced entry and that they had followed her home and maybe hit her on the head with a baseball bat is what he said."

"Is this the first time you knew anything about the assault on Natalie?"

"Yes."

"You are sure about that?"

"I am pretty sure, because it was pretty shocking and also stuck in the pages here was the newspaper article that I went and cut out after this conversation because it is an article that says, 'Bars visited in assault inquiry.' When you read the article, it doesn't have a name. The only way I knew this was because of the phone conversation."

"That same entry, dated October 15, does it address your relationship with the other man?"

"Yes. That he and I are finding a new unexpected connection and that we very much went on—we just had, like, a honeymoon period together."

"The days leading up to October 15?"

"Right, between those two entries, between October 11 and October 15, he and I had kind of just boarded ourselves up and just been together."

In other words, Ampie and the other man meant no Ampie and Dennis. But I needed to stress this point. "Is there any reference anywhere in there about you spending that night with Dennis Davis the night of October 13?"

"No."

"If you had spent the night with him, would it be in the diary?"

"Yes."

"How can you be so sure?"

"Because I pretty much chronicled every interaction I had with him. I mean, it was such a new, short relationship that that was clearly what I was doing."

"Having looked at your diary and what was going on in your life, do you have any independent reason to give the jury why you weren't with Dennis Davis?"

"Because my other boyfriend and I were boarded up pretty much. We had taken a deeper turn into our relationship."

"That was that weekend?"

"Yes."

My last few questions dealt with something Davis had said in his interview with Tom, about why he and Amparo broke up and then about the failure of the police to contact her. "Did the end of your relationship have anything to do with you being scared or freaked out about Natalie's death?"

"No, not at all. I mean anyone would be shocked, affected by that. I certainly was, but it had nothing to do with Dennis, in my mind. Those two things didn't correlate."

"Did you ever tell him, 'I can't see you anymore, because I am freaked out by Natalie'?"

"No, I wouldn't make that connection."

"Did the police ever ask you anything about Dennis Davis?"

"No."

"Never asked you about an alibi or anything?"

"No."

"Did you ever speak to police with regard to this incident?"

"No."

I paused and gave her a lingering look, signaling to the jury that what came next mattered. "I guess the ultimate question for you, ma'am, is: Are you telling this jury you were not with Dennis Davis on October 12 and 13?"

"That's right. I am pretty sure I was not."

"Pretty sure?"

"I am very sure."

I looked to the judge. "Pass the witness."

Wade's co-counsel handled the cross-examination. In his late forties, he had a wide open friendly face and blue eyes. He was highly respected and very good at his job. His manner was casual and relaxed.

"Hi, Ms. Garcia-Crow. I have some questions for you. First of all, you said you had one independent recollection back from the time around mid-October 1985 and that one was that Dennis had called you to inform you that Natalie had been assaulted?"

"Yes."

"That is the only thing that you can remember without having to refer to your journal?"

"Oh, no, no. I remember a lot of things. I am talking about dialogue and actual things. Those twenty-five years, you are not going to remember that, but I have a very good memory about that period."

"You said that you don't remember being with Dennis that night or the morning of October 13?"

I gave an inaudible sigh as she replied. "I am pretty clear I wasn't, just because of that phone call."

"That is, you would agree with me that is different than, 'I was not with Dennis that night or morning'?"

But Amparo came through strongly. "I will rephrase it. I was not with Dennis on that weekend."

"Now you are saying—"

"I am pretty clear I was not."

"What did you do the night of Saturday, October 12, 1985?"

"I was in rehearsal. We were about to open a play called *Into the West* and we were pretty much—weekends were significant for rehearsals because of the mixed cast that had day jobs and that sort of thing."

"You never told Officer Walsh that, did you?" the defense lawyer asked, referring to Amparo's first interview with Tom.

"I don't know. I don't remember if I said that in particular."

"That is important, isn't it?"

"I am not sure. I just know that is probably what I was doing on those series of weekends."

"It is difficult to remember what happened one year ago much less twenty-five, but you say probably?"

"Right. The reason I—yeah, because twenty-five years is twenty-five years, but the reason I am clear about the phone call is that days had passed since I had seen Dennis and that phone call shocked me on that morning and I am very, very aware a gap had occurred and he was giving me this information after many days of not seeing him."

"Yes, ma'am, but I'm sorry, I was talking about when you said, 'Probably I was rehearsing with that performance group.'"

"Uh-huh."

"You say 'probably,' so possibly not. See what I mean between probably—"

"Right, but I was definitely not with Dennis Davis on that weekend."

"But you don't know where you were?"

"I have a good suspicion. I think I just said that it is definitely the rehearsals, because you can document when we opened that show and you can pretty much know what a rehearsal schedule is going to be like. I am clear I was rehearsing. I was working on my thesis. I am clear I started a deeper relationship with my boyfriend and we did a little honeymoon period there."

"There is nothing in your journal about what you did the night of October 12, 1985?"

Amparo was starting to get defensive, speaking over the lawyer as he was asking questions so the judge stepped in to slow everyone down. The lawyer continued pressing her.

"You would agree with me that there is nothing in your journal, and when I say journal, I mean in that exhibit, in any journaling that mentions or discusses or details what you did the night of October 12, 1985 or the morning of October 13, 1985?"

"That's right, that's right."

Next he asked about her relationship with Dennis. "Where did you and Dennis go on your first date?"

"We—I was going to be moving in about two weeks and we went out to eat and I remember him picking me up in his vehicle and we spoke for a long time in front of the house, so it was like a food date."

"Do you recall where you went?"

"No."

"All right. Do you recall where you went on your second date?"

"I am influenced by what I wrote and I do recall…going to this party wasn't a date, because it was a big group of people, but the second date we ended up at his home, which is September 27, according to this."

They moved on and Wade's co-counsel used the diary to point out things that Amparo now remembered but were not in her writing. Her time with her new boyfriend, a party, a computer she borrowed from and returned to Davis. Amparo and the lawyer argued, but it was good natured and respectful and while she came across as less sure on some matters, she didn't waiver on that weekend, the weekend without Dennis.

When I began my redirect examination, I felt she was unscathed, but I wanted to zero in on a few more important points.

"You just testified that you wrote down things in your journal that were emotional to you?"

"Yes."

"If, hypothetically, you had spent the night at a new boyfriend's house and in the early hours of the morning, he had gotten up and dashed off to the scene of a bloody assault, would that have been emotional to you?"

"Absolutely."

"What about if you had spent the night at a new boyfriend's house and he got up in the early morning hours of the morning and left you there and not really explained why he was going anywhere, would that have been emotional?"

"Yes."

Amparo left the stand the way she entered, calmly, drifting past the counsel tables with a smile for me and a nod to Wade. From my perspective she was fantastic.

It was 4:30 P.M. and I was ready to call it a day, but we had two more witnesses in the hall ready to go. Two witnesses who didn't want to be there and who would be very upset if we made them come back tomorrow.

Fortunately, Efrain would be asking the questions for the first one and I knew there weren't many of them. The witness was the custodian of records at Brackenridge Hospital and she told the jurors about the hospital's policy of purging records after twenty years. Efrain got specific, had her tell of the subpoenas we served on her for records pertaining to Natalie Antonetti and Kellie Torres. She acknowledged getting them and repeated that because of the document-retention policy, any such records had been destroyed.

The last witness of the day was mine to question and once she was seated in the witness box, I began. "Would you state your name to the jury, please?"

"Deanna Cooley."

"Ma'am, my name is Mark Pryor. I am a prosecutor. You and I have spoken on the telephone?"

"Yes, sir."

"We have not had the chance to meet yet?"

"No, sir."

I took her through some preliminaries on her background and where she was living on Barton Hills Drive.

"While you were living there, after a weekend in October, you gave a report to the Austin Police Department; is that right?"

"Yes, sir."

"Do you remember why you contacted the police? What event prompted you to do that?"

"I think because it happened right there where I was at and I didn't know the girl who was hurt, but she had come into the club. A lot of people that I worked with on Sixth Street all lived in there, so it was kind of a small community. Even though we didn't know each other personally, we knew of each other."

"The 'it' that you refer to is an assault in your apartment complex; is that right?"

"Yes, sir."

"That report that you gave to police dealt with something that you had seen at about 4:00 in the morning on Sunday, October 13; is that right?"

She agreed. Then I asked the question I had been leading up to.

"The report that you gave to police had to do with a car that you had seen; is that right?"

"Correct."

"Something about the way the car was parked attracted your attention; is that true?"

"Yes, sir."

"What was it about the way the car was parked?"

"It wasn't in one particular spot. It was kind of across a couple of spots."

"Do you remember the color that it was?"

"From the statement that I gave, it was gray."

"Was it in good condition or beaten up?"

"I think it was beaten up."

"Do you remember seeing anybody inside the vehicle?"

"Two people, but I didn't see any faces."

"Do you know whether it was a man and a woman or two men or two women?"

"That was in the statement that I gave. I can't be sure why I thought that it was a man and a woman."

"Did you ever remember giving an actual written statement and signing something under oath?"

"Honestly, no."

"Were you able to get a license plate or anything?"

"No, sir."

On cross-examination, Wade had her go over the route she took to the convenience store, using the map he introduced earlier while examining Tom Walsh. She showed him and showed where the car was parked. But her memory was hazy and her story remained the same. Gray sedan, just like Davis owned. Right outside Natalie's apartment building and shortly before she was attacked.

Wednesday was over and, if all went well, we would finish putting on our case tomorrow.

If all went well.

Chapter 23

HOSTILE SPOUSE

I didn't say anything to Efrain, but on Thursday morning I felt good. All of our witnesses so far had delivered and it occurred to me that the only real hitch had come from modern-day equipment, which was kind of ironic given that our twenty-five-year-old testimony had flowed across the decades into the present relatively unscathed.

Today would be different, though. For two days we'd been shepherding friendly witnesses, guiding them through their testimonies and protecting them from real and imagined attacks of the defense.

Today we went from shepherding to wrangling and I signaled to the judge as we started the morning session, before the jury came in. "I was going to ask the Court's permission under Rule 611 (c) to use leading questions with this witness, Becky Davis, because obviously she is associated with the opposing party."

Judge Lynch frowned. "My general rule there is let's proceed normally until such time as it appears to be necessary to lead the witness."

"I was asking now, so I didn't have to do it in front of the jury." The truth was, I wanted to ask in front of the jury and have the judge declare her a hostile witness, but I wanted to play fair.

"I would suggest if you are having trouble getting straightforward answers, then you can do so. As long as you are moderate in your use, I will approve it. Mr. Russell, if you think he is exceeding that rule, you can object."

"I will," Wade responded.

"So I am giving you a partial yes," Judge Lynch said, turning back to me.

"All right. I'll take it."

"A sort of weak yes."

"Thank you, Judge."

So we began the last day of our case. "State calls Rebecca Davis."

She walked past the rows of people and across the courtroom, eyes straight ahead. She looked pale but resolute. I'd been waiting for this moment for a long time and when I glanced at the jury box I could see that this was a pivotal moment for them, too. I wondered if they were expecting animosity, because from my opening statement the jurors knew Becky had gone back to Davis's side. But I knew better than to be hostile with the wife of a man fighting for his life. I intended to keep a tight rein, as I did in the spousal privilege hearing, and I also intended always to be the calmer one.

"Good morning again, ma'am."

"Good morning."

"Could you state your name for the jury, please?"

"My name is Rebecca Davis."

"Could you please explain your relationship with Dennis Davis?"

"We have been partners for the last twenty some-odd years."

"During those twenty years, have you been married to him?"

"Yes."

"When were you married to him?"

"2001 through 2006, I believe."

"But as of right now, are you back together again?"

"Yes, we are."

"In fact, you are here kind of supporting him through this trial; is that correct?"

"Absolutely."

"Tell the jury when it was that you met Dennis Davis, please?"

"I met Dennis in December of 1990."

"What were the circumstances of that meeting?"

"It was at a Christmas party and we met and he asked me for a date and I told him he couldn't have a date with me unless he memorized my phone number. I asked a friend of mine and of his if he was a good guy to go out with and the friend said yes. We went out about a week later."

"Whereabouts was that party, that Christmas party?"

"It was the Brackenridge Hospital Christmas party and it was held at Steamboat."

"Were you working at Brackenridge at that time?"

"Yes, I was."

"How soon after you met did you begin living together?"

"Well, I went to Europe with my daughter about three weeks after we met, so as soon as we came home, which was the middle of January, he moved in with me right away."

"Probably within a month or so?"

"As soon as I got home, he picked us up from the airport and he stayed."

"Whereabouts were you living?"

"Tenth Street."

"Was he running Studio D at that time?"

"Yes."

"A music engineer, sound engineer?"

"Right. He was the owner of Studio D."

"I want to ask you about a statement he made to you a few months after you met, at the end of March in 1991. Could you please tell the jury what that statement was?"

"Are you referring to…what statement?"

Seriously? I thought. This was the kind of playing dumb juries despise. "I am referring to the statement that you phoned in to the police to tell them about."

"He said to me that he sinned against God and man." She said it matter-of-factly, as if he was asking her to add bananas to the shopping list. I didn't plan on letting her get past this momentous moment, the statement, so blithely.

"What was his demeanor when he was giving you that statement?"

"Well, we had been out that evening and we had had a few drinks and we came home and we had gotten in bed and we were talking and we had been in a fairly good mood and then he got really sad and started to cry and said he felt like that he had sinned against God and man."

"He was sobbing when he made that statement to you?"

"He was crying. He was upset."

"But fair to use the word sobbing, is that fair?"

"I am not sure what the difference between sobbing and crying is."

It was the difference between a sniffle and a whole box of tissues, between a second of watery eyes and minutes of chest-heaving, uncontrollable distress. I wanted the jury to understand which one Davis was suffering and I also wanted to make Becky understand that she shouldn't fight me on points I could win, she shouldn't try to lie or take back things she'd said before, especially when she said them under oath.

I stood. "Your Honor, may I approach the witness?"

Judge Lynch nodded: "You may."

"Ma'am, do you remember giving a statement to the police about this incident?"

"Sure do."

"Do you remember the name of the policeman you gave the statement to?"

"The written statement?"

"Yes, ma'am."

"Yes, Detective Walsh."

"Ma'am, show you what has been marked State's Exhibit 99. Do you recognize that?"

"Yes."

"There is a second page."

"This is an affidavit with the State of Texas, County of Travis with my statement at my attorney's office in front of my attorney and Detective Walsh and another police officer."

"This, in effect, is your statement?"

"Yes."

"It may be a small point to you, ma'am, but I would just like for you to read that sentence that begins. 'He started'."

"It says, 'He started sobbing, crying and he made the statement, "I have sinned against God and man".'"

"Thank you." I returned to my seat, point made and ready to resume. "At that time when you were in bed together and he made that statement, he didn't provide you with an explanation for what that meant, did he?"

"No."

"Either then or sometime soon after, you connected that statement with the death of Natalie Antonetti, didn't you?"

"It wasn't until we were getting divorced many, many years later that I realized that there might be a connection and I know in my statement I stated that I thought about it, but when I realized and went over the statement again lately, I realize that that wasn't true at all."

"Let me stop you."

"There was no way."

She was tugging against the reins, so I give them a loud snap. "There is no question right now."

"Okay."

"Thank you. You knew about a Natalie Antonetti by name, is that true?"

"Yes."

"You knew that she had been murdered?"

"Yes."

"Also that Dennis Davis had dated her?"

"Yes."

"Am I right in saying that he told you that he left a note on her doorstep the day she died?"

"He told me later that he had left a note, a letter to her, not a note, but a letter."

"Okay."

"He didn't say when."

"Well, ma'am, isn't it true that in the very first call you made to the police, the tip call, you told the police that he told you he left it that same day?"

"I may have."

"You are not going to disagree with that?" If she did, I had the tape recording of that call ready to play.

"I can't disagree with anything I said or not said. My memory has changed, my demeanor has changed, many things have changed."

"Okay."

"I can tell you what I believe now."

"He told you too, didn't he, that he knew she didn't lock her doors?"

"Yes."

"He made the statement in March of '91, correct, roughly?"

"Yes, roughly."

"Fifteen years later you called APD, the hotline, to tell them about that?"

"I did."

"Isn't it true that it was kind of your phone call that started this whole investigation again?"

"Yes, it is all my fault."

"You spoke to Detective Walsh a couple of times, is that true?"

"Oh, he called me all the time for almost two years."

"Well, one of the reasons for that was at some point you started lying to him, didn't you?"

"No, I never lied to him."

"Really, well—"

She tried to back up. "I don't think so."

"You told him at one point that you didn't know where Dennis was?"

"Oh, okay, yes, I did."

"Okay."

"I was trying to stop talking to him and I was trying to get away from him and I told him I didn't know where Dennis was and he changed his demeanor with me and told me he was going to have me arrested, so my sister called him back and—"

I raised my hand and my voice to cut her off a second time. "There is no question right now. Fact is, you remember trying to cover for Dennis Davis, right?"

"Yeah."

"I am almost finished. I don't have many more questions. When you first started going out with Dennis Davis, you and he knew the members of the Lotions band, isn't that true?"

"I heard of them when I worked—they had a baby where I worked, but I didn't know them."

"You told the police that you had hung out with them?"

"I did not. With the Lotions?"

"Yeah."

"If I said that, I didn't mean that at all. I don't even know who is in the Lotions."

"Do you deny saying it now? Because I can play the tape if it helps."

"I did not hang out with the Lotions."

"Now you are saying you didn't hang out with the Lotions?"

"I didn't."

"Okay."

"I don't even know who is in the band. I worked at a birthing center and one of the members of the band had a baby, so they were all there. I don't even know who had the baby."

I didn't need to play the tape. Her wriggling on the stand and jousting with words told its own story. I had what I needed. "Pass the witness. Thank you, ma'am."

Wade spent some time on Rebecca's background and her life with Dennis, filling out a picture of her as a person rather than a witness. It was a smart plan, but eventually I objected, as the homespun tales of their past were legally irrelevant. Wade moved on.

"Let's go back to the statement that you said that he made about sinning against God and man."

"Right."

"You don't know what he is talking about, do you?"

"I didn't know and I asked him and he wouldn't answer and so the only thing I could do was just try to surmise what he was talking about, because we didn't know each other that well. I knew that he was grieving over his mother who had just died suddenly of stomach cancer and I knew that he was really feeling guilty about not spending more time with her in the hospital."

"Let me just ask you questions about that. You said you had been out drinking, you came home, you were in bed. Were you talking about his mom?"

"We were talking about his mom, we were talking about my mom and dad, we were talking about how we were going to have our lives together. We were having this sort of general conversation about I don't even know what, just chitchat about how much we loved each other and what a good time we had."

"There were some discussions about the manner in which his mother had died and how much he had—how many times he had been able to see her before then?"

"Yes, yes. He said to me that she said, 'I knew you would come' when he did go over and he started crying about that and I cried too and so he felt terrible. I knew that he felt terrible about that."

Frankly, this was gibberish to me and I was quite happy for the defense team to run with it.

"Was it pretty soon after that he makes this statement to you?"

"Uh-huh, it was that night."

"You had not been talking about any assaultive behavior or past behavior of his in Austin?"

"Not at all."

"That wasn't the context of this statement being made?"

"Not at all. Not at all. We only talked about that once."

"You had heard something about a woman named Natalie who had been killed; is that right?"

"Yes."

"When had you heard about that?"

"Right after we started dating, a nurse friend of mine and her husband were afraid that I was going to have my heart broken again, because I had just been basically heartbroken."

"By somebody else?"

"Yeah, I had been pretty much left at the altar and I was vulnerable and not going out at all. When I met Dennis, they took me to lunch and they said, 'This guy may not be the best guy. He might break your heart; he is kind of loose; he goes up and down Sixth Street a lot; he stays out late at night. It could be that he is not going to be the one for you.' Then the man said, 'And then there was that girl' and I said, 'What girl?' and he said, 'Well, he had a girlfriend who died.' I said, 'I don't know anything about that' and they didn't go on.

"So I went home and I asked Dennis what did he mean, who that girl was and that is when he said he had a girlfriend named Natalie, he didn't tell me her last name, and that she had been too—what is the word—she had been too trusting and that she didn't ever lock her doors and that one night somebody broke into the apartment where she was living because the door wasn't locked and hit her on the head and she eventually died at Brackenridge and it was because she was too trusting. He thought that it was somebody who lived in the complex and so he said he had set up vigil at Brackenridge and that he was really sad about it."

Becky was talking too much, in my opinion, had again confirmed that Davis knew about the unlocked door and she'd even given evidence I would never be allowed to ask about, concerning Davis's somewhat unreliable character.

Wade and his witness kept going, because they had to give the jury a good explanation for not just the statement, but also why she called police and essentially turned Davis in.

"At some point you had some trouble in your marriage?"

"Yes, we did."

"You had some arguments?"

"Yes, we did."

"At some point, you had gotten into therapy?"

"Yes."

"For a while?"

"Yes."

"When you were mad, you were mad at Dennis?"

"I was extremely mad at Dennis."

"You told your therapist about these things that you knew about, this statement you had heard and this woman who had been killed whom you knew about in Austin?"

"Yes."

"Your therapist encouraged you to unburden your soul and tell somebody about what these statements meant?"

Becky sighed heavily as if these memories were uncomfortable to relate. But I felt the jury needed to better understand this witness and her mixed feelings toward the defendant. "Yes, we were both—he was

my mentor of Buddhism as well as my therapist and he suggested…
we went through my whole life, about why I felt guilty about things in
my life and that was one of the things that I thought of then."

"In your anger and your attempt to unburden this thing nagging
on you, you called APD and made the statement?"

"I made the statement to clear my conscience, not to turn him in."

"I understand that. But you didn't then know for sure—you don't
know now for sure—what he was referring to, right?" Wade asked.

"No, I never found out. I never asked him."

"All you knew was the context of this had come up when you
were talking about his mom?"

"Yes."

To me, none of this helped them. Rebecca didn't want to get
Davis in trouble, but she *did* want to clear her conscience. Why would
she want to do that unless she thought he was guilty of murdering
Natalie? If the statement was about Dennis Davis's failure to spend
time with his mother before her death, why would it weigh so heavily
on *Becky's* conscience?

Her next claim was, in my opinion, ridiculous and I assumed it
was offered to somehow cast aspersions on Tom. *Good luck with that,* I
thought, reflecting on Tom's thorough investigation and his demeanor
on the stand.

"You said Detective Walsh called you numerous times?"

"Yes."

"When did that start?"

"About six months after I made the supposed anonymous phone
call, he called me and he started calling me frequently and asking me
all about Dennis and all about his family. Then he started calling me
more and more frequently and I thought I had to talk to him. He
was nice to me on the phone and sometimes he would call me several
times a day. In fact, sometimes he would call me ten times a day and
he was always asking me all sorts of questions and always asking me,
did I have more to say, wasn't I sure that…didn't Dennis confess at
some point."

"He asked about that, if Dennis confessed to murder?"

"Always, over and over."

"Had sort of a beeline trying to get you to say something?"

"He sure did. He talked to my family as well as me."

I knew that was true; Tom talked once to her sister during the time Becky Davis was lying and trying to cover for her husband. But the idea that Tom called Becky ten times a day pressuring her to, what, make up a story? I hoped the jury found that as incredible as I did.

Wade asked Rebecca about the statement she gave to Tom, the emphasis being on how long it took, how many questions Tom asked. Suddenly, Wade asked her about an incident that I wouldn't have dared try to get into evidence. I was shocked.

"I want to ask you, one of the things you mentioned in your statement is an incident where you said Dennis was swinging an ax around the backyard? Did you have a project going on in the backyard that would require him to have an ax or a wood splitter out there?"

"Right. We had dirt delivered, a big truckload of dirt and we had one section of the fence removed and they were supposed to dump the dirt inside the yard, but instead they dumped it right in between the two gate posts, so Dennis was trying to put the fence back up with this mallet thing. To keep our dogs in, to keep our dogs from running out."

"That requires splitting wood and pounding wood together and rebuilding a fence?"

"Yes."

"Moving some dirt around?"

"Uh-huh."

"You say in your statement that he had been drinking too much, you were out there. Were you having an argument at that point?"

"We sure were. We argued a lot."

"I just want to backtrack a little bit. Was he also digging a trough back there? Was he having to dig a channel of dirt?"

"Yeah, we had really too much dirt, so we were trying to find ways to put it and so we made a berm, I suppose you want to call it, out of it."

"You were having an argument. Tell me about that. You had been having this argument that night?"

"We had been having this argument over and over about money and about him going back to work and I wanted to split up and he didn't. He wasn't well, he had been to doctors a lot and so he was taking medication and he was feeling bad. The doctors were just prescribing all sorts of drugs for him. They were making him act odd and he would get yelling more at me and I am really afraid of people who yell at me, especially men, anybody who is authoritative, so I got really afraid of Dennis."

"At that point?"

"At that point. He swung that around and the dogs got out and he started yelling and screaming and I got scared to death."

"Was he swinging this ax at you?"

"No."

"What was he doing with it?"

"He was swinging it around, yelling at the dogs and just venting. He was angry that the dogs got out and that I had not made the guys deliver the dirt and put it in the right place and that it was my fault and I felt like it was aimed at me, but he didn't swing anything at me."

"What was he swinging at? I mean, where was he swinging this ax?"

"Well, we had a fire going in the outdoor fireplace and so it was dark. I couldn't really see, but I just saw it going around, just saw it going around and then I saw him hitting on the fence and then the dogs got out and then we started chasing the dogs."

"He never threatened to or swung it in your direction?"

"No, no, but I am a big scaredy-cat."

"Then you went and looked for the dogs together?"

"Yes, we did and we finally found them."

"Did he threaten you along the way when you were looking for the dogs?"

"He didn't threaten me, but he was really mad at me."

"He was mad at you?"

"Yeah."

Angry at her and swinging an ax. Given how biased I felt she was, I was not just amazed that Wade brought this up, but also amazed she expected anyone to believe Davis wasn't swinging the ax in her direction, at the very least. Even though, in my mind, this was normally inadmissible testimony (it went to Davis's character, not to the events of Natalie's death), Wade had opened the door and now I could ask about it if I wanted to. I made a few notes on my pad.

Wade returned to the call Rebecca made to APD. "When you called this in, your intent was not to tell the Austin Police Department, 'I think my husband killed somebody back in 1985'?"

"No, they told me it was anonymous. They went into this whole big description of how it was anonymous and how it was a red telephone and there was no caller ID and they would never tell anybody and they were lying."

This made me fume. I'd questioned Becky Davis on the stand a couple of times and each time she'd demonstrated a willingness to lie and to make herself the victim. If Wade had continued to question her, I would have, most likely, bitten back my annoyance, but he didn't. He passed her back to me.

I started out blazing. "The important thing to you isn't a murder investigation getting off the ground, it is your conscience being cleared and it is your identity being protected. Is that right?"

The anger in my voice caught her by surprise. "When? What?"

"You seem real upset that this phone call wasn't actually anonymous, but the truth is they had an investigation to carry out, right, into a murder?"

"Well, I suppose so. I didn't know anything about it. I didn't know one thing about it."

I had gotten the anger out of my system, but who knew if I'd made a point or not. I took a deep breath. "Let me ask you just a couple of follow-up questions. Mr. Russell was asking you about an incident in which Dennis Davis was swinging an ax or a mallet in the backyard?"

"Yes."

"When was that exactly?"

"Oh, my. Well, it must have been in the fall. I don't know."

"What year was that roughly?"

"I don't know. I mean, I am all mixed up and I am scared. Probably—it was obviously before I called in that tip and before Dennis and I had split up. He was still at the house, so I would think it was five or six...and since we were having dirt delivered, it must have been in the springtime, but other than that, I'm sorry, I don't really know."

"About 2005?"

"Probably."

"How old would he have been in 2005 or 2006?"

"He was born in 1950, so you do the math."

"About fifty-five years old?"

"Yes."

This reminded me to get his height into the record. I planned to argue later that Davis fit the description of the homeless man arrested by Officer Cannaday, as pointed out to him by Donn Chelli as looking like the mystery "Lotions man." Before I could do so, there had to be evidence during the trial about his height. "How tall is Dennis Davis?"

The question seemed to catch her off guard. "About an inch taller than me and I am five-six."

"He is roughly five-seven?"

"Uh-huh."

"Going back to that incident in your backyard, the way you have described it, it sounds to me, maybe to the jury, that he was in a rage?"

"He was mad."

"Okay."

"He and I fought quite a bit."

"Okay."

"I yelled too."

"You also said—you also said at that point, 'He didn't threaten me; he was just really mad at me'?"

"That is correct. He never said, 'I am going to hit you' or point the thing at me or anything like that, but—"

"After you were separated, isn't it true he did make threatening phone calls to you?"

"He did."

"You feared him?"

"I did."

For a woman to be afraid of a man, someone she knows very well, she should have a good reason. People aren't afraid of those they know will do them no harm. I hoped it was apparent to the jurors that not only was she afraid of him, but also that she had reason to be.

Next, I indulged my urge to defend Tom. Rather silly, perhaps unnecessary, but Tom was a proud man who conducted himself professionally throughout this investigation and I wanted the jury to know it.

"I also want to ask you this. How many times are you telling this jury that Thomas Walsh tried to phone you? You said at one point he was calling ten times a day?"

"He called me for over a year."

"So he called you, what, 3,000 times?"

"I don't know."

But probably not 3,000 times. One more point to make and it was about Rebecca's statement that Davis was upset about his mother's death and that Natalie had nothing to do with the conversation that night. It had occurred to me that there was a very natural link between the two topics, a very good reason why a discussion of his deceased mother might bring Natalie into the conversation. I tried my luck. "Finally, Mr. Russell asked you about the context of when Davis made that statement about sinning against God and man?"

"Yes, sir."

"When you boil that down, Ms. Davis, the context of that statement—and tell me if I am right or if I am wrong—was that you guys were talking about a woman who died before her time and who was a mother, isn't that true?"

"I surmised that. Before he made the statement, he was talking about his mom."

"But Natalie Antonetti was a mother too, wasn't she?"

"She was."

"She died before her time too?"

"She did."

I sat back. "Pass the witness."

Chapter 24

ANOTHER VICTIM

Next up was the witness whom I believed the defense feared most. We had filed motions back and forth about her testimony; I myself had battled to get her in court, to cooperate. Unsurprisingly, there were a few minor issues to sort out before Kellie Torres took the stand and the main one was whether or not she could testify about Davis's assault on her. Wade and I approached the bench.

Wade Russell's voice hardened: "Any evidence of any assault by my client on Kellie Torres is inadmissible. It is not a signature crime. It only bears similarity. There are lots of people who have been assaulted by bats. Well, basically in 1989 it wasn't a bat. It was a fist and it transformed itself later after she knew about this death to being beaten by a bat and it morphed into being assaulted by a bat."

The judge looked at me. "Your argument is essentially contained in your material that you filed."

"Yes, Judge, but I would also add that given the testimony about him swinging around an ax in the backyard and being aggressive, that any—"

Wade interrupted, a half-smile on his face. "Aggressive with dirt."

"Any harm is tempered slightly," I finished.

Judge Lynch frowned. "What I am thinking about doing is sustaining the objection at this time to the assault until I hear evidence which may well make that admissible on rebuttal. The State has only circumstantial evidence to offer, so I will still give you a break, but at this time it may only go into other things as opposed to that particular assault. See where the chips fall. She may have to hang around for a while."

I went out to the hallway to talk to Kellie for the first time in weeks and her appearance impressed me: she was dressed in a forest green jacket and black slacks, her hair immaculate and just the right amount of makeup. She looked like a bank executive, like the head of her town's chamber of commerce. We talked for a few minutes and she seemed calm, eager to get this over as much as anything. I gave her my usual spiel about listening closely to all my questions and being as nice to the defense attorney as she was to me. Maybe nicer. I informed her, too, that as of right then the judge was not letting me ask questions about the assault and her outrage began to swell, but I calmed her by saying that it might come in at some point. If not now, maybe later.

She took the stand at 10:20 A.M. The jury was paying close attention. If first impressions counted for anything, I was confident they'd like what they saw. For her part, Kellie focused her attention directly on me, settling herself and waiting.

"Good morning, ma'am."

"Good morning."

"Could you state your name for the jury, please?"

"Kellie Torres."

Somberly I asked her about where she lived and whether she was married and how long. I had her tell about her career and her community activities in order to establish that she was a respected professional woman.

"Are you a little bit nervous this morning?"

"Yes."

"I want to shift to the 1980s. Do you remember when it was that you moved to Austin?"

"I believe I moved to Austin around end of '85 or '86."

"What was your reason for coming here then?"

"My fiancé at the time had a job with his family's company."

"Did that relationship end at some point?"

"Yes, it did. 1987."

"How old were you then?"

"Twenties. I don't recall exactly what age."

"Were you yourself working in Austin?"

"Yes, I was. I was travelling. I worked for a company where I was a district supervisor for several stores."

"Where were you living?"

"At that time?"

"Yes."

"Before I split up with my fiancé or husband?"

"Yes."

"We lived not far from Barton Hills Way." Short answers, each one a direct response to my questions. So far so good.

I could see that she was wound pretty tight. Most people had gone on a little more about the changes the city of Austin had seen, so I tried again, asking if it was a party town.

"Very much so."

"Some would say it still is." I said it with a smile, but my little joke fell flat and her demeanor didn't change.

Then it was time to connect her to the defendant. "Well, I want to ask you, do you know somebody called Dennis Davis?"

"Yes."

"When did you meet him?"

"1987."

"What were the circumstances? How did you meet him?"

"I believe—it is something that I don't recall—but I believe it was on Sixth Street and then I got invited to a party at a studio."

"What studio was that?"

"Studio D."

"That is the studio that he ran, owned?"

"Yes."

"Did you accept that invitation and go to Studio D?"

"Yes, I did."

"You saw him again?"

"Yes, we started dating and things progressed after that."

"Do you remember when it was exactly you started dating?"

"I want to say—it could have been around the fall of 1987."

"Fair to say that your memory from twenty-plus years ago is a little hazy?"

"Yes."

"How soon after—well, did you move in with him at some point?"

"Yes, I did."

I questioned her about moving in with Davis and then asked: "When did your relationship with Dennis Davis end?"

"1989."

"You were with him for approximately two years?"

"Approximately."

"Did your relationship ever get deeper than just boyfriend/girl-friend living together?"

"Yes."

"How far did you get?"

"It was far enough that we made an announcement that we were going to get married."

For almost this entire time she'd been looking directly at me, with occasional glances at the jurors. I noticed some of their attention was waning with this clipped, informational yet uncontroversial testimony. I decided to ratchet up one gear.

"The Dennis Davis that we are talking about, do you see him in the courtroom today?"

"Yes."

"Would you identify where he is sitting and perhaps something that he is wearing?"

"Beige shirt, brown and gray tie, gray suit, on the end."

I stood and addressed the judge. "If the record could reflect the witness has identified the defendant."

Judge Lynch nodded. "Record will so reflect."

"Thank you, Judge." I sat down and used my next question to signal to the jury that we were getting close. "Did you ever meet Natalie Antonetti?"

"No."

"You moved to Austin after her death; is that right?"

"Yes."

"When you were with Dennis Davis, had you heard her name?"

"Yes."

"Who had raised her name with you?"

"Dennis Davis."

"Had you talked to him about her?"

"Yes."

"Was it something he felt like he could talk to you freely about?"

"No."

More one-word answers and I could feel the tension flow across the courtroom to her, taking in the jury on the way. She knew the moment was close at hand, but I couldn't have her giving such short responses for this. I needed her to tell the story.

"What do you mean by that?"

"Because of some things I guess that happened to her, he never wanted to talk about it much."

It was time.

"Kellie, was there a time when he told you something very specific about Natalie's death?"

She shifted in her chair, straightened herself. "Yes, he did."

"When was that?"

"1988."

"Please tell the jury the circumstances of that statement and what that statement was."

"He had been out and I heard him on the front porch and when I opened the door, he was basically curled up and crying really hard. We had had a disagreement before that, so I guess that is why he was out, so I went out and he—I said, 'What is going on?' or 'What is wrong?' I was holding him. We were both basically on the ground. He was curled up. He said, 'I didn't mean to do it. I didn't mean to do it.' I said, 'You didn't mean to do what?' He said, 'I didn't mean to kill Natalie.' I didn't know what to do because of some history that we had and I was afraid."

"Was he crying when he was saying this?"

"Oh, yes."

"Okay."

"I just was dumbfounded looking at this big tree that was in our front yard. Because of the history, I was afraid not to—I didn't know what to say or what to do."

"Did it seem to you like he was letting something go?"

"Yes."

"He had been holding something inside?"

"Very much so."

"Did you believe him?"

"Considering the circumstances and the past history that we had, yes." *Past history*. It was an unsubtle allusion to what had happened to her and I suddenly worried she might blurt something out. I needed to cut it off now and I did so by putting her on the defensive a little, asking her a question I'd warned her would be coming.

"Why didn't you call the police?"

"Because at the time I loved him still and was hoping that maybe it wasn't true. I don't know. I don't know why. I didn't—I was afraid to call the police because if something would have happened, I had no place to go, no car, no nothing."

"After he made that statement to you, did you end up going back into the house?"

"Yes."

"Did you spend the night together?"

"No. He stayed in one room and I stayed in the other."

"Why was that?"

"That is the way I wanted it and that is the way he wanted it. I mean, it was just really weird."

"At some point after that admission, did you find anything in the house relating to Natalie?"

"Yes. I was cleaning and I found a box in the room where he had stayed. It was just a small wooden box."

Wade was on his feet. "Your Honor, may we approach?"

The judge waved us forward and at the bench Wade stated his objection. "Pryor is getting ready to go into testimony about how Kellie found a box that Davis kept that contained some trinkets and some women's underwear. It doesn't prove anything in this case other than characterizing him as somewhat creepy and he was protective of this box and he didn't want her looking in it. I think it is character evidence and not probative and it is highly prejudicial and the prejudicial nature under Evidence Rule 403 highly outweighs any probative value."

He was right about my intentions, but I thought it was relevant evidence. "Judge, one of the things in that box was a rabbit's foot that belonged to Natalie Antonetti. I think it is probative that Davis is keeping mementos and trinkets. It goes to his connection and how strongly he felt about her. It goes to guilt, hanging on to some memento of hers."

Wade didn't buy it, but he was smiling as he made his point. "He didn't kill all those other women. He hasn't admitted to them yet."

Judge Lynch looked at me. "You want to just get in the rabbit's foot, that is all?"

I wanted to discuss it all, especially the panties, but I knew when to push my luck and when not to and the judge was definitely not with me so far. "Yeah. I can do it with a leading question."

Judge Lynch turned to Wade. "So he is not interested in the panties."

"I am but—" I smiled and shrugged.

Judge Lynch's voice tightened: "I have trouble seeing the probative value of those in this offense. If it was involved with some sort of sexual fetish or on the edge of some sexual assault, that would make it much more probative, but I just—what it proves is he might be a little weird. A lot of people have similar; his just happened to be uncovered. I don't know. The rabbit's foot, perhaps."

"There is some sentimental value there maybe," Wade said. It was an argument, not a concession.

"I will get that in with a leading question." I could feel this slipping away, so my offer indicated I planned to help limit the testimony to this one item and not give Kellie the chance to mention the panties. But the judge decided against me, for now anyway, sustaining Wade's objection with the proviso that the contents of that box "might be something that would become more probative as we hear the rest of the case."

We returned to counsel table and with a glance at the jury I asked my imperative question. "Kellie, did you know Dennis Davis to own or possess a small baseball bat?"

"Yes, I did."

"Did he have that throughout your entire relationship?"

"Yes, he did."

"Did he play baseball?"

"No."

I paused and looked again at the jurors. They were watching this witness avidly. "Pass the witness. Thank you."

Wade had several files open in front of him and, I thought, of all my witnesses, she was the one he must have prepared for the most. My case didn't hinge on one witness, but it was fair to say that it was held up by just a few crucial ones. Kellie was most certainly one of them. Crack her and Wade would be a long way toward freeing his client. My biggest fear was not that she'd break down and confess to lying to Tom about Davis's confession. If I thought she was being untruthful, I would never have called her as a witness. No, I was confident her account would remain the same. But I was worried that Kellie might argue with Wade. The fastest way for a witness to lose credibility is to appear biased. The most common way that happens is when the witness argues with the defense lawyer over every little point or acts as though he or she doesn't understand very simple, direct questions. Being evasive, combative and defensive are sure ways for the jury to disregard testimony that is truthful.

As Wade started, I held my breath. "Ms. Torres, my name is Wade Russell. I'm Dennis Davis's attorney. Your initial involvement in this case started in September of 2007 when Detective Tom Walsh called you on the phone?"

"Yes, I was called."

"You received a phone call from Detective Walsh out of the blue; is that right?"

"Yes, I did."

"You talked for a while during this initial conversation?"

"Well, he told me why he was calling."

"What did he tell you?"

"He would like to come out and talk to me."

"What did he tell you about then?"

"That he was working a cold case."

"Did he tell you the nature of the cold case?"

"Yes. It was about Ms. Natalie."

"It was about Mr. Davis also?"

"Yes."

"You understood that?"

"Yes."

"Just as part of the introductions to each other, you chitchatted a little bit and you gave him a little background on yourself?"

"He wanted to know what I had been doing and wanted to know if he could come out."

"Did you talk a little bit about being back in Austin in 1989?"

"Yes."

"Did you know a man named Mike Gonzales in those days?"

"Yes."

"Did you know a man named Jimmy Rose in those days?"

"Yes, I did."

"How did you know these folks?"

"Jimmy Rose and Dennis were real good friends and I think at one point he actually stayed with us for a while."

"Jimmy did, right?"

"Yes."

"He stayed with you, you and Dennis, in a couple of locations, maybe three locations?"

"That I don't recall."

"You told the jury about the different apartments you lived in. The one where you said Mr. Davis made this admission, right?"

"Yes."

"Then you lived in the Barton Hills area?" She agreed. "Then another condo in the same area?"

"I did. He didn't."

"You did. Was that an apartment you had rented for yourself?"

"After I—after we split up."

"Yes, yes."

"I got offered to stay, because I was afraid to stay because of something that had happened at the other apartment in that same complex."

I flinched, because she was alluding to the assault, almost baiting Wade to ask about it. At the very least, she was letting the jury know that there was something there, something the defense didn't want to talk about. I don't like this type of cheating, because the rules are in place for a reason. I didn't want to win because a witness blurted out something she shouldn't and I didn't want to have to retry this case because Kellie insisted on telling the jurors about the assault.

Wade ignored the provocation and kept going. "In a couple of these locations, Jimmy—oh, you lived also in Perry Alston's house?"

"Yes, I did. I stayed there. It wasn't very long because of an incident that happened there."

There it was again, as if she couldn't help the story leaking out of her. I shook my head, hoping Kellie would pick up on it.

Again I felt Wade ignored her. "Who is Perry Alston?"

"He was a friend of a friend. He was going to be gone to New York at a play or something and had offered to let me stay in one of the rooms that he had."

"He was a musician, wasn't he?"

"Musician and playwright, I believe, or something like that. I didn't know him that well."

"Was your understanding that he was on the road?"

"A lot."

"A road show of some sort?"

"Yes."

"Do you recall the name of that road show?"

"No, I don't."

"Going back to this first conversation you had with Detective Walsh, just think back to that. He calls you on your cell phone. He was asking you questions about Natalie's death and how that related to Dennis Davis; is that right?"

"What do you mean? He was asking me if I knew her, ever knew her, and no, I didn't."

"But you did know that Natalie had been assaulted at some time in the past?"

"Yes, Dennis told me."

"You are aware of some of the details of how that happened, right?"

"I was only aware of what Dennis had told me."

"Did that include some details about how she was killed?"

"Do you want me to tell you what he told me?"

"I am just asking if you knew some of the details about how the murder had occurred?"

"Not all the details but some of the details in retrospect of what he told me."

"Were you aware of whom some of the witnesses were who were involved in that or associated with that assault on Natalie?"

"The only person that I knew that was aware was Jolene Wells who I was told lived there at the time."

"You didn't talk about any other potential witnesses or witnesses who were involved in that?"

"No."

"When you were in Austin living with Dennis Davis, what was your circle of friends? Were they people in the music business generally?"

"When we were living together, yes."

"Were you part of a group that would go and hang out at Steamboat on a frequent basis?"

"Me and him both hung out at Steamboat."

"Friends of yours, mutual friends of yours, would hang out there, right?"

"Yes, that was the place everybody hung out to listen to music."

"Was it a little different back then? It was easier to park on Sixth Street?"

"Oh, yes, definitely."

"It was an easy place for people to go and congregate and get to hear bands, some of whom the members of these bands were friends of yours and Dennis's and your other group of friends?"

"Yes."

"Any idea how many times a week you would go down to Steamboat?"

"I would say we were down there—he was down there more than me, but I would say we were down there three, four, five times a week.

To listen to bands, I guess it was, and people invited us to go down there and to listen to them because of his studio."

"In this circle of friends, it was common knowledge among them that this woman Natalie Antonetti had been murdered some years before, right?"

"Yes."

"People—I am not saying they talked about it all the time, but it would be mentioned from time to time?"

"Not a lot, but sometimes, yes."

"So a lot of people were aware of her murder and perhaps some details of how that murder occurred?"

"Actually, I never got any details from anybody. I was just told that she was murdered."

Wade's point, I assumed, was that people had talked about the case and so knew the details—including how many times Natalie had been struck. Apparently that wasn't the case and I was relieved, because this wasn't something Kellie and I had ever discussed.

"I am going to shift back to your first phone conversation with Detective Walsh. During this period of time, from the time you said Dennis made this statement to you, which was—can you put a date on that, approximate year on that?"

"I want to say it was spring, June-ish, somewhere in there, 1988."

"When did you move away from Austin?"

"When I left here, I moved in 1994."

"During all that period of time, you didn't tell anybody about Dennis Davis admitting to committing the murder?"

"No."

"There is nobody stopping you from making that report, was there?"

"No, only the—I was afraid to say anything."

Wade abruptly changed subject. I felt it diverted from whatever Kellie seemed determined to say. I wondered if I should ask for a break so that I could talk to her, warn her off. But I didn't; I just sat there and watched the powder keg smolder.

"Going back to this first conversation you had with Detective Walsh," Wade said, "you told him that Dennis had talked about Natalie, right?"

"Yes."

"More than once, right?"

"A couple of times, yes."

"Detective Walsh asked you if Dennis said he killed Natalie, right?"

"Yes."

"Didn't you tell Tom Walsh you weren't exactly sure what he said when he first asked you about it?"

I was momentarily lost so I was pleased when Kellie spoke up. "Would you repeat the question?"

"When Walsh first asked you about whether Dennis admitted killing Natalie Antonetti, your first response was, 'I don't know exactly what the words—what he was saying'?"

"I really didn't want to admit that Dennis had told me that, but I knew that now I had to."

"But you told him you weren't sure what he said, right?"

"At that time I couldn't recall. There was a lot of trauma at that time when Mr. Walsh called me."

"I see. And you told Walsh that you think he said he shouldn't have hurt her; is that right?"

"He said he didn't mean to."

"You don't know if he meant physically hurt her or emotionally hurt her, right, you don't really know, do you?"

"Well, I don't understand that question, because if someone said they killed somebody, you have me lost there."

"I am saying, before you got into describing Mr. Davis talking about killing her, before you got to that point, you are saying, 'Well, he said he hurt her' and I am saying, you don't know what that statement referred to, physical hurt, mental hurt?"

"It was one of the first statements Dennis had said when he was in that fetal position on the front porch or the concrete there in front of the door."

"Then Walsh, Detective Walsh, if you can recall this, he asked you again if Dennis had said he killed her and then you say, 'Well, I really can't remember'?"

"No, I don't recall."

"Then you said, 'God, this is so far back I really just can't remember what he said'?"

"I don't recall."

"But would you disagree if we played the tape back and that is what you said, would you disagree with that?"

"No."

"Detective Walsh kept asking you about this and you said, 'Well, I am pretty sure he said he killed her.' You made that statement, didn't you?"

"Yes, I did."

"From there on, you gave more description about how this event took place; is that right?"

"Yes, I did."

"You said at one point you asked Mr. Davis why he did it and he told you that he was having a baby; is that right?"

"Yes, he said that Natalie was pregnant with his baby and he was bawling."

"Was that something you had heard before?"

"No. Only from Dennis."

"Was not that a rumor you had heard circulating among your group of friends in Austin?"

"No."

"Then you said the defendant said he didn't mean to and you said you asked him who it was and he said he killed Natalie; is that correct?"

"Correct."

"This initial conversation ended with Detective Walsh and did you have a conversation again the next day or a day or two later?"

"With who?"

"Detective Walsh," Wade clarified.

"I don't recall."

"You don't recall talking to him again?"

"I just know that he called that day. He also called another time wanting to know if I would—if he could come down, where a good place to meet would be, et cetera, et cetera."

"Your testimony today was when you went out there and talked to Mr. Davis, you said, 'What is going on?' That is what you asked him, right?"

"It was something to that effect. 'What is wrong? What is the matter?' Something to that effect."

"You asked a number of questions beyond that. Do you recall asking Detective Walsh, 'Why did he do it?'"

"I probably was asking him a lot of those questions that night, because I loved Dennis at the time but we had a past history of violence in our affair, so I didn't know what to do. I was afraid."

"Now you are saying you asked him a whole lot of questions about what this was about?"

"I didn't say a whole lot of questions."

"Well, did you ask him a whole lot of questions or just asked him one or two questions?"

"Dennis?"

"Yes. When he was out there?"

"He was crying and I was trying to console him and I was trying to not get beat on again."

The tension was rising and both Wade and Kellie had sharpened their tones. I knew now that war was about to break out. Wade wouldn't stop her from saying her piece—no one would—and the only question was how much damage she'd do to his case and, quite possibly, to ours. Wade was visibly annoyed with her for injecting comments about Davis, but in my view, he made a mistake with his next question.

"Well, you say you didn't want to get beat on again, but you beat on him some too, didn't you?"

"I don't think so, not the way that I got beat on. I never beat on him."

"Is that right?"

"Yes."

Wade's anger dissipated and I suspected he knew to back away, that he couldn't win this point. Even if Kellie did physically fight Davis, no jury was going to believe that he was the victim in that relationship because, while it happens, it's very rare and not part of people's common experience. The jury already knew, thanks to Davis's wife, he was the kind of guy who would get angry and swing a sharp garden tool around. Moreover, the jury was not going to see Davis as a victim of Kellie's brutality when he was charged with beating another woman to death.

Wade continued. "You ended up giving a written statement to Detective Walsh about this incident, right, after he came up and interviewed you?"

"He interviewed me and then they brought a statement of what I had said, I guess, and I signed it."

"Did you read it before you signed it?"

"No."

"You just signed it, you took on faith that since the detective is handing you a statement summarizing what you told him—"

"I skimmed over it, but I didn't take time to read it word for word."

"You understood that was a sworn statement that you signed?"

"Yes."

"You later testified to the grand jury. You were brought down here to testify to the grand jury; is that right?"

"Yes, I was."

"When you testified to the grand jury about Mr. Davis' statement, you got into a little more detail about what you thought you heard, what he was saying and what you are asking him; is that correct?"

"I just said what I recalled."

"At some point you told Detective Walsh that this incident with Mr. Davis went on for thirty minutes or so?"

"It was a while, because he was crying really hard."

"You asked him a lot of different questions about what this was about?"

"Yes. I knew that we had had a fight and I hid in the attic."

"You said some of these questions were about what he said: 'I didn't mean to' and you said, 'What did you not mean to?' Is that right? Is that one of the questions that you asked him?"

"I am sure that was probably something that I asked."

"Did somebody in the grand jury ask you about whether he definitely said he did not mean to kill Natalie? Do you recall answering a question like that?"

"No, I don't recall."

"But you knew Natalie had been beaten really badly and didn't die immediately; is that right?"

"I only know what Dennis told me. I mean, that she was beaten with a bat."

"When you are asked if he definitely said he didn't mean to kill Natalie, did you not say, 'I believe he said he didn't mean to murder her' or something to that effect?"

"It was something to that effect. He said he didn't mean to do it and because of the history that we had and the times that I got beat on, I kind of was like, okay, maybe I am not going to say anything, because I didn't want him coming back to me."

"But you couldn't say that he definitely said—"

"He said that he didn't mean to hurt her; he said that he didn't mean to kill her. It was a conversation that went on for about a half an hour."

"Did you tell us earlier he first said he didn't mean to hurt her? You testified to that and after Detective Walsh has asked you numerous questions and you get in front of the grand jury, then you say, 'Well, I am sure he said he didn't mean to murder her, he didn't mean to kill her'; is that right?"

"Correct."

I didn't really understand Wade's point, unless it was to draw a distinction between *hurt, murder* and *kill*. Given what happened, I couldn't see why it mattered, but other than a defensive attitude and too many comments about her being Davis's victim, Kellie was holding her own.

"Is it fair to say that your story got more detailed the more Detective Walsh talked to you and by the time you got in front of the grand jury, you had more details to give to the grand jury at that point?"

"Well, now that it was brought up and I started looking at what had happened, yeah, I started recalling things that happened that long time ago."

"You started putting together what you knew about Natalie's death?"

"I didn't know any details about her death."

"I am saying you knew about her death and you knew about these statements Mr. Davis was making out there and you started to sort of piece it together in your mind about what this was about; is that correct?"

"I am not sure what you are getting at. I knew that he admitted to me, I knew that he was crying and I was trying to console him and he admitted that he didn't mean to do it."

"You didn't tell police back then? You moved away from Mr. Davis and continued living in Austin for how many years?"

Her next words were searing: "I got away from him in '89 after I was left unconscious."

"So you separated?"

"Big time, yeah."

"You kept living here in Austin for how long?"

"From '89 to '94. My mother lived here."

"Did you live with your mom?"

"Yes, I did for a while."

"Did you tell your mom about this?"

"Yes, I did."

"Okay."

"That is why she got me the gun and that is why he probably asked me about Perry Alston's house, because Dennis showed up. I woke up out of a dead sleep with that gun at my head."

The thin veneer of politeness between Kellie and Wade had been stripped away entirely and I was no longer surprised that she was dropping these tidbits into her testimony, accusation after accusation. I wondered why Wade wasn't objecting more, asking the judge to tell her to watch what she said. Maybe Wade wanted her to come across to the jury as an angry, vengeful woman. That was certainly a legitimate strategy. But I believed this required the jury to buy into the notion that after twenty years she was so vengeful that she was prepared to commit aggravated perjury. It also allowed the jurors to ask precisely *why* she was so angry at Davis and reach the conclusion that maybe she had reasons and maybe those reasons were that Davis was a violent and dangerous man. Either way, Wade was not objecting and Kellie was giving a verbal picture of Davis as a monster.

"You never called the police and told them here in Austin that Dennis Davis had admitted to this murder back in 1985?"

"No, I never told anybody here. I didn't know what this man was going to do to me."

"You moved when?"

"1994."

"And you didn't tell anybody there? You didn't report it then either, did you?"

"No, all I wanted to do was forget Austin."

"You didn't think it was important to report a murder that you knew about to the authorities somewhere?"

"Not when somebody is loose and he may come after me again. No, I didn't tell anybody."

"Even in another state when you knew he wasn't living there?"

"His dad had a lot of money. I didn't trust anybody."

"Then you moved again?"

"Yes."

"You eventually married?"

"Yes."

"Did you tell him about this—"

"No."

"—admission?"

"No."

"And—"

"I wasn't being abused anymore," Kellie interrupted again, "so I didn't want to relive any circumstances and I wanted to go on and live a nice and healthy life like I am doing now."

"As part of living that healthy life, it was to never tell anybody about a murder that you were aware of and aware of the perpetrator of this murder?"

"That was only because he told me. Why would I?"

"Why wouldn't you?"

"I guess I wanted to forget it all. I didn't want to bring abuse back up. When you are abused that long, you don't have very much self-esteem. I am just now getting that back. I still have trauma. I still won't shower when I am in the house by myself. I lock my doors. My curtains are still closed after that last incident with him."

"You moved and you lived with your husband?"

"Yes, I do."

His voice rose. "And you still didn't tell him about—"

"No."

"—this murder?"

"This was a past life and I didn't want to remember that life."

"The first time you tell anybody about knowing about who committed this murder was 2007 when the detective calls you up and starts asking pointed questions about it? Is that the first time?"

"I don't know if I mentioned any of it back at that time. I don't recall. It was too long ago."

When Wade finally said, "I will pass the witness," I exhaled and wondered how long I'd been holding my breath. I wanted to get Kellie off the stand as soon as possible, but I looked at Efrain to see if he had any questions he wanted me to ask. Apparently he was on the same page as I was, because the most thorough man I knew just shook his head. I stood up and said, "I have no more questions, your Honor. Thank you."

Chapter 25

POTENT BACKUP

Before the next witness could take the stand we had a legal issue to discuss at the bench. Efrain and I wanted to elicit important testimony from Linda Bless, a former friend of Dennis Davis, that she saw him with a bat while he was angry and that he told her he wasn't afraid to use it, because he'd used it before. We wanted to go into the incident in detail; Wade wanted to keep this testimony out.

As we made our respective cases at the bench, Judge Lynch noted Kellie's wayward testimony in a question to Wade and with a wry smile he asked, "What's your objection, given the last thirty minutes?"

"Well, correct me if I am wrong," Wade said, "I don't know if she clearly said hit her with a bat. She didn't say hit her with a bat, this testimony we just heard."

"No, but they are saying the bat is the murder weapon," Judge Lynch noted. "When was this incident?"

"A few years after 1985," Efrain replied.

"What is a few?"

Wade filled in some of the details. "They were at a party…The party where she saw the bat. They are saying that he—that Linda said, 'Come on, Davis, put that bat away' and that she said that Davis said, 'Well, I have used it before. You never know when you are going to use a bat.' Words to that effect."

Efrain nodded. "That is what she would testify to."

"What is the objection?" the judge asked.

It was Wade's turn to offer a wry smile. "It hurts my case tremendously." He knew that was not a valid objection, but he wanted the judge to know that any decision would impact the trial greatly.

Efrain remained adamant. "It goes to show a baseball bat is not a—he is using it for, using it for whatever, protect himself. I think the jury needs to—I think it is very probative. I think the jury can see."

Judge Lynch ruled: "She can testify at a party in 1988 the defendant displayed a baseball bat, but I think that is about it."

Efrain wanted to make sure he got it right, so he asked for clarification. "Not go into his demeanor? I will have to talk to the witness about the statement."

Judge Lynch looked at Efrain and me. "I am trying to keep some cap on this. I am assuming you are going to want to get in that other. I am trying to keep this—trying to keep sort of a balance. I mean, there seems to me to be direct evidence coming in of his propensity without allowing in close-call stuff."

Efrain somberly stated: "We can get into the fact that he had it in his hand at a party but not go into his demeanor or what he said or why he had the bat?"

The judge nodded. Wade, happy with the ruling, started to move away from the bench. "That's fine."

Linda Bless walked into the courtroom, an elegant figure in a black dress and black boots. She was tall, blonde and a very attractive woman.

The judge swore her in and we waited while she took her seat in the witness box. When she was ready, Efrain began. "Ma'am, would you please state your full name?"

"Linda Bless."

"Ms. Bless, where do you currently live?"

"Arizona."

He asked Linda about what she'd been doing—care giving and going to school to study medical insurance. Then he asked her about the time she lived in Austin and when she met Dennis Davis.

"Can you tell the jurors here how the circumstances were when you first met him?"

"I had another group of friends. We went down to a place called Steamboat a lot and we met Dennis there, became friends. He had a recording studio and we would go there."

"Is that recording studio Studio D?"

"Yes, sir."

"Did you ever come to date Dennis?"

"Never," she replied vehemently.

"How would you characterize your relationship with the defendant then?"

"Very good friends."

"Did you consider him like a brother at the time?"

"Oh, yeah."

"What are some of the things that you and Dennis did back then?"

"Oh, all of our friends together would go down to Steamboat a lot." She gave an embarrassed giggle, admitting what we were all thinking. "We just—we partied a lot."

"During that time, did you ever come to know a girl by the name of Natalie?"

"I never did know her, no, sir."

"You never met her?"

"No."

"How long did you stay friends with the defendant?"

"Well, I heard that he moved to Nashville and I lost track with him, but I have always considered him a friend."

"When did you lose track of him?"

"I guess when I—close to when I got married in '91. Maybe '90."

"After '91 or '90, did you ever see him again?"

"No."

"Did you ever meet a lady by the name of Kellie?"

"Yes, I did."

"How is it that you came to meet Kellie?"

"When I came back—I left for a year to stay with my brother in Ohio—Dennis and I talked on the phone a few times while I was in Ohio and he said that he wanted me to meet somebody, so he put a girl on the phone and it was Kellie and he said that I would meet her. So I met her after I moved back."

"How long would you say you have known Kellie?"

"From then until now."

"Have you all stayed in contact since after the mid '80s?"

"Off and on. She has a new life and I did too, but yes, off and on."

"I want to focus your attention to the time—let me just ask the question. Had you ever witnessed the defendant here, Dennis Davis, have a bat?"

"I did, yeah." The courtroom grew quiet.

"Where was this that you saw him with the bat?"

"It was in a house where they lived."

"You say 'they.' Who are you referring to?"

"He and Kellie."

"Who was present at the time that you witnessed this?"

"I am not sure. I am sure Kellie was there. We had parties there all the time, so honestly I couldn't name names."

"Was there a party going on at that time?"

"Yeah."

"When you saw him with the bat, was he holding it in his hands?"

"He came out of the bedroom, had it in his hand."

"What time frame would you say that you saw him with the bat? What year would that have been, Ms. Bless?"

"I think it was about '87 maybe."

"Looking around the courtroom, do you see the Dennis Davis that you knew back then?"

"I see Dennis, yeah."

"Could you point him out and describe something that he is wearing for the jurors, please?"

"A black and brown and gray—sorry."

"That's okay. Take your time."

"Tie and a gray suit coat."

Efrain stood. "If the record would reflect the witness has identified the defendant in court, your Honor."

Judge Lynch replied, "Yes, sir."

Efrain looked at me to see if he'd forgotten anything, but given the judge's ruling I didn't think so. I shook my head and Efrain said, "I have nothing further of the witness, your Honor. Pass the witness."

It had gone smoothly, but I was frustrated. The real story, about Davis losing his temper, threatening people, seemed, to me, highly relevant and legally admissible. I appreciated that the judge felt we already had evidence tying an angry Davis to the bat, but this additional story was from a credible, impartial witness. However, I also understood why the judge ruled the way he did; it was a tough balance for him ensuring that admissible evidence came in without unfairly prejudicing the defendant.

Wade took up the questioning. "Ms. Bless, you and I have talked before, haven't we?"

"Yes."

"Back in August last year?"

"Uh-huh."

"You came to my office and we discussed items that you had made in a statement; is that correct?"

"Yes."

"Just for a little background, you were part of this group that hung out at Steamboat quite a bit during that period of time?"

"Yes, sir."

"Dennis was there, Natalie. Did you know Natalie?"

"I never met Natalie."

"That was earlier than when you were going down there, right?"

"Honestly, I have no idea the time frame that she would be going down there."

"I mean, you started going down there about what year?"

"Well, '84, when I first got here."

"A lot of the people that hung out down there were musicians or they were associated with the music industry in some way; is that correct?"

"Yes."

"You also were connected with some musicians in certain capacities, right?"

"A bit, yeah."

"You knew a performer named Bryan Adams?"

"Yes."

"And a performer named Billy Squier?"

"Yes."

"These were popular musicians during, correct me, '84, '85? Later than that?"

"Yeah, about '84, '85."

"You went on the road with them, working as a wardrobe manager and what they call a product manager?"

"Production."

"Production manager, I'm sorry. Production manager?"

"Assistant."

"You would go out on tour with them?"

"Yes, sometimes."

"Then come back to Austin?"

"Right."

"When you would go on the road with these rock stars, it could be pretty stressful, couldn't it?"

"That too, but especially in Austin."

"You knew Dennis Davis in '84 and '85?"

"Yes."

"Isn't it true that he would wear a mustache in those days? Do you recall that?"

"I think so, I think so."

"Dark mustache?"

"I think so, yeah."

"Dark hair?"

"Yeah, uh-huh."

"Are you still friends with Davis to some extent, with Dennis?"

"Well, we haven't seen each other for a long time. Kind of had different lives, but the past is the past and you know…"

Wade spent some time asking about the music scene in Austin in the 1980s, the kinds of bands she used to watch, including Jimmy Rose's band. I wasn't sure what it all meant, but I didn't see it advancing his case much or harming ours. Wade moved on to the topic at hand.

"During this period of time—well, eventually after you got to know Kellie or sometime between meeting Dennis in the mid-'80s and meeting Kellie later, you had learned bits and pieces of how Natalie had been killed, Natalie Antonetti?"

"No. When I left I came back to Austin. I was hearing little things about one of Dennis's girlfriends getting hurt, but I never—it was never really elaborated to me."

"You just knew a little bit about it?"

"Oh, yeah."

"But it wasn't a secret, a big secret. People did mention it from time to time?"

"I did not know anything about that. I didn't know that there was any kind of a killing or a murder."

"You didn't even know that?"

"No, I didn't know that until—up until I believe the detective showed up a few years ago, in '07. I did not know any of that."

"You met Kellie about what year, do you recall?"

"I guess when I came back from Ohio, so it had to be '86 maybe, I don't know. I don't know the time exactly."

"From that time forward, after you had met her and you knew that she and Dennis were dating, you all would socialize and have parties and you would see her at Steamboat?"

"Uh-huh."

"You spent a fair amount of time in her presence, right?"

"Yes."

"You knew people who knew her?"

"Uh-huh."

"As part of your group of friends?"

"Right."

"Is it fair to say you got to know her pretty well during this period of time?"

"Yeah, I believe so, yes."

Wade paused. "Do you have an opinion about Kellie Torres' character for truthfulness?"

Linda seemed uncomfortable, but I knew she was going to be honest. She'd told me on the phone that she thought sometimes Kellie exaggerated her own importance, maybe even lied to build herself up. I suspected the jury had seen that for themselves, the way she had talked about her role in the community and her daughter's executive job. However, Linda didn't hear any of that and didn't want to speak ill of her friend.

"Well," she said, "I think that part of the time when I would hear her talk a lot about who she knew in the music business or who she had worked for, I kind of got the idea that maybe she was just trying to be part of the crowd, part of the music scene."

"Are you saying you discounted some of what she said?"

"I did sometimes."

"Is your answer that her character for truthfulness was not necessarily good?"

"Not all the time about certain things, no."

Not altogether helpful for us, but since it seemed Wade was going to suggest Kellie was lying about Davis's admission of murder, Linda's testimony struck me as pretty tame.

"Did you ever see Dennis Davis do anything violent to Kellie?"

Linda hesitated; she seemed to be almost as surprised by the question as I was. "See him actually do anything to her?"

"Uh-huh. I mean, we talked about this. Didn't I ask you about this?"

"Yeah. No, I can't say that I actually saw anything violent."

"But it is fair to say you know they had sort of a tumultuous relationship?"

"Yes, sir." Given Linda's tone, I thought it was pretty clear "tumultuous" wouldn't have been her word choice.

I also thought Wade had opened the door to the very testimony he had so far managed to keep out, testimony that could show his client to be a man who lost his temper in violent ways, with a baseball bat in his hand. Testimony from someone who once loved Davis like a brother.

When Wade finished with his questions we argued the issue, again at the bench, whispering so the jury couldn't hear us but loud enough so the court reporter could.

Efrain put our case. "During the relationship between Dennis and Kellie, this witness had—at various times Kellie had bruising on her… That was inflicted by the defendant. I believe Linda knew this."

"How?" Judge Lynch asked.

"I think that is what she was going to say, that during that relationship Kellie would tell her Dennis beat on her and Linda would see the bruises."

I chipped in. "At the party with the bat."

The judge looked at me. "What?"

"Well, she did witness a scene of violence when the defendant was attempting to get at Kellie and this witness got in the way. I think he opened the door to that particular incident."

Wade leaned in. "I don't think that is what she said, was it?"

"I guess we are going to go to lunch, but I don't know." Judge Lynch shook his head and looked at Wade. "You went awful close to the line here."

"Kellie sort of blurted all this stuff out," Wade responded.

Lynch shrugged. "Nobody objected. I figured it was part of your strategy."

"It was out before I could do anything."

"Well, I could have cautioned her, but I thought that was your strategy, to show her to be hostile and upset and blurting out whatever she came up with."

Wade grinned sheepishly. "It wasn't originally, but it is now."

"I thought it was the defensive theory, so I decided not to step in and try to alter her testimony, judicial fiat. If any party asked me, I would have restricted her, but I figured both sides were happy."

Efrain brought us back to the current issue. "I want to ask the witness, 'Did you ever see any bruising at the time Dennis and Kellie were dating each other?'"

Judge Lynch wasn't sure. He told us that unless Linda saw specific incidents that caused bruising, her testimony would be inadmissible hearsay. He also expressed concern about Linda making general statements about seeing bruises on Kellie without knowing how they got there, because bruising without a cause wasn't particularly relevant. Efrain looked over at Linda, who was still on the witness stand, and suggested to the Court that he ask her some questions outside the presence of the jury.

Efrain did so and Linda testified about the incident at the party, that Davis had the bat in his hand and at the time "he was very angry at Kellie" and that she was the one who took him outside and calmed him down.

Afterward, the judge said he was inclined to allow the specific testimony about that incident into evidence, but not let Linda testify generally about bruising she'd seen on Kellie. Judge Lynch told Wade what I'd been thinking—that Wade himself opened the door with his last question about whether Linda had seen Davis be violent to Kellie.

Wade continued to object. "I have not opened the door that he is a good guy. I have only asked in response to what Linda said whether she saw Dennis hit Kellie. I have not tried to characterize him as a peaceable citizen."

But the judge took the State's side, seeing this as rebutting Wade's attempt to portray Davis as being non-violent. He told Wade, "You can't offer that kind of evidence without taking—you just can't do that. I don't know that anybody has ever been able to do that in the law."

"I'm sorry, do what?" Wade questioned.

"You can't offer up that kind of evidence and expect the State to sit there and just eat it."

After lunch, Linda Bless took the stand again. Efrain asked the questions. "Ms. Bless, earlier before the lunch break you testified that you had seen the defendant here holding a bat at a party sometime in 1987. Do you recall that testimony?"

"Yes, I do."

"At the time that the defendant was holding the bat, was he angry?"

"Agitated."

"At the time that he was holding that bat, was he threatening Kellie with the bat?"

"Seemed to be, yes."

"What did you do at that point when the defendant had the bat in his hand?"

"I approached him, asked him what he was doing: 'Come on, Dennis, you got to straighten up. Let's go outside, talk about it.'"

"Did you in fact take him outside?"

"Yeah."

"Did he calm down after that?"

"Yeah, we just talked."

"At the time that this incident happened, Dennis and Kellie were living there at that house where this incident took place?"

"Yes."

Wade had no follow up questions; no doubt he didn't want to open that door any wider. Linda left the stand and I felt much better. The jury had heard a more complete story and had a better picture of the man with the bat.

Next I asked to admit two agreements I'd reached with the defense. Some of the things I wanted the jury to know about were not contested and Wade had saved me a great deal of trouble and the court a lot of time by agreeing that the information could be presented to the jury by way of written stipulation. We worked out the specifics together, Wade and I, so that both sides were happy with the language. The judge told the jurors: "These State's Exhibits are admitted and the stipulations agreed to by the Court and received. They can be received as any other evidence that comes before you just without a live witness testifying to these things. They will be read into the record and available as other exhibits."

I stood in front of the jury box and read aloud State's exhibit 100:

Comes now the State of Texas and the above named defendant on this eleventh day of April and hereby stipulates to the Court that the following matters are proven and true:

On October 14, 1985, a nurse with Brackenridge Hospital performed a sexual examination on Natalie Antonetti. She examined her vagina and found no evidence of trauma. She also collected vaginal swabs from Natalie Antonetti.

For purposes of DNA analysis, Detective Edward Balagia with the Austin Police Department submitted Natalie Antonetti's sexual assault kit, including vaginal swabs, couch cover, three couch pillows, teddy nightgown, pink T-shirt and jogging shorts to the Texas Department of Public Safety, DPS, on October 14.

A DNA expert with DPS analyzed these items for the presence of semen and detected no semen.

The second stipulation had taken a lot more work than the first, but Wade and his client approved the final version and I read it aloud:

Comes now the State of Texas and the above named defendant on this eleventh day of April and hereby stipulates to the Court that were he called to testify, Terrance Gilmore of Austin, Texas would testify to the following:

That he was the keyboard player for the band the Lotions, that he was a casual acquaintance of Dennis Davis, that as well as being a band member, like Dennis Davis he also worked as a sound engineer and had done some work at Studio D at the time, that the Lotions had numerous logos printed on T-shirts and were selling them and giving them away to members of the public, that the Lotions did not ever record at Studio D. After October 13, Dennis Davis requested that Terrance Gilmore provide a collection of Lotions T-shirts to the Austin Police Department to assist with the investigation of the murder, that he cannot say whether or not he gave Dennis Davis a Lotions T-shirt prior to October 13. He has no memory of doing so.

With that, I returned to counsel table where I remained standing and said the words that always cause a jolt to run through me.

"Your Honor, the State rests."

Chapter 26

THE DEFENSE SPEAKS

Dennis Davis didn't have to put on a case. No defendant in the State of Texas or anywhere else in America has to present any evidence whatsoever. The Constitution assures them of that. Most defendants don't, in my experience. They leave it to their lawyers to pick holes in the prosecution's case and trust the jury to abide by the "beyond a reasonable doubt" standard. But in bigger cases, again in my experience, either the defendants or their defense attorneys aren't content with that; they want to show *why* the jury should acquit.

And the defense had Donn Chelli's statement.

But Wade began with Davis's old friend, Jimmy Rose.

"Welcome back, Mr. Rose."

"Thank you."

"Just to recap a little bit. You were a drummer and you played almost every night down at Steamboat?"

"Correct."

"You knew this group of friends along with Dennis Davis and Kellie Torres among others?"

"Yes."

"Did you know Linda Bless also?"

"Yes."

"You have testified that you lived with Mr. Davis over a period of about eight months total, you think?"

"I would say between eight and a year. I am not quite sure how long it was."

"After Ms. Antonetti was assaulted and subsequently died, were you around Mr. Davis?"

"Yes, I was."

"During that period of time?"

"Uh-huh."

"Did you do anything with Mr. Davis in regard to this case?"

"I believe we went to the funeral together."

"Did you do anything in Austin? Did you go anywhere, try to do anything to work on the case?"

"Dennis and I discussed—there was mention of a T-shirt… Dennis and I decided we would go down to Sixth Street and just hang out down there trying to find someone who would be wearing that T-shirt and we went down there and looked for weeks, every day for a few weeks."

"Never found anybody?"

"Never. At that time, Sixth Street wasn't as crowded as it is now, so there wasn't as many people, so it would have been easier to find something like that then than it would be now. But no, we never did see anything."

"Were you looking for any other indicators other than just a particular type of T-shirt?"

"No."

"That was all you knew?"

"Yes, sir."

"Sounds like a silly question, but how much time did you spend around Kellie Torres during this period of time where you lived together?"

"Well, I believe I was around them from the time they got together until I left Austin."

"Which was about when?"

"In '87."

"Based on your relationship with her and being around her, did you ever form an opinion as to her character for truthfulness?"

Efrain didn't let Rose answer, jumping to his feet and asking to approach the bench. This specific objection was my idea and it had to do with timing. I felt that Rose's opinion as to Kellie's truthfulness in the 1980s was irrelevant. Back then, she and Davis, Linda and Jimmy, they were different people. They partied and were generally wilder. What they were like then bore no resemblance to the people they were now and so what Rose had to say about Kellie's character for truthfulness, in my opinion, was not helpful to the jury.

As Efrain put it: "He has no knowledge about her at the time she made the statement. I think her character should be relevant to the time she made that statement."

The judge considered the argument and pointed out that Wade needed to make clear his question related to when Rose knew Kellie. "Limit it just to that and the State then can fully cross-examine about the fact that he doesn't have the slightest idea today."

Back at counsel table, Wade asked: "Again, Mr. Rose, I am referring back to the time period in which you knew her, Ms. Torres?"

"Yes."

"Based on your relationship with her, dealing with her at that time, did you develop an opinion about her character for being truthful or untruthful?"

"I believed…" He paused and shook his head. "Kellie and I never got along."

"Let me just—"

"I would say that she would lie quite often."

As Wade continued asking questions, I thought how silly lawyers must seem sometimes, objecting to keep out testimony that the jury could evaluate perfectly fairly, huddling at the bench and talking in whispers when context made it plain what each side wanted. Trial always struck me as something of a performance, but every now and again, such as this moment, I saw how our roles could occasionally override common sense and make us appear somewhat ridiculous. I liked to think that seeing past the theater was what made me good at my job, that seeing a case, a trial, from the jurors' perspective was what made me an effective advocate for victims. But I was not above getting a clever idea and failing to see it for what it was—just a clever idea.

Wade ended his direct examination by having Rose describe Davis as he was in the 1980s. He was doing this so he could draw distinctions between his client and the man Donn Chelli described in his statement. But Jimmy Rose said something that made me sit up straighter. Rose compared Davis to how he looked that day in the courtroom and said, "Maybe his hair was a little lighter, but still dirty blond, kind of curly hair."

Dirty blond. I wrote the phrase down on my legal pad, put two circles around it and made a mental note to revisit that phrase in my closing.

On cross-examination, Efrain had just a couple of points to make. "One of the questions that counsel was asking you with regards to Kellie: it is true, Mr. Rose, that you and Kellie never got along?"

"That is true."

"You two just didn't care for one another?"

"That is true."

"This opinion that you are giving about her character for being truthful, I mean let's be honest here, you haven't seen her since the late '80s?"

"Correct."

"So you don't know what kind of person she was when she gave a statement with regards to this case in the year 2007?"

"I have no opinion."

"What was the height of the defendant when Natalie was assaulted and eventually died?"

"I'm sorry, repeat the question."

"Sure, I'm sorry. Do you recall the height of the defendant here when you knew him?"

"Five-eight, five-seven."

This was for our own comparison, so we could point out that Dennis Davis was exactly the same height as the man in the park whom Donn Chelli said so closely resembled the mystery "Lotions man" and felt compelled to call the police about.

We were in the guesswork phase of the trial, when the defense could put people on the stand with no notice to the prosecution whatsoever. People we'd never heard of or people who, in our opinions, had nothing to do with the case. But all we could do was sit and listen, object when improper testimony was being sought and hope we could come up with good questions come cross-examination time.

Neither Efrain nor I were prepared for Wade's next witness. As the man made his way to the stand, Efrain and I looked at each other and shrugged. *No idea what he has to say* was the message we were sharing. I could only assume Wade called him because he was going to offer an opinion about Kellie, because I didn't believe the man knew anything substantive about the case.

Wade began, "State your name for the record, please?"

"Perry Alston."

"Did you know Mr. Davis?"

"Yes, I did."

Back and forth the questions and answers flew, attempting to establish Alston's credentials and, to some degree, Davis's credentials in the music business. Wade also established that Alston traveled a lot and had many different roommates in Austin, including Davis and Kellie.

"When you were home for these, what, are they weeks or months at a time?"

"Usually only a week or two, three at the most. Usually we would go to the next place."

"You were around both Kellie Torres and Mr. Davis?"

"Yes."

"During that period of time, based on your relationship with her and knowing her and being around her, did you or have you formed an opinion about her character for truthfulness or untruthfulness, yes or no?"

"Yes, I have formed an opinion."

"What is your opinion?"

"I do not consider her to be a truthful or a reliable person."

Pretty emphatic, so on cross-examination I planned to try to soften Alston's view of Kellie, being careful to rely on what he'd already told the jury. I didn't believe Perry Alston would lie on the stand, commit perjury. But I did believe that friends were loyal and their views could be colored by those they know and like, especially in times of crisis. I wanted the jury to know that Alston didn't know

Kellie well, didn't know her now and what he believed about her came through Davis.

Before I began, Alston poured himself a glass of water from the jug beside the witness stand. I signaled my lack of hostility by saying, "I'll join you" and did the same at my table. Once we were both finished I said, "Mr. Alston, it sounds like you weren't actually around Kellie all that much because you were traveling, is that fair?"

"Yes, that is fair."

"When you were home, you were kind of hanging out with other people as opposed to Dennis and his crowd and Kellie. You were hanging out with other people?"

"Yes, I mean we slept at the same house every night when I was there. I still had my room."

"Sure, sure. When was the last time you saw Kellie or spent any time with her?"

"Probably when they moved out in 1990 or so. It is hard to remember those dates exactly."

"Sure."

"Especially with twenty-eight roommates. I can't remember who came and went when."

"But as we sit today, it is probably twenty years since you have seen her?"

"Oh, yes."

"Is that true too of Dennis Davis or are you still in contact with him?"

"Still in contact with him."

"Are you still friends with him?"

"Yes."

"Have you been friends with him for the last twenty years?"

"No."

"When did you stop having contact with him—in the '80s, '90s time?"

"Probably from the time he moved out, although I think he was a sound man at Steamboat or something. Then when he moved to Nashville in '95, between '90 and '95, I probably didn't see that much of him."

"But since you have rekindled your relationship?"

"Yes."

"Are you pretty close?"

"Yes, I would say so."

I wrapped it up and hoped I had achieved my small goals with him. Let the jury decide.

Wade's next witness was almost a carbon copy, a musician who knew Davis and Kellie. He offered his opinion about her poor reputation for truthfulness and Efrain handled the minimal cross-examination.

Then at 2:20 P.M., Wade recalled Tom Walsh to the stand.

He asked Tom about the composite drawing William Beechinor did under Donn Chelli's direction.

"You have looked high and low for that and you cannot find it?"

"I cannot find it. I even called Sergeant Beechinor when he was working for the police department."

"Let's just talk about this person that was subject to this causing you all to do this, the composite drawing."

"Uh-huh."

"You are aware that back right around the, let's say within minutes of the time that a 911 call was made in by Jolene Wells to APD, that a neighbor had called in just a few minutes after that, maybe say nine minutes after that, made a 911 call?"

Tom gave a small smile. "It was eleven minutes."

"Eleven minutes?"

"Yes, sir."

"Eleven, that's right, not nine. Your math is better than mine. And this person made a report about seeing somebody outside the apartments, right?"

"That's correct."

"It was determined that this person who called in was a neighbor, lived in the same apartment block as where the victim was assaulted?"

"That is correct, in the same building."

Wade elicited from Tom the fact that his client did not resemble the description Chelli gave, both from talking to Chelli and looking at old photos of Davis. Then Wade pressed hard on the statements Tom got from Kellie, his point being that when Tom first spoke to her she was less than certain about what Davis had said about killing Natalie.

Tom said, "I think if you look at the total context of the first conversation that I had with her and at that time I felt that as we progressed through that first conversation on the phone that she became stronger and her conviction became stronger as to what she heard."

"Let me ask you this. In these first conversations, she gets more detailed about what he said to her, right?"

"I believe so."

"Then she calls you back in a couple of days and is saying, 'I am not certain word for word what he said'?"

"Yes."

"She also says, 'I kind of remember this conversation, but I don't remember word for word what he said'?"

"That is correct."

"You visited her and you interviewed her and you took a more detailed statement; is that correct?"

"That is correct."

Wade continued to pursue, what I believed to be, two prongs of his trial strategy. The first was to make Kellie the bad guy, lying and making up stories about Davis to get him in trouble. The second was that Tom took her statement and ran with it, didn't bother looking for the real killer but instead focused on Davis and Davis only.

"Having this information," Wade asked, "I am assuming the first thing you did was check around with people who knew her credibility?"

"Not really, no."

As he finished up, Wade returned to an issue that I always feared might be a problem for us. "When you interviewed Ms. Torres and she gave you this information about a statement made by Mr. Davis regarding committing this offense, did you wonder why it had taken her so long to make this statement?"

"I did."

"Did you inquire into that? If you don't have an answer, that is fine. Wouldn't you agree with me it is a little bit odd that a person would wait seventeen years to report a person, an unsolved murder?"

A fair question and Tom answered it the only way he could. "Absolutely."

When it was my turn to question Tom, I tried to do some damage control, touching on several topics briefly but succinctly. I established that neither the Internet printout that the defense showed him yesterday nor the medical examiner's report said how many times Natalie was struck. I moved on.

"Regarding Becky Davis, how many times did you talk to her on the telephone?"

"Twice."

"Did you record all the phone conversations you had with her?"

"Yes."

"Was there a period where you were calling her ten times a day for a year?"

"Never."

"Did you ever call her ten times a day?"

He shook his head and looked at the jury. "No, I never called her ten times a day."

I covered this topic, because I wanted the jury to consider: Was Tom lying about this or was Becky Davis? One of them had to be lying and I thought it was a clear-cut answer. I also wanted to rebut the idea that Tom would harass someone until the person said what he wanted to hear.

Kellie's statements were the next topic. I wanted the jury to understand that if her account waivered in the early days of the investigation, there was a reason.

"Defense counsel asked you some questions about Kellie Torres's testimony. I am going to ask you generally if it is true that particularly in a cold case a witness the first time you talk to them will remember everything straightaway?"

"No."

"Is that ever going to happen?"

"I am not going to say it is never going to happen, but generally people have to warm up and just like interviewing somebody, sometimes it is easy for people to say things if you are very easy with them and just let it come out."

"You have already testified that it is unusual for somebody to keep a secret like this for seventeen years?"

"Yes."

"Would it be surprising to you that a witness like in this case would be a little reticent at first to give you this important information?"

"Not at all."

"Would you be surprised though if she kind of warmed up to giving you the big details?"

"Not at all."

"You would expect her to do that?"

"Yes."

When Wade and I were done, the judge called for a ten-minute break so the jurors could stretch their legs and use the restroom. While they were out of the courtroom, the lawyers talked at the bench about the defense's upcoming evidence, because we were approaching the Chelli moment. We all wanted to be absolutely sure how any information relating to him came in, step for step.

Chapter 27

ABSENT WITNESS

W hen the jury returned, Wade began by admitting into evidence
the 911 call Donn Chelli made and read our agreed stipulation that the call was made on "October 13 at 5:40 A.M., that this 911
call lasted two minutes and forty seconds, that this 911 call was made
from Chelli's apartment on Barton Hills Drive, Austin, Texas."

The tape itself was admitted, but Wade didn't play it. We'd tried
previously, but it was almost inaudible with the equipment we had in
the courtroom. Instead, Wade read to the jury what he called a "vir-
tual verbatim recitation" of the call that he and his second chair had
prepared.

With a nod from the Court he began to read into the record the
statement of Donn Lewis Chelli:

On Sunday, October 13, between 4:40 A.M. and 4:45 A.M.,
I noticed a white male about six foot zero inches tall, broad
shoulders, big belly, straight dishwater blond hair not quite
touching the collar. He had on a gray or dark green T-shirt
with, quote, The Lotions, unquote, written on back. He also
had on a pair of shorts. I am not sure what color they were,
but they might have been tan. He appeared to be in some
kind of rage. What I mean by this is that while he was calm,
he appeared to have a lot of built-up tension inside of him.

This man was carrying what looked like a child's baseball bat. It was wood and approximately twenty-four inches long.

I had been walking back from the store and noticed this man looking into my living room window facing the south side of my apartment. When I saw him, he said something to me. I can't remember his exact words, but it was something like, quote, you are the second person that has gotten into my shit, end quote.

I then asked him what he was doing there and he replied that he was looking at my cats. They sit up on the balcony. My townhouse is a two-story home with a balcony up above the living room.

We then walked alongside each other toward the parking lot. I then turned right so that I could enter my apartment. I noticed that he continued walking straight in the direction of the clubhouse. I then put my milk away in the refrigerator and then walked back outside to see if I could see this man again. I walked down in the area to where he had been heading, but I didn't see him again.

I went back into my apartment and was debating on whether or not I should tell my girlfriend [Fran Alcozer] about this. I had been up so early this morning, because I was going to catch a plane at the airport for a business trip. However, because I had seen this person looking in our apartment, I was worried about leaving her alone.

We then sat down and had some cereal.

About this time the morning paper was delivered. When it thumped against the front door, I decided I should tell her about the man I had seen. I then decided that I should call the police and report this suspicious person.

When I called the dispatcher, he asked me if it was the same incident that had just been called in. I told him I didn't know and he told me that someone was just beaten at my complex and he would have a police officer come talk to me.

Me and my girlfriend then went outside and saw John, last name unknown, approximately seventeen or eighteen years old. John is the son of the lady who was beaten. He told us that his mother was bleeding and he was looking for the emergency van. He told me somebody had beat her.

Shortly thereafter, EMS arrived and when EMS arrived, John asked them what had taken so long and then they went to the apartment. We walked up to the apartment and stood at the door and then walked back to the parking lot where we met the police.

After talking to the police at the scene, me and my girlfriend went back to bed. About an hour later, somebody knocked on our door, but we didn't answer it, because we wanted to continue sleeping.

About 9:30 or 10:00 A.M. someone knocked on our door again. People knocking on the door. The police advised us that they needed us to come down to the station and give statements to Officer Schmidt in reference to this incident.

Next, Wade read into the record another stipulation, the one that had been the most difficult for us to agree on. For the prosecution, though, it was vital, because it contained information that directly contradicted portions of Chelli's original statement.

The State and the defendant agree that if Donn Chelli had testified in person in this case the State would have elicited from him the following facts: One, that both the State and the defense spoke on several occasions with Donn Chelli and requested him to come testify in person and he refused. He also concealed his physical address from the State and from investigators for the defense making it impossible to compel his attendance through a subpoena.

Two, that during two telephone conversations with officers of this court, Donn Chelli made four statements changing those in his written statement, specifically: A) that the "Lotions man" he saw was not six feet tall but six feet three inches tall; Chelli stated that he himself was six feet and the "Lotions man" "towered" over him; B) that he had never had any discussion with the "Lotions man"; C) that a newspaper never hit their door and that in fact he and his girlfriend Fran Alcozer were not even having the newspaper delivered; D) that he never even saw, let alone spoke to, either Johnny Goudie or Jolene Wells on the morning of the assault.

This stipulation, I hoped, would start to show why we viewed Donn Chelli as an unreliable witness. The next witness would make that even clearer.

Because of the witness's schedule, Wade had agreed to let us call Charles Weaver as a rebuttal witness before the defense had finished putting on their case.

After the professor was sworn in, Efrain talked Dr. Weaver through his education, qualifications and experience before bringing him to his current specialty.

"I am what is called a cognitive psychologist. I study human memory, how people remember things, specifically, eyewitness identification."

"Sir, have you had the occasion to testify as an expert not only in the area of memory, but also eyewitness identification?"

"I have."

"Has that been on few or many occasions?"

"I have probably testified in forty cases, fifty cases over the past fifteen years."

"Have you had the occasion to testify in courts here in Travis County?"

"I have."

"As a matter of fact, have you testified before this judge in this court?"

Weaver looked to his left, toward the judge. "I don't know if he remembers it or if I remember it wrongly, but I believe this was the first court I ever offered testimony in about fifteen years ago."

"You have testified for the defense before, have you not?"

Other than his actual expertise, this was what made him such a good witness for us. He nodded. "In fact, all of the expert work I have done up to this point has been for the defense."

Efrain moved to the substance of his testimony. "Let's talk about memory for a minute. Can you share with the jurors what are some of the most common mistakes, mistaken beliefs about memory?"

"Most of them, most of the mistaken beliefs fall from the most common belief, which is that memory works like a video recorder, that we have this device in our heads that passively records our lives as events transpire and later we have to rewind the tape, push play and the memories flow back perfectly. That is a poor understanding of memory.

"One of the things we have discovered in the past fifty years or so is just how reconstructive memory is, how easy it is to distort, how easy it is for inaccurate facts to influence our memory and so forth."

"Can you share with the jurors how is it that memory works?"

"Memory is best thought of as a reconstructive process, not a reproductive process that would be 'rewind the tape, press play.' Memory is better thought of as a situation where we combine our memories for bits and pieces of the event that might still be there, but we combine those with all other sources of information, with information we learned since the event, with the manner in which questions might be asked of us, with beliefs that we might have that can alter our memories really quite dramatically.

"It is really not fair to say those are flaws of memory. Those are simply features of memory. That is how memory works. We often make inferences, suppositions. We let new information influence our memories for old events. That is simply how memory works."

The jury was rapt, all their attention on Dr. Weaver who, like Tom, was directing his answers at them, educating them.

"Let's talk about eyewitness identification for a minute. Based upon your experience and the research that you have done in that area, can you share with the jurors some of the factors that might affect one's identification of another individual, for example?"

"Sure. We can break factors that influence eyewitnesses into two categories of variables: those variables that we don't have much control over as investigators, the time of day, the lighting conditions, fatigue or other kinds of factors like that that simply happen to be present when a witness sees an event. There are other situations, other factors that we do have some control over. How it is we question witnesses, whether we use photo lineups or in-person arrays, whether we question witnesses one at a time or in groups. All of those, those kinds of factors can influence not just what a witness remembers, but also how confidently the witness testifies with respect to what he remembers."

"What about an individual's emotions or fears?" Efrain continued. "How does that influence the ability to be able to remember an event?"

"Most people would think that in situations of extreme stress, our memory would get very, very good. 'I will never forget the face of the person who was there' and so forth. In reality, like most things, a little bit of emotion is a good thing, but too much of it is not. It is situations of extreme emotion, especially in ones where there is fear or where there is a weapon involved, we recognize what we call the weapon focus. When people feel themselves under threat, their attention tends to be drawn to the weapon and, as a result, witnesses can usually give a very good description of the weapon, but at the expense of the other details of the event."

"Can you share with the jurors what it is that you are here to testify about?"

"Sure. I am not here to testify whether a witness is right or wrong. I don't have any special abilities to determine that. Neither am I going to testify that a witness is credible or not credible. That is the jury's job. What I am here to do is to provide a little bit of background on the scientific understanding of how memory works, identify some of the factors that we know influence eyewitness memory to assist the jury as they go about evaluating the eyewitness testimony in this case."

That was important. We wanted the jurors to know that we were giving them information, tools to evaluate testimony (specifically Donn Chelli's), but what they actually did with it was up to them. We were looking to empower the jurors, not spoon-feed them the answer.

Efrain approached the witness stand, handed Weaver a pen and paper and said, "I'm going to give you a hypothetical and I want to talk about that hypothetical with you as it relates to memory and eyewitness identification."

Weaver nodded. "Sure."

The hypothetical consisted of the facts of our case, given in great detail. As Efrain talked, Weaver listened intently and made notes. At one stage, he held up a hand. "Can I ask you a clarifying question?"

"Yes, sir."

"The T-shirt that you said had a logo, was it a logo or a name?"

"It was a name actually."

"That actually matters quite a bit."

"It was the name of a local band."

The hypothetical Efrain gave him included a statement given to police describing a burly, six-foot man. "Later, a month after all that, he gives a description of an individual whom he believes was the person he encountered and that individual was determined to be about a five-six to five-eight individual." And the question itself: "Given that hypothetical, I want to ask what factors do you see in that hypothetical that you think may influence the reliability of that witness identification of what he saw that morning?"

Weaver nodded again and looked up from his paper. "I am not surprised by those discrepancies. Our ability to identify perceptual factors like that, height, weight, is notoriously bad.

"The other factor I would point to as an exception to this—and this is why I asked that—when it comes to recognizing something like a name, a name that may have been on the T-shirt, that is a very different process.

"A good analogy, a good distinction would be the difference between me trying to remember someone that I met for the very first time, which I would have great difficulty doing after a brief encounter, but I can recognize someone I do know almost instantly.

"In one case I am recognizing; I am tying something that I am experiencing to something I already know. In another situation, I am having to form a new memory of something I have never seen before under really poor conditions. Those would be the factors that I would point to. Late at night, brief encounter, conditions less than ideal. I am not sure what the lighting conditions would be. I would not expect them to be good. And the presence of the club, the bat, as you mentioned."

"Going back to the name on the T-shirt, is it your opinion that someone being able to identify a name on a T-shirt would be more reliable than someone trying to recall that person's facial features, height, weight?"

"It tends to be. When we talk about witnesses being unreliable or eyewitness memory being unreliable, it is really not a blanket true statement. Everybody's memory is probably accurate in some details but not others. We may remember gender quite well, we may remember ethnicity, things like that. We may remember other details like that which would be reliable. In other cases we might not.

"The ability to name—and I would assume from the description you gave that the name of the band was volunteered by the individual who saw that. In other words, they were not asked, 'Did you see a logo on the T-shirt?' That was a detail that was volunteered."

On cross-examination, Wade was smart enough not to challenge Dr. Weaver on the science of eyewitness identification. As a trial lawyer, one of the quickest ways to embarrass oneself is to take on an expert witness on that person's area of expertise. The expert has spent years studying it and writing about it and no matter how smart a lawyer is, unless the witness is a charlatan, the lawyer is most likely going to lose that debate.

So Wade had Weaver confirm that if the underlying assumptions in Efrain's hypothetical were different, the result might be different. If the lighting was actually good and the witness wasn't tired or afraid of the man with the bat, his recollection might be better.

Wade Russell drew an analogy: "If a person were to walk alongside a person in medium lighting and he later describes that person as having a big belly and he walks side by side with him for five or ten paces, then an hour later he calls in and says this fellow had a big belly, do you have an opinion about whether or not that could or could not be mistaken?"

"It certainly could be mistaken. I don't know that it necessarily would be. Again, if the identification was given as soon as possible without any kind of prompting, assuming that the lighting conditions didn't cast shadows or anything like that, there is no reason to suspect that it could not be reliable."

That was in our favor, in my view. Then Wade asked Weaver about the second identification, a month later, of a smaller person.

Wade had argued to me several times that Chelli was probably some distance from the homeless man he identified as looking like the "Lotions man," which explained the mistake. For my part, I'd pointed out that we had no idea how far away he was. Wade went with his theory and asked, "Wouldn't the distance away affect his ability to accurately describe this person he is now seeing as being like the person he saw close up a month earlier?"

"In some respects, probably not with height. Height we usually judge relative to other objects. The moon when it rises seems like it is really big, much bigger than it is when it is in the sky. It is actually the same distance in both cases. It is the relative size that it appears on the horizon with the trees that gives it the illusion of looking bigger."

Wade wasn't ready to abandon his theory. "What if he is 200 yards away? Are you still saying perceived height is really not affected by that kind of distance?"

"Sure, as long as there are objects around that one can get relative distance from. If he is standing next to a window or standing next to a tree. We have no trouble at all judging height of people from considerable distances as long as we have something relative to judge it to."

Wade moved on, but into another sticky patch, asking Weaver about a topic we didn't think to broach with him ourselves.

"The question would be, can an individual have paranoid tendencies yet still have a fully functioning sensory memory?"

"It would depend upon the nature of the paranoia. If they were schizophrenic to the point where they were hearing voices, seeing hallucinations, almost by definition one can't trust their sensory experiences. If it is simply a paranoid tendency, that can sometimes influence how people perceive events—I shouldn't say perceive. How they interpret events."

"At a later time?"

"At a later time, right. Again, I would presume those effects would be much greater at a later point than they would be immediately after an event."

"So paranoia doesn't necessarily affect perception," Wade continued, "but it can affect a person's processing of things that he had seen earlier in his life when he thinks about them in a distorted manner?"

"I think I use the word interpret rather than processing, but one can reinterpret events in light of the paranoia, sure."

We hadn't put on evidence about Chelli's paranoia, but maybe it had become apparent to the jury. If so, Dr. Weaver had just given jurors another reason not to trust the man's testimony. He left the stand and the defense resumed their case.

Cliff Byers, Wade's investigator, was next. He was a former police officer and veteran of the FBI.

Byers began by telling the jury that he timed the drive between Natalie's apartment and Dennis Davis's home in Onion Creek: twenty-one minutes, he said, done at five in the morning with very little traffic. That sounded about right to me and I didn't think it undermined our case any.

Then Wade started asking about how investigations were run and I suddenly realized why he called Byers to the stand: to second-guess Tom's entire investigation. I objected and we conferenced at the bench. I told the judge that my objection, simply put, was that the witness planned "to bad-mouth the investigation." Wade essentially confirmed that I was right, but the judge wasn't having it. As he pointed out, that would require recalling Tom and nit-picking every single step he took, effectively having a second trial about the merits of the investigation itself. Instead, Judge Lynch permitted Wade to ask two specific questions.

"Mr. Byers, based on your experience as an investigator having worked in the police department for a number of years and the FBI, is it possible—are there occasions where investigators can get what we call tunnel vision, focus on, say, one fact, one thing someone said to them to the exclusion of other factors in a case?"

"Yes, sir."

"Is it proper investigative technique if a person has told you something of greater interest and perhaps tends to incriminate someone, is it proper or expected for the investigator to inquire into the credibility of the person who is giving them this information?"

"Yes, sir."

Next, Wade introduced through Byers the registration documents for the automobile observed at the scene of the attack. "Does that document tell you when the registration was issued to this person right here?"

"Yes, sir."

"Who is that person?"

"Dennis Davis."

"What does it say as to when that registration was given to Mr. Davis?"

"August 13, 1987."

Wade asked to approach the bench. He said somberly, "I would like to ask him one question about why police officers would give someone immunity in a case."

I shook my head. "Police officers don't give immunity."

"Sustain the objection."

Wade replied, "Okay" and we headed back to counsel table. I gave Wade credit, though, because there were a great many defense lawyers who would have happily asked that question regardless whether it was legally improper. It was a rare moment when my respect for a lawyer rose because a judge had ruled against him.

During cross-examination, I structured my questions carefully, knowing that Byers would give me honest answers.

"Have you ever worked on a cold case?"

"Yes, sir."

"Would you agree with me that if somebody gives you a piece of information that you deem to be important, it is a good idea to spend your time checking out the information rather than checking out the person or maybe as well as checking out the person?"

"Yes, sir."

"In terms of credibility, people's opinions of credibility will vary depending on who you speak to?"

"Yes, sir."

"Credibility itself isn't a measurable item of evidence that you can put in a bag and tag and show to a jury, is it?"

"No, sir."

"Referring to that exhibit that Mr. Russell just showed you about the registration, does that document tell you when a registration was issued?"

"Yes, sir."

"Does it tell you when a vehicle was transferred from one person to another?"

"No, sir, it was just that it was Dennis Davis's."

"So if Mr. Davis had testified that he was in possession of that vehicle two years earlier, that document doesn't necessarily negate that testimony, does it?"

"No, sir."

The last witness of the day was Mark Thomas Lewis, Jr., otherwise known as Buster. After the formality and professional detachment of Dr. Weaver and Cliff Byers, Buster was a breath of air. His ruddy face was sweating a little and his eyes peered around the courtroom checking us all out. It was one of those faces you instantly liked.

Wade established that Buster was a musician, a drummer who had known Dennis Davis since the early 1980s. He asked about the evening before the assault. "Were you there at Steamboat that Saturday night, I guess that would be the twelfth of October?"

"Yes."

"About what time did you arrive?"

"Oh, I would say probably around 9:30, 10 or it could have been 10:30. I really don't recall."

"You were drinking that night, right?"

"Yes."

"You drank maybe a little too much that night?"

He got a few titters from the jury as he admitted, none too sheepishly, "I am sure I did."

"But you do recall what night it was, right, because you got that phone call the next day?"

"I got a phone call the next day, the next morning. I assume, I guess that was the Saturday night and the phone call came I guess that Sunday morning."

"Do you recall seeing Ms. Antonetti at Steamboat while you were there the night before?"

"Yes, I do."

"When do you recall seeing her?"

"Oh, later that night, I guess probably around eleven or twelve. It was getting pretty late in the night. I just remember her being there, being by herself."

"Did you see Dennis Davis there that night?"

"I don't remember seeing Dennis Davis that night. I do not."

This was interesting to me, because it directly contradicted the testimony of Davis's friend Jimmy Rose. Given Buster's admission to being drunk and Rose's unwilling but certain observations, I was not too worried by Buster Lewis as yet.

Wade continued. "Do you have any recollection of whether you danced that evening with Ms. Antonetti?"

"I probably did. I can't sit here and say yes, I do remember, but I probably did."

"People would just typically dance, get up and dance, with different people while the band is playing. That is not unusual, right?"

"Yes, yes."

"Do you have a recollection of whether Ms. Antonetti ever appeared to be upset that evening or not?"

"I don't recall her being upset at all that evening."

"About what time did you leave Steamboat?"

"I am going to say we left probably—I think it was at closing."

"Which would be what, 2:00 A.M.?"

"Close to 2:00 A.M. Bands quit usually before 2:00 A.M., probably when the band quit. Close to 2:00 A.M."

"Did you and Mr. Kane and Ms. Antonetti all leave about the same time?"

"Yes, we did. As I recall, Davey and I and Natalie, I guess her first name was, walked out together to the corner, the west corner, which is right in front of Paradise. We said goodbyes and Davey and I walked to our cars, which was south off of that corner street and Natalie walked west down Sixth Street toward Congress and we didn't know where she was going."

He'd already said that he'd not met Natalie before; this was the first time and his memory didn't seem too solid. To me this was unsurprising, given the passage of time.

"Did you recall seeing a fellow named Jimmy Rose down there at Steamboat?"

"Actually, I guess he was there. I honestly—as I said before, nothing on that evening really stood out. Jimmy said that he was there. I guess he was."

"Is that what you are going by, what he said?"

"I can't sit here and say I could tell the court that, 'Yes, I saw Jimmy Rose that night.'"

"That is not your independent recollection? That is based on something you heard from him?"

"Right."

More guessing, so Wade circled around to finish. "Your testimony is, when you saw her, you didn't—she seemed perfectly normal to you that night?"

"Well, she seemed—she didn't seem upset. She didn't seem sad. She didn't seem scared. She seemed just fine, like nothing was wrong; cheerful, ready to party and have fun."

I'd let Efrain know I wanted to handle Buster's cross-examination and I started by establishing that he was first contacted about this case by the defense twenty-three years after the assault, more than two decades after that night in the bar.

"I think you testified that you were drunk that night?"

"Uh-huh."

"Is that fair?"

"Sure."

"I mean, are you guessing or do you remember being drunk?"

"I had too much to drink. I wasn't stumbling drunk. I was able to drive myself home, sober enough to do that."

More smiles from the jury and without thinking about it I gave him a big grin and said, "You know you're talking to a prosecutor, right?"

He laughed along with most people in the courtroom. "Yes."

"Okay, statute of limitations is past on that one." I got us back on track. "Did you spend the whole evening with her or were there times when she was off doing something and you were off doing something else?"

"Oh, I assume so. We were just acquaintances. I may have bought her a drink or two. She was alone. I think we danced."

"Okay."

"I was told."

"You don't remember dancing with her?"

"Not exactly."

"Who told you that?"

"Somebody at the club said I was dancing with her."

"Your memory of this whole evening, to be fair, is probably pretty hazy?"

"As I said before, nothing about the evening stood out tremendously, but I do remember seeing her."

I was pretty sure his entire memory of the evening had been reconstructed, in good faith, by information provided by others. In other words, he had probably been a lot drunker than he was letting on.

As Buster Lewis headed out of the courtroom, Wade stood. "Your Honor, at this time the defense rests."

This surprised me, as I'd been expecting the defense to raise one of the biggest issues that we wrestled with pretrial: Marty Odem.

That morning before court, I had been shocked to see Marty Odem in the hallway outside the courtroom. I approached him and asked why he was there. He showed me the subpoena from Wade Russell. We talked for a moment and it was evident he wasn't happy about coming up from Houston, but it was also clear to me that he didn't want to do anything to foul up his parole, which would include ignoring a subpoena.

With the defense resting, it now looked like the issue of Odem testifying had withered away entirely. The parties had talked about it with the judge numerous times in chambers and submitted our briefs, but we had never really hashed anything out on the record. Informally, the judge's opinion had run parallel to mine: Without something specifically tying Odem to Natalie's murder, Wade couldn't get to present him as an alternate suspect. In my mind, the proper way to force the issue was to have a hearing on the record, put on witnesses (including Tom Walsh and Odem himself), try to make that connection and have the judge rule. To date, the defense hadn't done that and now it seemed they weren't going to.

Chapter 28

CONCLUDING TESTIMONY

We were so close. It was Friday morning and the weekend ahead of me seemed like an actual event, something that I might get to enjoy, rather than a theoretical bookend to what had become an exhausting case.

The morning session began without the jury and with an argument. We were ready to put on the witness stand the officer who took Donn Chelli to the park after he called 911 claiming to have seen the "Lotions man." Wade objected, arguing that we were trying to introduce hearsay evidence, Chelli's words through the officer. I stood ready to rebut the objection, but Judge Lynch did it for me, debating the legal issues with Wade as I watched and did little more than nod. Eventually, we were underway.

Efrain handled the questioning. "Sir, would you please tell us your name?"

"My name is Kenneth Cannaday."

"What do you do for a living?"

"I am a police officer with the City of Austin," he said, adding he'd worked for the department for over twenty-five years and was currently a lieutenant.

"I would like to focus your attention, if I may, Lieutenant, back to November 2 of 1985. At that time were you working with the Austin Police Department?"

"I was."

"In what capacity, sir?"

"I was a patrol officer."

"On that date, did you have the occasion to arrest an individual by the name of Seth Pickett?"

"I did."

"Can you tell the jurors here the circumstances surrounding that arrest?"

"I was contacted by some homicide detectives who probably needed a uniformed officer to go with them. They had received information from a person named Donn Chelli that a person fitting the general description of someone that was seen in the area of the homicide, that he saw him again, so he had called and contacted or got ahold of them and told them that he had seen this person in the area again and they were going to go look for this person."

"Why were you called out there?"

"I guess—it is most likely those guys were in suits. If they go out and go out in public or do something, often they will take a uniformed officer to be with them so they have the presence with them, maybe an extra set of eyes, something like that."

"Did you in fact make contact with Seth Pickett?"

"Yes, sir, he was arrested by me."

"What was he arrested for?"

"Public intoxication."

"What was his height at that time?"

Cannaday reached for a piece of paper. "I have the booking sheet if you will allow me to read that."

"Sure."

"It says on that date that his height was five-eight."

"What was his weight?"

"Approximately 180 pounds."

"The color of his hair?"

"Hair is black."

"The color of his eyes?"

"Reflects that they were green."

"To your knowledge, did detectives with homicide interview Seth Pickett?"

"Yes, sir. I booked him into jail for the public intoxication and placed a hold on him for homicide and found out that Sergeant Balagia did interview, talk to him and eliminated him."

"Was he eliminated as a suspect for the murder that this defendant is on trial for?"

"As far as I know, yes, sir."

"Nothing further, your Honor. Pass the witness."

Wade didn't have much on cross-examination; he just confirmed with Cannaday that he had no idea how far away Chelli was when he spotted Pickett. The answer didn't matter as much as the question; Wade was giving the jury a reason to explain away Chelli's mistake and believe the original description, the one that didn't fit his client.

We had one more witness, the man who would tie the car to Davis. I went through the preliminaries quickly: His name was Dale Streiker and he was a businessman who'd lived in or around Austin for several decades. He'd been married for almost thirty years and had adult children. He looked the part, neatly attired in khakis and a conservative shirt, but I had spoken to him enough to have detected an undercurrent of electricity that ran in him, a sense of humor and fun.

"What were you doing back then?"

"Mostly trying to make it big. I was in a rock band."

"Tell the jury about that band."

"I was the son of a preacher, a Baptist preacher, and he really didn't really like what we were doing much, but we decided to start the first-ever Christian heavy metal band, one of the first two and so we started working on songs, writing songs and music and recorded."

"I apologize for not having a picture. I wish I did. Could you describe to the jury kind of what you wore, what you looked like back then?"

He grinned. "We were often referred to as the Kiss of the Christian market, so we had white faces, dog collars, long hair dyed black, stuff like that, wore armor." The jurors were smiling, liking this amiable man and enjoying the vision of him white-faced and in body armor.

I asked him a few more questions about the band and then about his recording a hit song, "Rock On." I moved on to this recording session's connection with Dennis Davis.

"Sound—it was actually co-produced by Dennis Davis. He also, as I recall, he did the engineering work, although he may have had somebody else come in, but I don't recall if somebody else was involved."

I stood. "May I approach the witness?"

The judge nodded. "You may."

I showed Streiker a copy of the recording we'd been talking about and it came into evidence so the jury could look at the dates for themselves.

"You testified this recording was made at Studio D with Dennis Davis as one of the producers?"

"That is correct."

"How did you pay him for studio time?"

"A lot of ways."

"For this EP?"

"It wasn't uncommon for us to pay some cash, but I don't recall if we gave cash in this particular case. Certainly a check and in this particular case, what I recall—I went back and looked, because I wanted to make sure that the timing was right, but Dennis needed a car. He asked us for a car, he said, 'I need a car.' I said, 'Okay, that is cool' and I went outside with the drummer, I don't know whether the bass player was there. I said, 'I have this great idea. Why don't we give him your car, one of your cars.' He said, 'That is a great idea.' Anyway, so we paid, we paid for that and we traded some studio time to Dennis for that car."

Moment of truth. "What was that car?"

Streiker identified the make and model, same as the one seen the night of the assault.

"Do you remember the color?"

"Yes, it was blue." Which, it seemed to me, in the dark could easily be mistaken for gray.

"Do you remember exactly when that transaction took place?"

"No. I mean that is like when my wife asks me, 'What was I wearing the day we met?'" The jury laughed. "Probably—it would have had to have been before the EP was finished, but again, I'm guessing."

Wade stood. "Excuse me. I object to any speculation about when this transaction occurred."

My heart beat faster, because this was the point of this witness's testimony. And I was surprised, too, because Streiker was sounding a lot less sure than when we talked on the phone. We waited for the ruling.

Judge Lynch sat back in his chair and looked at Dale Streiker then us. "Overrule it, as long as he bases it as best he can on his memory. Just about everybody has been doing that here. As long as it is not just pure speculation but you are attaching it to some event, you may proceed to answer the question."

"Yes, sir," Streieker said. "Do you want me to explain the logic or tell you—"

"Just tell me when you think," Judge Lynch interrupted.

"Mid '85."

It had turned out well and in my relief I took advantage of Dale's easygoing nature to make a joke. "Just for the record, when you met your wife I think you were wearing a dog collar." Streiker and the jurors laughed and I passed the witness to Wade.

Wade had Streiker go through the history of his band, when they formed and changed their name, then showed him a printout from the Internet. It was a history of the band but written by someone else and for some reason that irritated the witness. I saw the businessman in him and he was firm when Wade challenged him on the dates of the trade.

"You are telling us you did some recording at Mr. Davis's studio, but you can't say exactly when you traded this car for studio time, right?"

"Other than it was 1985."

"And that is all you can say. You can't say early '85, late '85, you have no clue?"

"I said mid '85. You might look at your notes."

Streiker also helped clarify the paperwork issue.

Wade asked, "Generally when people buy or sell vehicles, part of the transaction is, 'I give you money, you give me the car, we transfer the title, people get new plates'?"

"That is not the way it was done back then. Pretty much people would take the car. This is my experience anyway. Sign the title and you give it to the person. They were responsible for transferring it. It wasn't as tight as it is today."

"You don't have any knowledge of how that transaction was finally completed?"

"I don't know if Dennis transferred it to his name. I don't know if my bandmate went with him to the title registration office. I doubt it."

At that point, Dale Streiker was finished.

Dennis Davis had decided not to testify, although right until the end I held out hope that he would, but I assumed that Wade, very sensibly, advised him not to. There was too much he couldn't explain and he'd have to stick to the story he told Tom as well as the statement he gave police at the time. A disappointing choice for me, but from the defense perspective the right one.

All that was left now was for the judge to read the charge to the jurors and then for the lawyers to argue our closing statements. The charge was the list of instructions that would guide the jurors during deliberations. They set out the law, defined legal terms like "intent" and "knowledge" and contained the constitutional protections afforded every defendant, like the right not to testify and the presumption of innocence. The charge also included the verdict form, on which the foreman would write either "guilty" or "not guilty."

When Judge Lynch was finished reading it, he turned the floor over to Efrain.

For closing arguments, which Judge Lynch liked to keep brief with time limits, we'd all agreed to twenty-five minutes for each side. Efrain and I agreed that he'd take twelve of our twenty-five and I'd have thirteen minutes. The order was the same as in any jury trial: Efrain first, then Wade and I would finish.

Opinions vary on the importance of closing arguments. Research shows that most jurors have made up their minds long before the lawyers stand up to argue. But to me, closing arguments still play a crucial role. First, I feel that not every juror has come to a firm conclusion by this point. They aren't supposed to and I can't imagine every single one has done so. Which means there's almost certainly one person who can be convinced by my argument.

Second, I know that some people who *think* their minds are made up can be persuaded to look again. I know this, because I've seen juries deadlock, but when told by a judge to keep working, some come around and reach a verdict. I have personally spoken to jurors who changed their minds during deliberation. My argument, then, is to provide a basis for that change. In the same vein, it also lets a juror who agrees with me address a concern expressed by another juror: "I hear what you're saying," a juror might say, "but do you remember when Mr. Pryor said that…" I want to arm those who agree with my perspective with tools they can use in the jury room to augment their own persuasion if necessary.

Third, argument isn't just for the jury. In this case especially, it was for Natalie's family and her friends, for Johnny and his friends. I wanted them to see that I cared, that the system cared and that the passion and logic of my closing argument showed how much we cared.

As ever, Efrain was methodical in his approach. I could see the soldier in him as he questioned the witnesses and discussed the evidence during the trial, reminding jurors of the important things that showed Dennis Davis to be a murderer. I knew what his focus would be; for him there was one thing that had always told the story of this case and I knew he'd hammer home our first and best evidence: the crime scene.

Efrain stood directly in front of the jury box.

"Ladies and gentlemen of the jury, justice is ageless. The passage of time has in no way diminished the guilt of this defendant for the murder of Natalie Antonetti." He surprised me; there was real emotion in his voice, real passion and feeling and it ran over the jurors like fresh, pure water. I thought maybe they were a little surprised and impressed, too. "The evidence that you have heard throughout this week, I submit to you, speaks loudly, as if you heard it for the first time.

"Let's talk about the crime scene. What does the crime scene tell us about the person who committed this murder? Johnny took the stand, as painful as it was for him to go back to that time period and look at those photos of that apartment. What did we learn from those photographs? We learned: One, that there was no forced entry into that apartment. Two, Johnny told you that as he walked through that apartment, not only the first floor but also the second floor, everything seemed in place. Nothing was out of order. 'Johnny, was anything taken?' 'No. Nothing was taken.' You have to ask yourself, 'Was this a burglar coming in who burglarized this house? Some guy trying to take a guitar or trying to take some money, trying to take something from that apartment?' No, it was not a burglary, folks.

"Then you ask yourself, 'Well, was it a sexual predator, someone preying on Natalie to satisfy their sex?' What did we learn about that? At Brackenridge Hospital when Natalie was taken to the hospital, they did a SANE exam, sexual assault nurse examiner exam, to determine whether or not there was any trauma to her vaginal cavity. Nurse tells you no trauma. That is the first indication there was no sexual assault and then Dr. Bayardo told you, 'We examined her genitalia, we examined the vaginal cavity, we looked at the organs and there were no signs of a sexual assault.'

"Not only that, but also DNA. They collected vaginal swabs of Natalie. They examined that couch cover, those pillows, things around the couch looking for semen and they found none, so I submit to you that this was not a sexual predator."

Efrain was ticking off the boxes, eliminating the possibilities and the jury was focused on the intense and eloquent man walking before them, leaning slightly forward as he made his points.

"What did Dr. Bayardo tell you? He told you there were no defensive wounds on Natalie. All the injuries that she sustained were to the head, all of them. No broken ribs, no broken hand, arm, leg. He also told you that the skull itself was fractured, that the blows were, I think he counted them, maybe five. He said it could have been more, because there was one that he knew had more in there just because of the fracture that occurred at that particular location.

"You have to ask yourself then, 'If it is not a burglar who went there looking to take something and it is not a sexual predator, what is it?' Tom Walsh, seasoned investigator, told you when you look at the autopsy photos, when you study the crime scene, he concludes that this was a crime of passion, that the person who went in there and inflicted these injuries on Natalie had it in for Natalie, had a beef against Natalie, wanted to hurt Natalie. Not take something, not sexually assault her."

After a week's worth of testimony, I fervently believed only one person fit that picture. Efrain continued:

"What do we know about Natalie and this defendant? Well, we know they dated, they started seeing each other. We know at one point during that courtship, a new guy came into Natalie's life and that guy, as you recall, was Andy Stout. We know from the defendant's own words when he talks about Andy and Natalie and he says, 'I think Natalie started hooking up with that guy to get me jealous and you know what'—these are his words—'it worked.' Not only that, he leaves a note close in time to the murder of Natalie and he was questioned about this on that videotape. I invite you to go back and listen to his words. But on this note he says, 'Natalie, you can go to hell and take Andy with you. If you don't have the brains and the self respect to see this is bullshit, then fuck you.' Signed DD.

"Again, a crime of passion. Who had it in for Natalie at that time? You heard from Jimmy Rose, good friend of the defendant back then, roommates. What does he tell you? He kind of quibbles a little, was it a Friday night or a Saturday night, Saturday night being the night before Natalie was murdered, that he witnessed, observed, heard an argument between this defendant and Natalie and how did he describe that argument? It was emotional. They were yelling at each other.

"When I questioned him, I asked him, 'Jimmy, in this statement here that you gave authorities, you say it was the night before Natalie was murdered.' I submit to you that the argument took place right before Natalie was murdered. Remember what Jimmy told you. Timing is always crucial. He told you, 'Steamboat closes at 2:00 in the morning. That argument took place as we were walking out. We don't leave that place until it closes.'

"I submit to you that argument took place closer to 2:00 A.M. that morning, the morning Natalie was murdered. Then what do we hear about Natalie? She gets assaulted sometime around 4:30, 5:00 in the morning. A crime of passion, folks. Remember Jolene Wells? Jolene Wells said, 'Dennis Davis, he was like a little brother to me.' Jolene also told you that at that time Natalie had no enemies, none whatsoever. You heard Johnny talk about his mother. She was outgoing, sociable; she was a landscaper, into art. No enemies whatsoever.

"Everything points back to this defendant. The defendant in his statement told authorities, 'I have an alibi. Amparo Garcia-Crow, that is who I was with that night, the morning of the day Natalie was killed.' No one ever checked that alibi and here we are today.

Tom Walsh goes knocking on Amparo Garcia-Crow's door and says, 'Remember this Dennis Davis guy?' 'Yes, I remember Dennis Davis.' 'Were you with him the morning that Natalie was killed?' and she told you, 'I was not with Dennis Davis that morning. I would have remembered something like that, because I kept a diary about my life.'

"Does she write about trivial stuff? 'Today I am going to have a hot dog as opposed to a hamburger.' No, she is an emotional person, very earthly individual. She wrote about emotional things that impacted her life. You don't think that if this defendant was with Amparo that morning that Amparo would not have reflected that in her diary, whether it would have been that day or two or three days later? 'Hey, I remember Dennis Davis woke me up, that Natalie was hurt and bleeding because he had received a call from Jolene.' She writes on October 14 that she learns about the death of Natalie and she puts that little article in there from the newspaper. His alibi holds no water."

Now Efrain moved on to discuss the murder weapon and tied the defendant to it. "We also spent a lot of time talking about the bat. What is the big deal with the bat? The defendant in his statement tells you he never owned a bat. Very trivial point, fact, question. 'Hey, did you ever own a bat, a bat back then?' 'No.'

"Really? You heard from Jimmy Rose, who came in and testified that he found a bat underneath the bed that he was sleeping in when he was rooming with this defendant and underneath that bed was all of Dennis's stuff and included in that stuff was this bat and he described it to you, an eighteen-inch bat.

"Linda Bless tells you the same thing. 'I recall a time where not only did he have the bat, but also he was threatening Kellie Torres with the bat and he was angry,' or 'agitated' is the word I think she used, 'to the point where I had to intervene and take him out of the house so that he could calm down.'

"But this defendant wants you to believe him when he tells Detective Walsh, 'I didn't own a bat back then.' Why? Go back and listen to his words, because it is there, this person being the killer of Natalie.

"Then we spent some time talking about Donn Chelli, the gentleman who, around 4:30, 4:45 in the morning, he is about to take a flight out, encounters an individual that morning around the time of Natalie's death. I submit to you that the person Donn Chelli saw that morning is this defendant. We brought you Dr. Weaver who shared with you his knowledge as it comes to eyewitness identification. He gave you some factors you should look at about whether or not certain things may influence somebody's reliability when they tell you what they saw.

"He talked about things like how long did you see the person for, what was the lighting like, were you fatigued at the time, what time of day was that, the distance, but he shared something that I think is very important that you should take with you when you go back and deliberate. He talked about two things that I think are important. Weapon focus. Remember what Donn Chelli tells you in that statement, how he describes that bat. He describes it as a child's bat. Wow. Wait a minute. Jimmy Rose tells me that this defendant, amongst his stuff, had a bat that was eighteen inches long."

The judge interrupted: "Eleven minutes."

Efrain didn't hear him, he was so deep into his argument. He turned to the bench. "Sir?"

"Eleven minutes," the judge repeated.

Efrain, immersed in the flow of his points, nodded, barely acknowledging his one-minute warning, and turned back to the jury. "Think about that. Then Dr. Weaver tells you that when you are encountered in a threatening situation like that—remember what Donn Chelli said that the person he encountered said: 'You are the second person that has gotten into my shit.' I submit to you that the first person that got into this defendant's shit was Natalie and she paid dearly for that. She paid with her life.

"But Donn Chelli also tells you this other thing, because remember what Dr. Weaver says: You have to be careful, because people are going to be off on height, facial features, weight and Donn Chelli is everywhere. He is all over the place as to height. He is at five-six. At one point he is at six-three. Color, he is a little bit off on that, build and what have you.

"One thing that Donn Chelli never wavers on is the bat. Got to wonder, what is a person doing at 4:30 in the morning walking around with a bat. Two, that he saw the Lotions on the back of that shirt as that person was walking away. What did Dr. Weaver tell you?

The Lotions shirt, the name of that band, that person would have re-membered that and that is more reliable than that person giving you a description about facial features, height or weight, because that was encoded in Donn Chelli's mind already, that whole thing about the Lotions." He looked searchingly at the jury. "That is why he was able to remember that quickly and always stick to that about the Lotions.

"How did he know about the Lotions name? Well, we know that Dennis Davis was in the music industry. We know that the Lotions was a big band at the time, around the time of Natalie's death. You also heard from Jimmy Rose, the roommate to this defendant, who said, 'I knew the lead singer to the Lotions. I would go there routinely to hear him play.'

"Question. 'Jimmy, would the defendant go with you?' 'I don't remember.' I mean really, your roommate? You are hanging out, you are going to see the Lotions, you don't think he would have gone there? This guy owned Studio D. You don't think he knows everybody in town, you don't think he is connected to everybody in town?

"I submit to you he knew the Lotions and you also heard from one of the band members who tells you that in fact he knew Dennis Davis. In fact, Dennis Davis came to him around the time or days after Natalie was murdered and asked for T-shirts so he can go around town asking people, 'Have you seen someone wearing this shirt?'

"I submit to you that those two things that Donn Chelli gives you, that Dr. Weaver said are pretty solid, are reliable, more than any-thing else. That bat, which he denies he owned and of course that shirt. That band, that logo. Remember, the threat is no longer there, because he describes it as the guy is walking away and on his back, 'I saw the Lotions' and he recalls that and he has stuck with that. He has never wavered on that."

Efrain took a breath and stood very still before the jurors for a quiet moment. "Folks, my time is up. I submit to you that the per-son who murdered Natalie sits with us here today and that is Dennis Davis and I ask you to find him guilty of murder. Thank you."

Chapter 29

CLOSING CONTRASTS

Now it was Wade's turn and I readied my pen. It was my job, my responsibility, to pay close attention to what Wade said and, where appropriate, rebut his argument.

"Ladies and gentlemen of the jury, when we first talked in *voir dire*, we talked extensively about reasonable doubt and you now know why that is important in this case. That is because this is a largely circumstantial case.

"Mr. De La Fuente was just up here and he was going on about probably—the defendant *probably* could have done it, he could have been there, he could have worn the Lotions T-shirt. Maybe, maybe he was there Saturday night having an argument with Natalie Antonetti.

"Their whole theory of the case, Dennis Davis is a jealous, jealous, vengeful man, went into this entire rage. Yeah, he wrote a note; he vented. We don't know when he wrote this note. We don't know if it was Saturday or weeks before. He was a little pissed off at her. She has a new boyfriend. He doesn't think. Half of this note is, 'I am mad at you' and the other half is, 'He is not good for you.' Is that the kind of motivation that would spur, in their theory of this case, that he went into a jealous rage and kept this jealous rage inside of him and it built and built all the way from weeks before, days before that Saturday night that he went over there? It ate at him all evening and he went over there and he knew her door was unlocked and he went in there and bludgeoned her to death because—because of something like this?"

Wade's voice resonated through the room as he emphatically made his arguments.

"That is outrageous. That is way beyond any of the evidence that you have heard in this case. Reasonable doubt. The highest burden, highest burden possible. We talked about this. They have to overcome every, every reasonable doubt in this case. 'Maybe, could be, probably' don't fit in. It is not reasonable doubt. I mean, it *is* reasonable doubt. It is not *proof* beyond a reasonable doubt.

"You have heard more about what this case is not about than what is there, really. You have heard all these circumstances that are suggestive. I mean, this could be the clearest case of reasonable doubt that I have ever heard of and you may ever hear of in your life.

"I told you in the beginning there is no DNA, there is no direct evidence of any kind, no blood, clothing, no physical evidence of any kind, any kind, connecting Dennis Davis to this crime."

As always in a defense attorney's closing argument, there came a point when I wanted to shake my head or show some outward form of displeasure. But I tried not to and hoped instead the jury was thinking what I was: *Of course there's no DNA or other physical evidence. What would that even look like in this case?* All I did was note it on my pad, for when my turn came to speak.

"You look at all the evidence," Wade continued. "Think of it how they looked at it back then. There is nothing connecting Dennis Davis to this crime, nothing whatsoever.

"They investigated a while. They can't determine who committed this crime. The investigation fizzles out. It sits there for years and years. Then you shift forward thirty years. How does it all change? People's memories have changed. People have forgotten things, people remember some things differently. Basically, he had the same body of evidence. All that has really changed at this point is now, after twenty years, an ex-girlfriend of Mr. Davis who came in here and demonstrated her temper tantrums to you, demonstrated to you her concerns were more about her relationship with Dennis Davis than anything else, she for the first time ever three years ago up and says, 'oh, now that you ask, Detective Walsh, yeah, I think he said it to me one time.'

"She waits all that time and her first words when he asks her are, 'I am not really sure what he said.' Detective Walsh, being a good detective, he is on the case now, he is on the hunt. He said, 'Come on, tell me more about it, tell me more about it.' She has an opportunity. She sees her opportunity. 'Well, maybe he said more about it. I asked him.' I mean, she gave different versions: 'I asked him this question, I asked him this question.' It went from, 'I am not really sure what he said' to this elaborate story. 'This went on for thirty minutes, we talked back and forth, on and on about this.'

"Her version just grew and grew. Reasonable doubt right there. From the get-go she says, 'I am not sure what he said.' Reasonable doubt. Every time she gets off Detective Walsh's page, his mission, he directs her back to it and she gets more details. He brings her back to the story.

"Reasonable doubt.

"You will notice that her questions and her description of what Dennis Davis was saying changes every time she talks about it and she couldn't even quite get it straight when she testified on the witness stand. Walsh talks to her a couple of times. She starts to equivocate. She calls and leaves him a message on the phone saying, 'I am not sure what he said; I am not sure what he said. I think he said something like this' and Detective Walsh, not going to take no for an answer, he arranges an interview, goes up there and interviews her, gets her back on track, back on the story.

"She left a message saying, 'I am not sure what he said. It was such a long time ago. I don't want to be the person to do that.' That is reasonable doubt right there. Walsh pursues her. Knowing—he knows the entire time, he admitted to you on the witness stand, all this time he is aware that Donn Chelli had made a statement describing a man who doesn't look anything like Dennis Davis. I asked him, 'You knew he didn't look like Dennis Davis now and he didn't look like Dennis Davis then' and he said, 'Yes.' You can see what is going on here. We have a detective who has tunnel vision. He is in the cold case unit. He wants to be a hero. He wants to solve this case. That is his job as he sees it. He has an opening, he is going to exploit this opening and he starts going down this tunnel and he doesn't want to see any other evidence that disagrees with his theory of the case.

"You heard from Cliff Byers, experienced FBI investigator. He says that is not how you do a proper investigation. You don't take one little bit of evidence that you want to believe and then you exclude other bits of evidence or you try to make these other bits of evidence conform to what this one person said. That is not how you do a proper investigation.

"Another interesting thing that Kellie said at some point was that Dennis said that Natalie was pregnant. Well, that is really interesting. He said that she was pregnant and that is the motivation for the murder now. Is that it or is it their jealous rage theory of the case?

"When I was in law school, they started talking about theory of the case and I was a little offended. I thought, theory of the case. Aren't you supposed to be in here trying to find out what actually happened and pursue justice and tell what really happened? Well, ladies and gentlemen, they have a theory of this case and it is based on the testimony of one person whom you have plenty of reason to doubt. I think it is pretty clear from her testimony. The minute I started asking her questions about what she said earlier to Walsh about not being sure about what Dennis Davis said, she immediately jumps into this tirade about Dennis Davis and their relationship and how he beat her up all the time. I mean, she just went off like a Roman candle.

"You see what kind of person she is. You understand what kind of person she is. She didn't want to talk about what she actually told Detective Walsh or when she told him or the different versions. It was all about her and Dennis Davis. That is what it was about. I mean, it is clear that she had an ax to grind and she has an opportunity to get back at Mr. Davis and she took her opportunity to do that. Why didn't she tell the police? I asked her, 'Why didn't you tell the police thirty years ago or whenever it was that he committed this crime?'

"Did Detective Walsh ask her that? I don't think so. I asked Detective Walsh, 'Don't you think that is a curious thing that somebody would thirty years later, twenty some-odd years later, for the first time ever say, "Oh, yeah, this guy told me he committed a murder"?' Detective Walsh turned and looked you all in the eyes and said yes. I asked Detective Walsh, 'After Kellie Torres told you that Dennis told her he committed this crime, isn't the first thing you did was go out there and try to figure out if she is a credible person and start asking everybody you could find about her credibility?' What was his answer? 'Well, no, I didn't do that.' 'Did you talk to people who knew her here in Austin back when she was living with Dennis Davis going down partying on Sixth Street? Did you ask those people what they thought about her credibility?' 'Well, no, didn't do that.'

"Well, I brought them to you. You heard witness after witness who knew Kellie Torres from that period of time when they were dating and when Dennis Davis and she and others were down there at Steamboat partying. What they thought about her credibility, her reputation as a truth teller, either personal experience or her reputation and person after person, including one of her best friends, Linda Bless, said, 'Well, she is not very good with the truth.' It is a polite way of saying, yes, she is a liar. She exaggerates. That is exactly what you saw and heard here during this trial, ladies and gentlemen. So I asked Kellie, 'Why didn't you go and tell somebody that Dennis Davis committed this crime?' 'Well, I was afraid of him. I was just so afraid of him I couldn't tell anybody.' What does she do after that? Well, she keeps living with a guy she believes is a known murderer. She keeps living with the guy, keeps partying with him, keeps hanging out with these musicians, doesn't tell her friends Dennis Davis admitted committing murder. She continues to hang out, so how afraid of him is she at that point? I think it is questionable.

"I asked her, 'Where did you go after you left Austin?' 'I moved out of state.' 'You are afraid of him?' 'Well, his dad is rich. I don't know what could happen.' Do you have any evidence his dad is like a Mafioso or has ties to organized crime or would hire a hit man to come after her? Of course not. It is a fabrication, it is an exaggeration, it is an excuse and it fits right in with what all these people said about her credibility and her ability to tell the truth. It is just a pure excuse. 'Well, he might come get me.' She moves, she lives with her husband. Does she tell him? Doesn't tell him. 'Are you still afraid?' 'Yeah, I guess I am still afraid. I don't know what could happen.'

"Fabrication, excuses, you can see the pattern here. When I first talked to you at *voir dire*, I said this is not the OJ trial. This has been a short trial. Our trials don't go on forever. Our rules of evidence are different. We don't elaborate, we don't go down every possible rabbit trail that exists to have you consider. We focus on whether this person did it or not. That is what you get to hear about. But it did remind me of a phrase from the OJ trial. You may recall this phrase. If the glove doesn't fit, you must acquit. You all may remember that from then if you were paying attention to that trial. I submit to you we have another appropriate phrase here. If the facts don't fit, you must omit. If the facts don't fit, you must omit."

I looked searchingly at the jurors, but I couldn't interpret their expressions. I couldn't tell whether they were buying into Wade's comparison.

Wade continued. "Detective Walsh wanted to omit what Donn Chelli described. Donn Chelli has stood by this description of the man. Medium to tall man, heavy, 200 to 220 pounds, broad shoulders, rather straight, blond, dishwater blond hair. He has never wavered from that. You heard from Dr. Weaver. He said under certain conditions people can have not very good memories or their memories could fail a little bit or be weak about identifying a particular person. Dr. Weaver, you probably know, testifies in cases mostly for the defense where a victim of a crime has identified a particular person as being the person who committed an offense.

"That is not what we have here. They brought him in to try to suggest that Donn Chelli had somehow wavered or had gotten wrong this description of the man he saw outside that apartment with a baseball bat and Dr. Weaver said there are certain conditions where their memory might be weak, such as the victim of the crime is in a heightened state of alert or fear.

"If you remember Donn Chelli's statement, he doesn't say anything about being afraid of a man. He sees a man looking in his window and the guy says something to him and at some point they are walking along the sidewalk, the man walks the other way,

"Mr. Chelli walks back into his apartment and he has to think about it for a while and discuss it with his girlfriend whether he thinks it is important enough to call the police and he finally does. This is right exactly around the same time that Ms. Antonetti was assaulted in her apartment.

"Mr. De La Fuente suggested when the mystery man said, 'You are the second person that got in my shit this night,' did Natalie Antonetti get in his shit? Maybe he got in her shit. I mean, that is ludicrous, that she got into something with him. Of course not. She was assaulted in her sleep, most likely. We are not sure, but we think that. You go by this sophisticated spatter evidence trying to figure out where these blows took place. We don't really know. There is no spatter here. We don't know how many blows there were, we don't know how heavy they were, but if they were repeated blows to the same head many times, there could be blood on the bat, there could be spatter going off on the walls. We don't really know how the assault took place. You have heard a lot of suggestive evidence, you have heard a lot of inconsequential evidence, you have heard a lot of plainly wrong evidence. But there are really two important pieces of evidence in this case. There are just two, the most important pieces.

"One, Kellie Torres, twenty-two years after the assault says for the first time that Dennis Davis did this offense. Two, Donn Chelli, a neighbor, sees someone outside the apartments at the same time as the assault three doors down with a bat in his hand peering in the window and this person he saw doesn't look anything like Dennis Davis. Those are the two most salient pieces of information in this case. The first one is by a person who has a clear bias and has demonstrated in front of you her bias and sat on this evidence for twenty-two years, approximately, before reporting it to anyone.

"The other bit of information, this most salient piece of information, is a man who saw somebody out there, a man who was not under any duress. Don't know for sure about the lighting, but it is by an apartment parking lot. They are usually well lit. He clearly describes this man, gives a very vivid description and, by the way, he comes down and he cooperates with the police. He comes in, they do a composite drawing.

"If you had that composite drawing you could see the man Donn Chelli described very shortly after he saw this guy, when his memory was fresh. Where is that drawing? Well, they have lost it. They can't find it so you don't get to see it. I'm sorry. I would like to see it myself."

He looked from juror to juror and then went on.

"You have a choice to make. You can believe a biased witness who claims at various times that my client admitted to committing this crime or you can believe an unbiased witness who saw somebody out there who does not and never did look like Dennis Davis. I ask you, why would Dennis Davis, once he is called on the phone, I don't care where he is, is he at Studio D, is he out there all the way on the other side of town where it takes twenty minutes to get there, why would Dennis Davis, when called, come back there? Why would he come to the scene of this horrendous crime and be there, except for Jolene Wells was his friend and he wanted to help and Natalie was in trouble. Why would he come back there to confront the victim of this crime who could point to him and say that is the guy?

"We now know that she couldn't talk, but he didn't know, he didn't know. He gets a call she has been assaulted, she is bleeding. He gets a call. Why would he come back there if there is any chance that she would point to him and say, 'That is him; that is the guy that did it.' Do you think he is completely stupid? He would have to be utterly stupid to do something like that."

Once more I scratched a note on my pad, because while it seemed, on its face, a fair argument, I was pretty sure that I knew the answer.

"In order for Dennis Davis to meet this description of the man Donn Chelli saw, he would have had to shave his mustache. He wore a dark mustache back then. He would have to put on a blond wig or have dyed his hair blond, straightened it. He would have to put on seventy-five pounds in a real hurry. He would have to grow by five or six inches. He would have to bulk up his shoulders and throw on that Lotions T-shirt and look like a man with broad shoulders and he would be sure to wear a Lotions T-shirt so he could be connected to the music community so everybody could find him eventually because he is involved in the music business. Yes, that would be a smart move. That would be the way to do it.

"Ladies and gentlemen, this is ludicrous, it is ludicrous. It is reasonable doubt after reasonable doubt.

"You heard another statement. I want to talk about it a little bit. Becky Davis, Dennis's ex-wife, they are still together, who called in a statement. You heard that statement and the statement was, 'I sinned against God and man.' I probably could have objected to that statement. There are rules of evidence that say when things are more inflammatory than they are probative; that means they tend to raise suspicion, but they don't really prove anything and the courts do these weighing processes. I mentioned that rule a couple of times. Maybe I should have objected to that, but I wanted you to see how this whole thing got started. You can see, people seize on these suggestive things."

My brow furrowed, because this surprised me. I couldn't imagine any scenario where this powerful statement would be kept out of evidence. The words came from the defendant himself, so they were not hearsay and just because evidence hurt his client it wouldn't be excluded as "prejudicial." The legal standard is "unfairly prejudicial." If merely prejudicial evidence were kept out of trials, the video footage of an armed robbery would be excluded, for example, as would the DNA results identifying a rapist! Both of those things "prejudice" a case against the defendant, because they are bad for his case. But they don't *unfairly* prejudice him.

Wade's voice dropped to a quiet but determined tone: "When he made that statement, they were talking about his mother. They were in bed; they were talking about his mother. He was sad about that. He may have been sad about some other things in his life. He had a pretty bad relationship with Kellie. You may surmise that their lifestyle wasn't all-American during that time. He may have been saddened about some things he had done in the past."

To my ears the vague reference to "some things he'd done in the past" indicated that the "sad about my mother" story was a weak one. Why else would he move to other justifications for the statement? Either it was an adequate explanation or it wasn't and if it wasn't…

"That does not equate to 'I went out in a vengeful rage and killed Natalie Antonetti, because I was so angry at her that she was dating somebody else.' Well, he was dating other people too. That is what you heard. Jolene said Natalie was more interested in Dennis Davis than he seemed to be in her, so where is all that jealous rage the State said they were going to prove to you? Where is that? You have a nasty note and that is about it.

"He vented. He vents when he gets angry. He vents. That is what that note is about. So they get started. They get this ambiguous statement. Becky, bless her heart, thinks she is doing the right thing and what she did comports exactly with what Dr. Weaver told you people do. They take bits of information, they put them together in their heads, start to synthesize them. 'Look, I know he told me years ago that he sinned against God and man after we had been out drinking and I know that he had a girlfriend who had been murdered' and it was eating at her. That was her understanding, a misunderstanding of even that fact.

"She synthesizes these things in her head, feels like she has an obligation to call somebody. She calls somebody with this ambiguous statement, puts it together in her head like Dr. Weaver says people do. It gets misconstrued…it gets misconstrued by Becky, by Detective Walsh and they are off to the races down this tunnel, going to be heroes, we are going to solve this case for the community. That is how it got started and that is how it continued."

Judge Lynch interrupted. "Two minutes."

Wade barely paused for breath, building on his insights and arguments in favor of Davis's innocence. "All right. We know Natalie wasn't upset. We don't have any evidence she was upset Saturday night. She went out to Steamboat to see her friends. She knew Dennis Davis was going to be there. Was she afraid to go out there? Was she afraid to go see this vengeful, jealous, crazy man? No, she was not.

"Sometime they had an argument and they yelled at each other. Boy, that is incriminating. How many couples breaking up do you think have had an argument and yelled at each other? I submit to you that it is probably more than just politely agree to part ways and go their separate ways. We don't know when this argument took place. Was it Saturday, Friday? It wasn't Saturday. Buster Lewis didn't see them. He was there the whole time. Maybe Friday, maybe earlier, maybe sometime after he saw her with Andy Stout. Nobody really knows.

"Walsh is a very good interrogator and he got Dennis to start thinking that he left that note Saturday and Walsh also got Dennis thinking that he had a gray car when this happened and John Goudie and Jolene Wells said Dennis Davis had a different car. He didn't have two cars at one time. He doesn't even own a gray car at the time of this crime. That's based on testimony that came from the State's witnesses.

"We talked a little bit in *voir dire* about your role in this and I talked to one gentleman who said, 'We have to reach a consensus, don't we?' No, that is not what the law says. The law, as the judge read it to you, says you have to believe, each and every one of you, unanimously believe Dennis Davis committed this crime. That is the only thing required by law to agree to. Nobody has to go back there and cave in to someone else if they think that there is inadequate evidence here and that is your duty as a citizen.

"I told you this was going to be hard. You may not all agree on this, but your duty is to determine whether Dennis Davis committed this beyond a reasonable doubt and you have to agree and you have to be convinced beyond a reasonable doubt. That is the only thing that you are required to agree upon.

"I want to touch a little bit on Amparo Garcia-Crow. What a precise mind that woman has. She recorded everything, didn't she? Everything important. When she says, 'I was not there,' well, she prefaced that with, 'I am pretty sure.' Then after she said, 'I was not there,' she said, 'I am pretty sure.' She writes down everything important. She was with her other boyfriend that weekend. That is not in there. Read that journal. That is a very interesting journal. You see what kind of mind is at work there and what an accurate scientific mind, as it were.

"Finally, ladies and gentlemen, I want to remind you about a parable you may all know about and it is from the Bible. I know I am maybe taking it a little out of context, but it is applicable to the situation we have here. My version comes from Mark, the gospel of Mark, and Jesus is talking about a sower. A sower went out to sow and as he sowed, some seed fell on the path and the birds came and devoured it. Other seed fell on rocky ground where it had not much soil and immediately it sprang up since it had no depth of soil. When the sun rose it scourged it and since it had no root, it withered away. Other seed fell among thorns and the thorns grew up and choked it and it yielded no grain. Then other seed fell into good soil and there was rain and it grew up, increasing thirtyfold and sixtyfold and one hundred fold.

"We know he was talking about the spirit of God when he is talking about that. I am not trying to profane this, but the principles involved here are important, because this is a very wise saying.

"The State has thrown their seeds, scattered their seeds on stony soil, thorny soil. It has not produced fruit. It is weak, weak evidence, certainly not proof beyond a reasonable doubt."

Judge Lynch was annoyed now. "Time."

"May I have thirty seconds?" Wade didn't wait for the answer. "Ladies and gentlemen, you are aware of other cases from the State of Texas where people have been convicted of crimes and later exonerated. Texas is getting a reputation for the kind of justice we are meting out here. Don't let this be another case of Texas justice gone awry.

"There is not going to be any DNA to resolve this case at a later date. You have all the evidence you are ever going to hear and you have it now and I submit to you, there is not enough here to convict Mr. Davis of this crime. There is not proof beyond a reasonable doubt and every one of you knows that as you sit here. Don't let this be a runaway train. Don't let this be a miscarriage of justice. I ask you, I plead with you, come back with the only kind of decision that is just and that is, Dennis Davis is not guilty of this crime."

Wade finished and sat down. He'd gone way over his time and irritated the judge by doing so. I didn't blame him; Wade felt passionately about this case and had an obligation to defend his client as vigorously as he could. An obligation he properly saw as more serious than irritating the judge. But now it was my turn and there were some parts of that vigorous defense that needed my attention.

I stood and moved to the front of the jury box, my yellow legal pad in my right hand. I wanted to make my points calmly and intelligibly, but my own strong feelings about bringing justice to Natalie came to the surface.

"Good morning, ladies and gentlemen. I want to address a couple of things that Mr. Russell touched upon. First one is the way this investigation was carried out. One of the first things Tom Walsh told you when he got that case file, he read through it four or five times. He did that not to focus on any one person but to learn as much as he could. He told you also that he interviewed every single witness he could find. Everybody who was still alive, anybody he could talk to, he would.

"Then he gets a tip by talking to Kellie. Dennis Davis has admitted killing somebody, killing Natalie. How often does that happen? What would you have Detective Walsh do? Look into Dennis Davis or just spend a couple of weeks asking about credibility?

"Unfortunately, that is what we have seen here. We have seen from the defendant's case, 'We can't rebut the evidence, so here is what we will do. We will badmouth the witness. We will make it look like Tom Walsh had tunnel vision,' whereas, in fact, he was as thorough as you would want a detective to be. The problem for the defense is everything he found *did* lead to a tunnel and that tunnel led to the defendant.

"He badmouthed Kellie too. Said she changed her story. Defense elicited testimony that she testified before the grand jury and she gave a written statement. Do you think if she had changed her story between those two times and yesterday when she testified, those wouldn't have been shoved under her nose? No, she told the same story every single time, each time under oath. Do we really think, do we *really* think that a woman who has been abused like that, has been beaten and has moved on in her life has nothing better to do than come down here and get difficult questions from me and hostile questions from the defense? Really? What is her motivation? Doesn't make any sense."

I glanced down at my pad and then heard my own voice and fervor rising.

"Why did Dennis Davis come back that morning? Because he had to. What happens when Jolene phones and says, 'My God, something has happened to Natalie' and Dennis says, 'I am busy, sorry, can't come, sorry.' He has no choice. He has absolutely no choice. But remember the testimony. Not one single witness remembered him going into that apartment. He stayed away from Natalie. He stayed away from her until he knew she was in a coma and she couldn't identify him. He stayed out with Johnny. Did Johnny keep him out or did he keep Johnny out? He did not go into that apartment.

"The defense talked about reasonable doubt and said that we have too many maybes, possibilities. Let me give you some things you can take to the bank, one hundred percent absolute facts.

"Dennis Davis knew that Natalie Antonetti did not lock her door at night. He knew she was in the habit of leaving her door unlocked. How do we know that? Because he said so. That is a fact. Did he own a gray car? Deanna Cooley said she saw a gray car. She couldn't remember the specific details, but she saw it parked funny, parked crosswise outside that same apartment building. Did Dennis Davis own one? Well, he said he did. Cross-examination is trying to elicit maybe he didn't, maybe he didn't have two cars. Listen to the statement, listen to the interview. He says he did. Then Dale Streiker, our Christian rocker. Yeah, he knows he did because he timed it with the release of the album. Dennis Davis had that car back then.

"What else is a fact, hard, solid fact? This man used to go into rages. He admitted that in his interview. He used to go into rages. Linda Bless saw one of those. Becky Davis, his own wife, saw one. Even at age fifty-something, he is swinging an ax, she said at one point aiming it at her but not really trying to hit her with it. I don't know what that means, but that is a rage and a rage that he admits he used to go into back then.

"We know for a fact, because he said so, he was jealous of Andy Stout, 'the listless loser' I think he called him, which is sort of ironic because they were in the same business, but see, anybody who isn't controlled by Dennis is a listless loser. Even Natalie, poor Natalie. At the end of Dennis's interview, 'Oh, Detective Walsh, she was yelling at me; she was shouting at me. I am the victim here.' Really?" I turned away from the jury and faced Dennis Davis and the room turned pin drop quiet as my words rang out. "Where is that in your statement? Who else did you tell that to? That came up for the first time in that interview." I turned back to the jury. "Take those facts. Those are beyond a reasonable doubt.

"What else is a fact? He lied in his statement. He lied in the interview. Didn't have a bat. Says it twice. Watch the tape. Jimmy Rose says he did, Jolene Wells says he did, Linda Bless says he did, Kellie says he did. Maybe he forgot?" I shook my head. "He didn't forget. His ex-girlfriend was beaten to death with a bat. He owned a bat. He didn't forget. He *lied*.

"What other lies did he tell? Look at his statement, State's Exhibit No. 93. When was that argument with Natalie? Was it Friday night or was it Saturday night? If it is Saturday night, that backs up Amparo's story, but his alibi is gone. Gone, gone, gone. But even if it is Friday night, look at his statement and find it in there. He talks about Friday night. There is no mention of that fight. According to him, everything is rosy. You know what? It wasn't. His best friend said so. So that is a lie.

"What about Amparo? What motive does she have to come in here and lie? None. She knew him a couple of weeks. They parted, things fizzled out.

"He lied about that too. 'Oh, she left, didn't want anything to do with me because she was scared.' No, that is not true. Find that in the diary. She talks about the end of their relationship. Go, read that. And look, look hard at the tone of that October 14 entry where she mentions almost in a detached way that Natalie, Dennis' friend, has been assaulted. Not, 'Holy cow, that is why he left that morning, that is why he got up and abandoned me,' which is what she would have written if he had been with her. No, that entry is detached, it's remote and it is because she had not seen him for days, for days. His alibi, untested at the time, fell apart real fast twenty-five years later.

"Kellie. Important piece of evidence, because he confessed to killing Natalie. Why was Kellie telling the truth? As I have said, she is not going to come down here and perjure herself for some vengeful motive. But think about small details that she remembered, the concrete of the step they were curled up on. She remembers looking at that tree thinking, 'What do I do? What do I do?' Mr. Russell is right, she didn't tell anybody. She kept it close until a detective came knocking and then she told the truth. She has told the truth ever since. Is it outrageous, is it ridiculous that she kept it bottled up for so long? Would most people, when a murderer confesses a murder, would they do that?"

I paused and then went on. "Probably not. But somebody else kept something locked up inside. The defendant's wife, who admits she is here supporting him. She wants him to be found not guilty, but she kept bottled up inside of her his statement that he had sinned against God and man. She kept that bottled up for sixteen years and then she called the police.

"She called the police, because she knew what it meant and who is going to know better than the wife of the defendant what a statement like that means? She has never retracted it. She has never ever said, 'He didn't say that.' Be clear about that. What they want to do now is give it some spin, give it some explanation, but did you ever hear from this witness stand a definitive explanation of what that statement meant? 'I have sinned against God and man'? You never did; you never did. Some explanation about his mother dying. Well, put those two things together. How is the death of his mother a sin of his against God and man? It's not. It can't be. It makes no sense.

"There isn't but one explanation for that statement and Rebecca Davis knew it and that is why she called the police. That is why she told them about it and that is why this investigation started."

Judge Lynch spoke from over my shoulder. "Two minutes."

"Thank you, your Honor. Ladies and gentlemen, as Mr. De La Fuente said, when you go back into that jury room to deliberate, go back to the crime scene. Go back and look at those photographs. Look at what happened, look at the kind of person who did this.

"See what this case is really about. It's about jealousy. It's about rage." I looked at the jurors but pointed back to the defense table. "It's about holding Dennis Davis accountable for the murder of Natalie Antonetti twenty-five years ago."

I took a deep breath to control the emotion coursing through me and my last words were calm and quiet, spoken to the jurors and to them alone. "And you know what? It's about time."

At 11:38 A.M. the jurors retired to begin their deliberations.

Chapter 30

THE VERDICT

It was a beautiful, sunny day and I walked to a restaurant near the courthouse with Efrain and Tom. We were joined by the entire cold case squad, including Ron Lara. They were all in court for the closing arguments.

I felt a sense of relief. I knew I'd done all I could and now it was in the jurors' hands. Ron and Tom assured me that my closing was awesome, but then they would say that.

As we ate, Efrain and I checked our phones constantly and, conversely, tried to unwind a little. But eventually I felt the need to sit in my office and be alone. I walked back to the courthouse with Tom and stopped by the witness waiting area on the ground floor to see Johnny. He was there with his cousins and members of his band, loyal friends waiting patiently, giving him the same support they'd given throughout the trial. We chatted for a few minutes, then I headed upstairs and closed my office door.

And I waited.

These hours of waiting for a verdict put me in a state of suspended animation. I felt like a cartoon drawing waiting to get slipped into its sequence, to be part of the action again. There was plenty I could be doing, should be doing, but inertia took me over. After a while, I tidied my desk, but mostly so I could put my feet up on it.

After an hour I opened my door and people stopped by to say nice things about my closing or just to chat. Every now and again I stuck my head into Efrain's office next door and each time he smiled wickedly and said, "Not yet, brother. They'll get there."

Suddenly, at 3:15 P.M., my phone rang. It was Tony the bailiff and he said simply, "Englishman, we have a verdict."

Like generals rousing their troops, Efrain and I notified our victim counselor Lynn Cragg, so she could bring Johnny and his supporters up. Then we called Tom, Ron Lara and our investigator. We crowded into the elevator with others from our office who wanted to be in the courtroom for the verdict and I looked at Efrain.

"Not even four hours. That's quick." I was suddenly worried. "Maybe too quick."

He shook his head. "Nah, brother, we're good. We're good on this one."

It took time for everyone to assemble, for Wade and the defense team to get there with Dennis and Becky Davis, for the sheriffs to place themselves in the courtroom. No one was expecting trouble, but these men had no intention of being surprised.

At 3:44 P.M. Judge Mike Lynch took the bench and went straight to business. "All right, thank you. We are back on the record in 09-900185, *State of Texas vs. Dennis Davis.* Court has received word through the bailiff that the jury has reached a verdict. All parties are present." He looked at Wade and then at me. "Anything before we bring the jury in?"

"Not from the defense, your Honor."

"Nothing from the State, your Honor."

Lynch nodded and looked at Tony, who was waiting by the door. "You may bring the jury in."

All eyes turned to the twelve men and women filing into the jury box for the last time. A few looked over at Dennis Davis but not for very long and most of them didn't. This moment was torture for me; my stomach was twisting itself in knots and yet I had to sit still as if I was waiting for a bus, expressionless and calm. I thought, as I always did, how much worse it must be for the defendant, because in reality there was nothing at stake for me. No one in my office cared about win/loss records and I knew I'd tried the case as well as I could. If Johnny wasn't getting justice today, I would be upset and lose sleep, make no mistake. But I'd done my best and no one could ask for or expect more. I was going home to my family tonight, no matter what the jury said.

Dennis Davis, on the other hand, would find out in the next minute where he was going to spend the rest of his life; out in the free world or in prison.

When the jurors were settled, the judge spoke again. "Ladies and gentlemen of the jury, speaking through your foreperson, have you arrived at a verdict in this cause?"

The foreman stood. "Yes, your Honor."

"You may surrender it to the bailiff, please, sir."

The foreman handed the verdict form to Tony, who walked it to the bench. I could hear the pages rustle as the judge checked that it was properly filled out. After a few seconds, Judge Lynch looked up.

"The defendant please rise." As Davis stood, so did Wade and his second chair, who put a hand on Davis's shoulder. Judge Lynch cleared his throat and began reading. "Cause No. D-1-DC-09-900185, *State of Texas vs. Dennis Davis*, in the 167th District Court, Travis County, Texas. Verdict of the jury. We, the jury, find the defendant, Dennis Davis, *guilty* of the offense of murder—"

A woman in the audience audibly gasped.

"—as alleged in the indictment. Signed by the foreperson." He had emphasized the word guilty only for clarity, so there was no mistake or misunderstanding in the courtroom. He looked to the jury. "Mr. Foreperson, is this the individual, personal verdict of each of the twelve jurors in this cause?"

"Yes, sir."

"Thank you. Verdict will be received and entered in the record."

As soon as the jury left the room almost everyone stood. The people behind Efrain and me were thrilled with the verdict, patting shoulders and shaking hands. Becky Davis was distraught, sobbing. When she tried to stand she collapsed back in her seat. I reminded myself of what had just happened to her world.

Davis's friends and family left the courtroom quickly and I stood receiving hugs from Johnny's family and handing out tissues. I was thrilled, exhausted, elated and spent. I palmed one of those tissues for myself, because the next hug could be the one that had me spilling tears, too. Twenty-five years of not knowing who killed their Natalie, her life remembered but her murder seemingly forgotten, twenty-five years of waiting for this moment that meant so much to them. I was pleased to see Johnny give the stoic Tom Walsh the tightest hug he'd had in years, maybe ever.

I went over and got one for myself, glad for that tissue in my hand.

On Monday, April 18, 2011, we held a short, half-day sentencing hearing.

The jury was gone and it was for one man, Judge Mike Lynch, to decide the fate of the defendant. I put on just two witnesses, Johnny and Olga Antonetti, Natalie's sister, who talked about Natalie and what her loss meant to them. Wade put on Dennis's brother, Buster Lewis and Becky, all of whom asked for mercy. Then the judge spoke.

"I have said this before in this situation and I guess I will say it again as a preface. In many ways it is really an impossible, almost a ludicrous task the law puts on a jury or, in this case, a judge to try to assign a number to a terrible act such as this rage that ended the life of an individual who had so much left to live. It is an impossible task, because what number could possibly do that situation justice? There is none, but yet the law requires us to do it and there is not a better system.

"The Court has tried to consider the factors involved in this case. It is a difficult and unusual case given its age, but I have tried to look at what the law requires the punishing entity to do and that is to look at the evidence both at the guilt-innocence phase, to look at the punishment evidence and to look at it from both the State's perspective and the defense's perspective. Having done that, I am prepared to go forward, so if the defendant would please rise."

Again Dennis Davis and his two lawyers stood. Judge Lynch continued. "As I stated earlier, based on the jury's verdict, a judgment of guilt has been entered. The Court has heard punishment evidence and argument of counsel. It now becomes the Court's duty to assess punishment in this case.

"At this time the Court assesses your punishment at a term of thirty-six years in the Texas Department of Criminal Justice."

Epilogue

I rose before dawn and made coffee quietly in the kitchen, because my family still slept. It was October 13, an important day because it marked two anniversaries. The first was my wedding, which took place eleven years ago and was an event that I would celebrate with my wife when I returned home later that day.

The second was an anniversary I needed to mark alone, because October 13 was the perfect day to fulfill a promise I made three years ago. I was going to visit Natalie's grave.

I poured my coffee into a travel mug and walked outside, breathing in the cool air, its chill a delight, because the Texas summer had lingered past September this year.

When I started the car's engine and drove away from my home, it was twenty-seven years to the day, almost to the hour, since Natalie Antonetti's world was taken from her as she lay sleeping. I felt an odd sensation in my chest as I thought of my family, safe in their beds, of leaving them behind. It was just for a day, half a day really, but even so I had a powerful urge to turn around and give them each one more hug. Then I smiled as the streetlights flickered past the car's windows and I told myself to drive carefully so I would come home safely to my family.

I headed east out of town. After a dozen miles Austin fell away and I entered a bleak stretch of road. The darkness on either side of my car thickened, because one year ago fire covered the land, destroying more than a thousand homes and turning thousands of acres of forest into blackened, twisted ghouls. Yet, despite the savagery of those flames, the car headlights showed me glimpses of life rising up, fighting back and, in some places, starting to reclaim the land. I saw fresh wooden frameworks settling into newly cleared plots and I thought about the resilience that lives in man's own determination to overcome, to survive.

The burned forest gave way to trees that had escaped the fire and then to wider pastures as I headed farther south and east. The drive was pleasantly solitary and as I reached the freeway to Houston, the dark of night transitioned to a silvery morning. For once I didn't mind the companionship of more cars alongside me.

As I drove I reflected on my arduous fight to find Natalie's killer and bring him to justice. My mind flashed back to following the trail of Dennis Davis, to his trial and conviction and, more than a year after the jury returned its guilty verdict, to the filing of an appellate brief by Davis's defense lawyers. It alleged five legal issues for consideration by the Third Court of Appeals in Austin.

First, the brief stated that the trial court should have granted Davis's motion for a new trial, filed soon after the verdict, because there "was sufficient evidence to establish a nexus to a third party perpetrator." Second, Davis claimed his lawyer, Wade Russell, was constitutionally ineffective. Third, Davis stated that Judge Mike Lynch should not have allowed Linda Bless to testify that Davis had threatened Kellie Torres with a bat. Specifically, his dispute was with the judge's ruling that a question from Wade "opened the door" to that testimony. Fourth, Davis's lawyers argued that Judge Lynch was wrong when he ruled pretrial that the spousal privilege did not apply in this case. Fifth, the appellate brief made an overall claim that the "evidence is legally insufficient to prove beyond a reasonable doubt that the identity of the assailant was Dennis Davis."

The most recent docket note at the Third Court of Appeals read simply: "9/28/2012—Case ready to be set." There was no timeline for when the appeals panel would review the case; it could be months or a year from now. I felt ready to defend our view and that of the jury that Dennis Davis was guilty.

It took me three hours to reach the cemetery. Suddenly, as I got nearby, I began to worry that it would be closed to visitors; it was a weekend and still very early. But when I pulled up to the entrance the gates were open. Breathing a sigh of relief, I turned the car into the entrance and drove slowly along the narrow paved lanes, manicured grass and heavy stone markers passing by on either side. It was quiet again, peaceful. Normally, I didn't like cemeteries—they offer cold comfort to the living and the dead don't care—but today I felt differently, because Natalie lay there.

Getting out of my car, I walked to her graveside. I kneeled beside her grave marker, remembering my last trip. When I visited her grave the first time, the sun beat down on the back of my neck and the humid air pressed in on me. This time the air was cool and my knees were soon wet from the dew on the ground. I traced my fingers over the letters of Natalie's name and, below them, the dates that she lived. Out loud I recalled my promise to bring her justice.

I looked around as if someone might be near, as if someone might find it strange to hear a man talking to a gravestone, though I knew nothing could be more commonplace here.

Then I told Natalie that I did it, that I did everything I could. They weren't the words I thought I'd use, partly because I wasn't going to script this moment and partly because over the past few years I'd come to view my responsibility to her differently, as if my sense of duty had evolved since I first knelt beside Natalie three years ago.

So I told her that I knew Dennis Davis's capture and sentencing couldn't help her now but that maybe the arrest, trial and sentence would help the people she loved so dearly, the people I had come to know and care about, to find peace. I admitted to her that I would have liked to have done more, made it easier on those good people, perhaps made it more certain by achieving some kind of admission or even apology from the man who took her away from one of the most close-knit families I'd ever met.

And then I told her something I didn't intend to say, hadn't even thought to say: that, in my opinion, Dennis Davis wished with all his heart he'd not done what he did and not just because he was caught.

It was a secret buried deep inside him, hidden from the world by a façade of stone that was finally cracked open by his own guilt and by an ultimate truth that was too powerful to remain hidden. I wanted her to know that, because I wanted her to know that no one truly wanted her to die. I wanted to believe that myself.

It was time to go. I stood up and walked away, leaving Natalie at peace to sleep some more.

Acknowledgements

This is my first non-fiction book and I am grateful to many people for helping see it through to publication: my agent, David Nelson, for being excited enough about the project to take me on as his client and for finding a home for it so fast; likewise, the folks at New Horizon Press for being so professional, responsive and moving from manuscript to publication so efficiently.

There are many people I need to thank for allowing, permitting and encouraging the creation of this book. My friends at the district attorney's office, especially Marianne Powers and Amy Meredith, great trial lawyers who taught me (almost!) everything I know. To my first mentor, Corby Holcomb, who taught me that one of the greatest assets a trial lawyer has is a sense of humor.

Special thanks to those involved, directly or indirectly, in this case. Kelsey McKay and Geoffrey Puryear, who covered for me in court for weeks to let me concentrate on the trial, as did Jackie Wood who is now in private practice. I am grateful to Sergeant Mike Henderson for his tireless efforts to put up with me before and during the trial, for making sure my witnesses and evidence arrived intact and uncompromised and for helping me keep a (relatively) healthy perspective throughout. To Jim Young, for being willing to take the case on in the first place (much less work with me on it!) and to Karen Kiker and the many support staff who lent a hand when needed: Jessica, Doli, Sissy, Rachel, Vera, Mary Beth and Leah. Lynn Cragg, one of the nicest human beings ever: thanks for everything you do for victims of crime and to help your team of prosecutors.

My thanks, always, to the wonderful team that kept the 167th District Court running and made my time there so enjoyable: Tony Casarez, Ben Castoreno, Steve Goertz and the Queen of the Court herself, Melissa Moreno.

To Efrain De La Fuente: I am fairly certain my portrayal of you fails to do you justice. I had no idea, when you agreed to try this case with me, just how lucky I was to have you by my side. I will continue to take credit for the good things that happened, but I will always acknowledge that our successes were because of you. I learned a huge amount from you, my friend, and more importantly, from my perspective, I enjoyed every minute I worked with you.

I would also like to acknowledge a debt of gratitude to two other men who made this trial a good professional experience. Wade Russell, one of the nicest and most honorable people I've worked with, I continue to be grateful for your professionalism and cooperation. Judge Mike Lynch, my sincerest thanks not just for the way you conducted this trial, but also for the incredible experience of working in your courtroom for almost three years before you retired. I have never seen a wiser or fairer judge and I am eternally grateful for your sense of humor, your advice and the books you lent me (none of which I intend to return).

This book would not have happened but for the Cold Case Unit of the Austin Police Department. These men and women have never received enough credit: Sergeant Ron Lara, Richard Faithful, Angel Hernandez, Jerry Bauzon, Scott Ehlert and the detectives who retired recently, Manuel Fuentes, Mark Gilchrest and Steve Meaux. You guys work magic, plain and simple; you bring closure to people who thought they would never see it and you bring to justice bad people who've lived too long thinking they got away with murder.

Which brings me to Tom Walsh, a man of humility, integrity and high intelligence and to whom I will say one thing: You owe me a martini.

I would also like to thank the friends and family of Johnny Goudie. I have never seen such love, support and unity over so prolonged a period of time and while I know Johnny is a very easy man to love, support and unify over, you deserve so much credit for being there with him and for him when he needed it. I hope that I'm not forgetting any of you: Olga, Maria, Emily, Chuck and Christina, Paul, Jessi, Kyle, Michael, Scott and Brenda, Natalie, Ben, Darin and Trish and Corey.

My thanks to Johnny himself. In our very first meeting I should have known that we'd become and stay friends.

Finally, to the person who's supported me the most in every way, in my writing career, as a prosecutor and as a dad. Thank you, my Sarah.